P9-ASB-848

MEXICO

By
STUART CHASE

THE TRAGEDY OF WASTE
MEN AND MACHINES
THE NEMESIS OF AMERICAN BUSINESS
MEXICO: A STUDY OF TWO AMERICAS

———•———

And in Collaboration with
F. J. SCHLINK
YOUR MONEY'S WORTH

BOSTON PUBLIC LIBRARY

MEXICO

A STUDY OF TWO AMERICAS

BY STUART CHASE

IN COLLABORATION WITH MARIAN TYLER

ILLUSTRATED BY DIEGO RIVERA

PUBLIC LIBRARY
OF THE
CITY OF BOSTON

1816.253
B

NEW YORK
THE MACMILLAN COMPANY
1931

F1215
.C49
1931
Copy 2

COPYRIGHT, 1931,
BY THE MACMILLAN COMPANY.

All rights reserved — no part of this book may be reproduced
in any form without permission in writing
from the publisher.

Set up and electrotyped.   Published August, 1931.

Aug. 25. 1931

PUBLIC LIBRARY
OF THE
CITY OF BOSTON   Dup.

Printed   nited States of America by
J. J. LIT   ES COMPANY, NEW YORK

aaa I/24/45

FOREWORD

WE went to Mexico on the advice of our friend George Biddle, the artist. He said that Indians had no time sense and that we ought to see the murals of Diego Rivera. Having just completed two moderately exhausting if not exhaustive studies of life in the machine age, I was impressed by both observations. I wanted a rest and I wanted to see paintings to which no process of reproduction in black and white can do justice. I went, then, for relaxation, but it is difficult to relax at seven thousand feet above the sea, the traveller's mean altitude. I stayed—and a few months later went again—because so many things excited me—volcanoes, the raw violence of the scenery, pyramids with plumed serpents marching across their bases, great crumbling cathedrals, native handicrafts, the frescoes of Rivera and Orozco, gold mines at the end of burro trails; and above all the way of life in the free villages, where I saw a handicraft economy functioning much as it did in the middle ages, and so a bench mark with which to compare my machines.

We remained altogether about five months. One of us learned to talk some Spanish and the other to understand it, after his fashion. We went wherever we chose in perfect safety—our only fear the wildness of *mestizo* drivers on certain motor roads. Bandits were reported from time to time, but, somewhat to our disappointment, never bothered us. Once we drove to Puebla with some friends, and that night on the way back alone they clipped their

[v]

Auburn clean through a wire cable strung from tree to tree. There may have been highwaymen behind the trees; that was our nearest contact with *bandidos*. We liked the food and drink; we lived hard but well, our greatest discomfort the bitter cold of the nights on the high plateaus after the blazing days.

We kept away from the border states, and so far as possible, from Mexico City. The interest and excitement lay in the smaller towns and villages of central and southern Mexico. Here the Aztec and Maya traditions prevail with least corruption; here a handicraft culture may be best observed. We went to the peninsula of Yucatan and visited the ancient Maya cities of Chichen Itza and Uxmal. We cut across the spinal column of the continent from Vera Cruz on the Gulf to Acapulco on the Pacific; with many side excursions and stops, including Orizaba, Puebla and Cholula, Pachuca and Actopan, Teotihuacan and the great pyramids, Tenayuca, Tepoztlan, Cuernavaca, Cuautla, Ameca-meca, Taxco, Xochicalco, the silver mine at Xitinga, Iguala, the Balsas, and the Nevado del Toluca, fifteen thousand feet above the sea. We saw the great spring fiesta at Tecalpulco, the eve of the patron saint's day at Guadalupe, and the Tiger Dance at Taxco. Our transportation included train, plane, motor car, motor boat, horse, burro, and human feet— no little of the latter.

Turning south from the capital we went down into Oaxaca (pronounced Wah-háh-ca) and explored with Ford and saddle part of that amazing state. Turning west from the capital we went into the lake country of Michoacan to Patzcuaro, Tsintsuntsan, the ancient Tarascan capital, where fishermen still wield their lollypop paddles in dugout canoes, and to Uruapan, whence comes the finest lacquer work. Finally, we flew from the capital

[vi]

to Brownsville, Texas, on perhaps the most admirably operated air transport line in the world.

We were met everywhere with courtesy and kindness, from poorest Indian to highest official. Even Americans and Europeans grow mellower in Mexico. Of the many who gave us invaluable assistance, both material and spiritual, I desire to thank particularly William Spratling, Dr. and Mrs. Eyler N. Simpson, Ambassador Reuben Clark, Rene d'Harnoncourt, Ernest Gruening, Moises Saenz, Dr. Manuel Gamio, Frances Toor, Frank Tannenbaum, Mr. and Mrs. B. C. Hill, Carleton Beals, Emma Reh Stevenson, Dr. and Mrs. Hugh Darby, Frederick Davis, Mary Doherty, Eyvind Verner, Salvador Bonilla, Martin Bazan, Salvador Solchaga, Paul Van der Velde, Franz Blom, Jose Reygadas Vertiz, Porfirio Aguirre. Without their help, this book would have been infinitely the poorer.

CONTENTS

MEXICO

CHAPTER I

MOUNTAIN VILLAGE

IN Tepoztlan one does not say "north" or "south" when giving directions; one says "up" or "down." This holds true for most of Mexico. It is a country set on edge; where straight lines and plane surfaces are virtually homeless. One goes up, in loops and zigzags, and one comes down. Topography is the despair of railroad and mining engineers. Topography, more than any other single factor, has saved Mexico from becoming Hispanicized, westernized, mechanized or Americanized; saved it, by and large, from becoming anything but itself.

We loop up from Mexico City to the 10,000-foot pass which divides the central plateau from the valley to the south, the pass over which Mr. Dwight Morrow was wont to drive his car to his charming country seat in Cuernavaca. We loop down the southern wall to a tiny railroad station and disembark. For an hour we see the smoke of our locomotive descending towards Cuernavaca. We take a burro road which also twists downward but at a different angle, and come finally to a place where beetling cliffs wall us on every side. The burro trail proceeds, finding its way somehow between the precipices. We turn left on a foot-path, soon to be lodged, like ants in the crack of a tree, in a perpendicular crevice which splits the eastern rock wall. Ladders help us from time to time. Climbing at 8,000 feet one's breath comes shorter than it should. We wriggle and crawl, and at last emerge on

[1]

the little *mesa* which crowns one of the lower pinnacles of the cliff. The main mass still towers above us to the north.

We come out upon a tiny field of grass, a thatched hut where somebody has recently slept, a ruined pyramid which seems to grow from the living rock, and one of the fairest views which it has ever been given mortal eyes to see. Before us lie a good many hundred square miles of Mexico; a great section of the land which mothered the Aztecs and taught them to build pyramids, weave cloth of humming birds' feathers, and read the stars with almost Greenwich precision.

In this temple lived a god named Tepoztecatl. He was the presiding deity of *pulque,* a drink made from the milk of the *maguey,* or century plant, to which the Aztecs were much addicted, and which their descendants still drink in enormous quantities. It is about as intoxicating as strong beer. He was also the god of Tepoztlan, the patron and protector of the little town which lies below us, as the stones of Broadway lie under the Woolworth Tower—except that it is 800 feet to Broadway and twice as far to this red-roofed village. Looking down as from an airplane, we see the roofs as red pavements on the ground; the only structure which actually rises is a great white cathedral at the head of the green square which must mark the plaza. Yes, there is the tiny circle of the bandstand.

About the town lie cornfields, with here and there a patch of vivid green which may mean an irrigation ditch and sugar-cane. Near one of these green strips, a puff of smoke rises lazily, and two seconds later, a dull report. Another rises, and another. "A battle!" we cry. "Bandits; a revolution!" "No," says the friend who has brought us here, "rockets. It's probably the beginning of a fiesta. I understand they are always having one in Tepoztlan."

Directly opposite us, perhaps five miles away, the village fields terminate in another sheer rock wall, castellated and carved as though by human hands. Here is a sculptured chasm which looks like a huge fortified gateway, there a turret which would dignify any castle on the Rhine. The whole mass is perhaps four miles long and 2,000 to 3,000 feet high. It blocks the valley to the south, but above it rise, in waves of blue and lavender, higher and fainter mountain ridges. To the west dreams Cuernavaca, twenty miles away, faint white towers in an opal haze, and beyond them the fields and mountains of the state of Morelos. To the east, the village lands dip to a throat between more of the fantastic cliffs. We catch a glimpse of a long rolling plain below, and then, springing half-way to the zenith, the snowy masses of Popocatepetl and Ixtaccihuatl, the Mountain who Smokes and the White Woman. Hand in hand these great mountains stand, the one in his glittering cone like Fujiyama, the other a broader, serrated peak. Where their hands join in a lofty pass, Cortez caught his first glimpse of the city he had come to conquer.

A fitting place for any god to live. With what an infinity of consecrated labour must men have toiled up these precipices to build a house for Tepoztecatl. Small wonder that their descendants in the village, despite the shifting centuries, the ruined walls, the encroaching forest, the graven image overthrown by the good Dominicans, feel his brooding presence, and in solemn pantomime and dance still celebrate his divinity.

We turn to the pyramid. Like all Mexican pyramids it is terraced rather than straight lined. The great pyramid of the sun at Teotihuacan—with a total mass said to be greater than that of Cheops—has four indented terraces before the broad top is reached, 200 feet above the plain. Tepoztecatl's house is tiny in comparison. It is perhaps 100 feet square at the base, with three low terraces; and in its ruined state rises nowhere more than forty feet. An enclosed altar rests on the flat summit, and here we find great stones with curious and still beautiful carvings replete with undeciphered words. There is a date which corresponds, according to the German archeologist Seler, to 1502, about twenty years before the Spanish conquest. The temple covers every foot of the pinnacle upon which it is built (the little field lies somewhat lower to the east), yet carries on the design of nature with flawless rectitude. It seems to have been born with the stony hills, and will remain until they too crumble.

We place a flagon of wine on the altar stone, and eat our lunch in the holy of holies. Tepoztecatl will not care, for Mexican gods are notoriously worldly. It might have been more courteous to have replaced the wine with pulque, but none of us can abide the milky brew with its abominable smell. No more rockets rise from the fields; the village looks infinitely peaceful sleeping in the sun; a green shelf set in a mountain side. "How do you drive in to it?" we ask, perplexed, disclosing the naivete of the newcomer. "You walk," our guide replies, "or go on horseback. Mostly, if you are an Indian, you walk."

"But how does one get supplies?" As an economist, I cannot repress a base interest in the means by which people eat.

"They carry them on their backs, or on the backs of burros; chiefly on their own."

"And no wheel has ever turned on these streets?"

"Never. There are hundreds of villages in Mexico where no wheel has ever turned."

I toss the empty wine bottle to hear it crash in a gulch 1,000 feet below, and ponder this remark. Indeed, questions have been growing ever since we set foot in Mexico, some weeks before. The buried cities with their white pyramids which we saw in the jungles of Yucatan; the spotless Maya Indians with their carved, fine faces; the great calendar stones in the National Museum in Mexico City; Mexico City itself, part Seville, part Atlanta, part indigenous Indian, embroidered with billboards, electric lights, tabloids, Tom Thumb golf courses and taxicabs; the eye-shattering spirals by electric engine from Vera Cruz to the rim of the plateau 7,000 feet above (and how did Cortez ever negotiate the ascent without annihilation?); these great churches, monasteries, palaces in the most dramatic and inaccessible places, decaying with such charm; and these massive temples of an earlier age which bid fair to long outlast them. . . .

In the country that I call home, the Atlantic seaboard of the United States, we have dignified and moderate mountains, not these fantastic crags. We have modern buildings, Victorian buildings, and a few colonial buildings which we call old. There the record stops. Here, on the other hand, are a few modern buildings in the cities; a vast architectural wealth of Spanish colonial structures, invariably in stone, not only in cities but on plain, hilltop, mountain side, already older than anything in my country; and underneath it all, solid and eternal, these pyramids and temples built 1,000, 2,000, unknown thousands of years before.

At home we have Americans, Negroes, and assorted immigrants, more or less naturalized. Here we have Indians, a reasonable number of *mestizos*—half and quarter breeds, most of them living like Indians—and a few whites in the cities. The Indians built the pyramids, the

Indians built the churches and the palaces for their Span-ish masters, the Indians and the mestizos do ninety-five per cent of the nation's work today. This is their coun-try; they have always lived in it; and, as the traveller looks about him, it is evident that they always propose to. In my nation, the old world has wiped out the Indian and made a totally new culture. Here, despite onslaught after onslaught for 400 years, the Indian has withstood the Old World. It has twisted him, changed him, but it has not broken him. Europe and Africa have taken over the land north of the Rio Grande. South of it the indigenous continent of North America sturdily survives. Suddenly my heart warms to these Indians for the fight that they have made. Mailed chargers and gunpowder, money changers and Christian crosses, prime movers and high-pressure sales talk have not prevailed against them.

How would this village have looked today if Cortez had never come; if his stout lieutenant, Bernal Diaz, had not reported "fine women and much loot" in Tepoztlan? What was Aztec civilization really like, and how much of its culture persists? When the forebears of these villagers marched out to meet the Spaniards, how were they dressed, how did they deploy, how did they fight? Would that we might see the meeting from this cliff. How did the Spaniards change the country, and how did it change them? What did Tepoztecatl do to the trinity and to the Saints of Rome? There in Cuernavaca, where water tumbles in every street in the driest season, royal viceroy after viceroy maintained his palace. Cortez lived there for a time, building the first sugar mill in Mexico; after him, 300 years of grandees and dons. What legacy did they leave, and why were they at last so summarily overthrown?

Among other bequests it is certain that they left a

century of revolutions, nor is the end in sight. In a romantic interlude, an emperor and an empress, Maximilian and Carlotta, worshipped in one of these hazy towers across the plain. Why did they come, and why was an emperor murdered who meant so well? This valley knew the peace of Porfirio Diaz, and the march of the grey-clad *rurales,* and anon, of all the valleys in Mexico, it flamed most violently when that peace was ruptured. Through it Zapata stormed, shouting Land for the landless! And Tepoztlan became a town of the dead, its citizens living in caves here in the cliffs, "coming down in the night to rob their own fruit trees." What is the meaning of that wild cry, and what sort of peace was that of Diaz, that ended in such a holocaust?

What do these people want? Only to be left alone? What has a roving American, watching a soaring *zopilote,* to learn from them; aye, what has America itself to learn from them, and what has it to give them? And why, in the face of this timeless pyramid, should we arrogate to ourselves the name "America" at all?

It is pleasant to lie here in the sun, to commune with gods and philosophize at random, but if we would sleep in a bed tonight we must somehow march on our own feet to Cuernavaca, and that is twenty and something miles away. We retreat gingerly down the crevice with its ladders, take the burro trail again, and drop, at say seventy degrees instead of eighty-nine, to the foot of the cliff, a tiresome descent and very hot. We emerge, perspiring and thirsty, in a miniature garden of Eden. A stream of water gushes from the rock face, filling a masonry pool which proves to be the town water supply. Only by the most rigorous concentration on the sublimities of sanitation, can we restrain ourselves from diving in. For a fellow citizen of Colonel Goethals to corrupt an Indian's

[7]

drinking water would hardly do. So we drink, and wash circumspectly in the overflow. Above us are mulberry trees, *ahuehuetes,* and the great green *machetes* of banana trees. It is divinely cool. Here is a little clearing with a stone bench or two, and a globe of stone, five feet in diameter, surmounted by a cross. It marks the spot, according to hearsay, where the image of Tepoztecatl was shattered when the Dominicans hurled it from the pyramid, thereby proving to the benighted natives that their god was not omnipotent. What the good monks did not quite understand was something the Indians were well aware of—and still know for that matter—that a god does not die when his man-made image is broken. It shows deplorable manners, hardly more.

The fragments were borne away to be incorporated into the walls of the church, and the natives were baptized according to a sort of ecclesiastical mass production, in the fountain which flows from the rock. That was in 1575 or thereabouts. As the conquest of the Mexican plateau was well concluded by 1525, it seems to have taken the Church some fifty years to bestow the blessing of baptism upon Tepoztlan. Thousands of villages are more remote (Tepoztlan is only about sixty miles from Mexico City) and presumably took even longer to be baptized. Indeed it is a matter of record that to some the true faith has not yet penetrated, so high on the mountains are they, or so deep in the jungle.

Refreshed, we follow the iron water pipe down to the town, a distance of only a few hundred yards. It has been said, and I think with some truth, that Mexico is slightly in the general, and messy in the particular; that it looks clean and tidy, but does not always survive a closer inspection—say the inquiring nose of a New England housewife. Or to put it another way: in Mexico, the community is always fair, while the individual may be untidy. In the United States, the individual is often clean, while the community—say the average Main Street—is a blistering eyesore. Mexico is easier on the eyes and harder on the nose. Which is worse I do not know.

Tepoztlan, then, is very good to look at. Here are some 700 houses—the total population is 4,000 souls—arranged along little shaded streets, many of them bowered in flowers. Flowers are more important to Mexicans than are motor cars, radios, and bathtubs combined, to Americans. The houses are small and very simple. Their walls are of adobe brick, sometimes whitewashed; their roofs are of red tile or of thatch; they have no chimney, frequently no windows, no glass; very little woodwork. In the front yard stands the circular corncrib made of cornstalks, precisely as it stood in the days of Montezuma; behind there is often a vegetable garden. There may be a shed for horse, cow or burro, while turkeys, chickens and pigs wander introspectively over the foreground. Dogs invariably take their siestas in the street. As why should they not? Wheeled vehicles are unknown.

We are beginning to meet people. They are stolid but polite. To each one of our party they give a *"Buenas tardes"* and receive one in return. Our somewhat bizarre tramping costumes excite them not at all; the quiet children stare gravely, a woman looks curiously from a doorway. A little boy asks "What *pueblo* do you come from?" We answer Mexico City, and he is filled with awe. What Spanish blood there is, is admirably concealed; men, women and children look pure Indian, with beautiful bronzed skins, high cheek-bones, black straight hair, and a haunting touch of the Mongolian. Señor Bernal Diaz reported many beautiful women in Tepoztlan in 1521. In 1930, most women are comely, but few are pretty. In all

[9]

Mexico there are few pretty women judged by northern standards. In the cities one finds a certain number of ravishing *señoritas*, creole or mestizo, but the Indian women are rarely beautiful save in the matchless grace of their carriage. Some of the older women have that carved, serene beauty which one associates with the face of a philosopher. And it is only fair to say that Charlot, the French artist, after seeing the flowing garments of the Indians, compares them with the virgins of the Parthenon, and holds the fitted clothes of western women to be absurd.

The men are mostly in white pyjamas, sandaled and sombreroed. Many carry, almost as an article of dress, a long, murderous-looking machete. This ferocious blade, however, is rarely used on human beings; it is in constant demand for the humbler uses of wood chopping, bush clearing, carpentry, agricultural and household tasks generally. In Tepoztlan, the blade curves at the end. In other parts of Mexico it may be straight. In Acapulco, on the Pacific, it is frequently as long as the boy who carries it. The women are in some such clothes as up-country farm women wore a generation ago in the United States, petticoat, skirt, and blouse—save for the *reboso*, or blue shawl, the vivid colours, the earrings, and save the fact that most of them are barefooted. Everybody looks reasonably well fed, and nobody is hurrying. Unconsciously we moderate our gait. Here are some men and boys making adobe bricks in a back yard. Tall ochre piles of finished brick and tile are drying in the sun. Here a man and a woman are spinning rope of horsehair, employing a curiously whirling wheel. And here through a cottage door we catch a glint of metal, and going nearer find a sewing-machine. Thus the machine age makes its breach in the Aztec wall. The town also boasts,

Diego Rivera, 1931

BOSTON PUBLIC LIBRARY

we are told, a phonograph, and a rickety steam flour mill which the housewife, pounding her own cornmeal, is usually too proud to patronize.

We turn a corner, no children following, and advance upon the *zocalo,* or plaza, a little grass-covered park with flowers and shade trees and a small Victorian bandstand (doubtless erected in the days of the Diaz peace). About it are several two-story houses with wrought-iron balconies, belonging to *los correctos,* the quality of the town. Here too is a little general store which puts me in mind somehow of the general stores I used to see in the White Mountains of New Hampshire. It smells the same; but of twenty bins of dried seeds and berries I recognize only three.

Beside the plaza rises the great church, cream coloured and streaked with grey and rose. It is clear that every iota of surplus wealth—labour, materials, artistic ability —of the entire community has gone into its construction; even as in Aztec days it went into the temple 2,000 feet above. Like many Mexican churches, it has two towers flanking the entrance doors of old carved wood, and a long nave, terminating in a big dome which rises almost as high as the towers. The dome is tiled, and the towers are full of bells. As everywhere, part of the structure is decomposing—but with what charm and grace! To the right are the ruined arches of a long cloister, where Dominicans once told their beads. In front of the doorway stands a stone cross whose arms end in symbolic Aztec serpents. On the screen inside the door is suspended a sign to the effect that a lottery for dead souls is in progress. The names of departed parishioners are listed, each with a lottery number, and a mass is promised the soul of the winner on a given date. But the loser need not despair; a sort of blanket mass will be

[13]

celebrated a few days later for all the remaining luckless candidates together.

Two pigs are asleep in the churchyard among the graves. A hen approaches, with some misgiving, the church door. A pony with a resplendent silver-studded saddle waits patiently in front of the store. Men, women, children, and animals are sunk in a divine lethargy. It is the siesta hour, which even the northerner on schedule must come to respect. We shall drink our beer here in the shade, watch the sleepy zocalo, admire the old rose and ivory of the crumbling church, try to believe that the cliffs from which we have descended are authentic and not a Hollywood backdrop, and presently, when it is a little cooler, ask an Indian boy to guide us over the *pedregal*—a heaving waste of lava rock—to Cuernavaca.

I stayed in Tepoztlan but a short time in the spring of 1930. Some months later there came into my hands a book by Mr. Robert Redfield, an American ethnologist from the University of Chicago, who had remained there nearly a year, studying every phase of the town's life. With this invaluable document, I was able to check my own impressions, and still better, to draw evidence for a more serious study in comparative civilizations. Robert Redfield's *Tepoztlan,* laid upon Robert and Helen Lynd's *Middletown,* provides as exciting a series of parallel columns as any sociologist could wish. One can compare item by item the work habits, play habits, religious habits; the food, houses, clothing, education, social organization of two communities, one north, the other south of the Rio Grande, but a whole world apart. The one is still following the leisurely pattern of the handicraft age, with many cultural traditions from the greatest indigenous civilization which the Western Hemisphere produced; the other is firmly locked into the culture of

[14]

the machine age, deriving most of its traditions and *mores* from the Eastern Hemisphere. The machine has entered Tepoztlan, as we have seen, but it is as yet the shyest of visitors. If it and its products were barred to-morrow, the white pyjamas of the men would have to give way to native cloth woven from a local tree fibre (the old looms still survive). Otherwise the village life would proceed largely unimpaired.

Tepoztlan is far more American than Middletown, when all is said and done, but it is alien to everything we regard as typically "American." Nor does the irony end here. Middletown, you will remember, is the pen name for Muncie, Indiana. If there is an Indian in Muncie, Indiana, he belongs in a museum. Of the 40,000 people in the town, ninety-nine per cent are of European or African stock. It has been estimated, on the other hand, that no more than fifty Spaniards ever settled in Tepoztlan. After 400 years this Hispanic strain does not amount to much. The southern community is ninety-nine per cent Indian. Thus in race as well as in culture, Tepoztlan is almost pure American, while the northern community, in the state called Indiana, is an omelette of English, French, Poles, Italians, Czechs, Russians, Negroes, Germans, Irish, and heaven and the Bureau of the Census know how many other nationalities.

The Lynds estimate that of all the great tonnage of factory goods which Middletown produces, only a tiny fraction—perhaps one per cent—is locally consumed. The rest takes rail and moves to the ends of the earth. The city grows a somewhat larger fraction, but still a negligible one, of its food supply. With its railroads and highways cut, Middletown would very shortly starve to death. It exists only as a cell in a vast interdependent industrial structure. About both towns stand fields of corn—that maize which the forebears of the Aztecs learned to domesticate. Middletown does not eat corn in any quantity, and most of its enveloping crop is used to fatten steers. But the cornfields of Tepoztlan take on a sacramental dignity. For centuries these *milpas* have been cultivated from father to son, and their sowing and harvesting are the outstanding ceremonies of the year. It is said that no Mexican revolution can survive the harvest season. The army deserts in a unit to tend its ancestral milpas. From this corn, from the squashes which grow between the furrows, the beans clambering on the cornstalks, and the wild fruits in the hills, Tepoztlan can feed itself if it must. Probably nine tenths of its food comes from within its own boundaries. It trades with the surrounding villages, the storekeeper buys cotton cloth and a few notions from Mexico City, but by and large, in dramatic contrast with Middletown, it is not a cog in the wheel, but an economically independent community. This costs something to be sure in terms of the efficiency of specialization, but it also gives something, as we shall see.

Indeed there is no end to the dramatic contrast. The typical community in the United States is urban and industrialized; the typical community in Mexico is rural and lives from the soil and the forests. The gospel of Middletown is work, and the gospel of Tepoztlan is play —one day in three, the year around, the southern community is celebrating a major or minor fiesta. Yet for all their hard work, a fraction of the men of Middletown is constantly unemployed and bowed down with fear and worry. Unemployment is unheard of in Tepoztlan, and fear stalks only when earthquakes rumble, or a Zapata comes riding over the mountains, federal troops at his heels.

Middletown is essentially practical, Tepoztlan essentially mystical in mental processes. Yet in coming to terms with one's environment, Tepoztlan has exhibited, I think, the superior common sense. Middletown has its due quota of neurotic and mentally unbalanced individuals. In Tepoztlan a Freudian complex is unthinkable. The men of the south are craftsmen—many students call them artists—they can put their hands to almost anything, fashion it, repair it, recreate it. Their popular arts, their weaving, pottery, glass work, basketry, are as authentic and delightful as any the modern or the ancient world has seen. (Tepoztlan has not a craft specialty, as have many other villages, but every boy is taught to work with stone, wood, metal, clay and thatch.)

I fear I am tipping the scales. In this dreamy haze, amid snow-capped volcanoes, it is all too easy to become sentimental. Let us endeavour to right the balance. There is not a bathtub in Tepoztlan, or a telephone or a radio (to the best of my knowledge), or a movie palace (but the village band boasts one saxophone), or a pair of silk stockings, or a refrigerator, or an electric light, or a spring bed, or a newspaper, or an overstuffed davenport, or a cocktail shaker, or a decent cup of coffee, or a baseball team, or a dance hall (they dance in the church), or running water from a tap, or a straight eight. Children do not sit on trees and establish records; nobody sends copy to confession magazines; to three districts in the town the postman never delivered a letter in the months of Mr. Redfield's residence. There are only two small schools, and the majority of the population is illiterate. All speak two languages, however, their own Aztec and Spanish.

There are thirteen native herb specialists and ten midwives, but not a doctor in the town. A lawyer would have nothing to do. The people look healthy, but according to Dr. Ernest Gruening, commenting on Mexico generally, the question of public health has been seriously neglected. Particularly appalling is infant mortality. I suspect—Mr. Redfield does not help us here—that despite its neurotics and its industrial and automobile accidents, Middletown has a better health record than Tepoztlan. Certainly in the matter of health and sanitation the pointer swings sharply to the north, and here we touch upon one of the harshest features of Mexican village life. The weak die early. Only the strong survive.

There are other harsh features, as we shall see in due time. Nowhere in Europe, not even in Russia, have I seen a community so alien to the way of life in my own country. Yet we are both members of the same continent, a muddy river between us. It is the purpose of the following chapters to generate a modicum of understanding between—shall we say?—old family Americans and their parvenu cousins. Ordinarily I am proud of the nine generations of New England behind me, but I feel like the rawest immigrant compared to the little brown boy up there in the belfry, who, with all the gusto in the world, is tipping one of the great tower bells in full somersault to announce the hour of vespers.

CHAPTER II

EARLY AMERICANS

THE SETTING

TEPOZTLAN is a green shelf set in a mountain side. Frank Tannenbaum has characterized all Mexico as one great mountain, rising from the sea to a final cone of 18,000 feet, with the best conditions for man in valleys and pockets a little less than half-way up. Once Mexico, when it first became independent, was larger than any country in the world save Russia, China, and Brazil. North of its present boundaries it extended from the Red River in Arkansas to the Pacific and up to the Canadian border. But some gentlemen in Texas, and other ladies and gentlemen in covered wagons, decided that the Rio Grande would make an admirable southern line for the United States. Indians were relatively scarce in that great district and Spaniards even scarcer, so they had it their own way.

The area of Mexico today is still a sizable parcel of land. The total runs to 767,000 square miles. On it one can place comfortably Germany, France, Great Britain, Spain, Portugal, and, for good measure, Holland and Belgium. It is shaped—save for the thumb of Yucatan and the tail of Lower California—like a cornucopia, and the figure is not without significance. I select at random four quotations from as many authorities, beginning with Cecil Rhodes. Later we shall seek the evidence for their enthusiasm:

Mexico is the treasure house of the world.

Most enormous and diversified wealth ever bestowed upon a single people in a single area.

Most highly mineralized region on the globe.

A greater variety of soil, surface and vegetation than any equal extent of contiguous territory in the world.

The horn of plenty is 1,900 miles long, 1,833 miles broad at the rim along the Rio Grande, tapering to 134 miles at the Isthmus of Tehuantepec. A wedge-shaped plateau, with plenty of mountains on its surface, starts south of Mexico City and runs north to the border, decreasing in average height and increasing in width as it runs. It accounts for one third the area, and most of the population—in ancient times as well as today. The majority of Mexicans live well inside their country around 6,000 feet above the sea. Born in this air, they become used to it. But let the newly arrived traveller try to run up a flight of steps, as I did the first night in a Mexico City hotel. The results are as painful as they are astonishing. The whole character of the blood stream must change before the oxygen shortage can be equalized.

Along the coast of either sea lies a low plain, some forty to seventy miles broad, before the national spinal column begins to rise. These regions are called the *tierra caliente,* hot country; and steamy they are, jungle bound, and often deplorably unhealthy. Yucatan is low and hot, but like Florida, with winds from both sides of the peninsula, it is not miasmal. In the tumbled valleys of the plateau, from 3,000 to 6,500 feet, lies the *tierra templada,* temperate land; and higher on the great mountain's sides, the *tierra fria,* cold country. Indian villages will be found almost up to the tree line at 10,000 feet or more.

From November to May the cloudless sun is shining

nearly every day over all these three kingdoms. This is the dry season, and a paradise for sun bathers. From May through October the rains come down, often in torrential bursts, but normally only in the afternoon. In Mexico City it is said that one can set one's watch by the afternoon shower. The mornings are usually sunny, and the whole world is bright and green. If you desire to study temperatures, take a thermometer with a wide scale. Lumholtz, on Christmas Day in the Sierra Madre, noted 150° Fahrenheit in the sun at noon, and 23° Fahrenheit at night!

There are four peaks 15,000 feet or more in height. Orizaba rises to 18,225. On a clear day its snowy cone can be seen as one sails in to Vera Cruz, and for many years it was thought the highest mountain in North America. Popocatepetl comes next, at 17,794 feet. One sees it from Puebla, Cuernavaca, and all parts of the valley of Mexico, as well as from Tepoztlan. It is known affectionately as Popo. Sometimes smoke climbs lazily from its crater—and sometimes it belches. There have been ten major eruptions since 1519. The Aztecs held it to be "the abode of departed spirits of wicked rulers, whose fiery agonies in their prison house caused the fearful bellowings and convulsions." One of Cortez' captains climbed it at the time of the first invasion, though the natives declared that no man could climb the Mountain who Smokes and live. It was climbed again in 1521 and sulphur collected for gunpowder. The next ascent was three full centuries later, in 1827, when Mexico had shaken off the hand of Spain. These figures are not without significance. The Spaniards who followed Cortez and his immortal 600 were of a less hardy breed.

Beside the graceful cone of Popo is Ixtaccihuatl, the White Woman. She lies on her back, with head, breast

and feet silhouetted against the violet blue sky. To climb
her cliffs and glaciers, though they are slightly lower, is
a harder task than plodding up the snowy planes of Popo.
The Nevado de Toluca touches 15,000 feet. Just up from
sea level, I struggled to within 300 feet of the top—
a spiny little pinnacle—before I gave up from oxygen
shortage. Its great crater, with frozen lakes and multicoloured walls, is one of the most striking and awesome
spots imaginable.

Mexico is a violent country, more remote and strange
than any I have ever visited. Violent are the contrasts,
the colour, violent the landscape and storms, and violent
the pressure on the membrane of the ear as one ascends
or drops 2,000 feet an hour—a normal travelling ratio.
Only the people and the long-suffering burros are gentle.

I say people advisedly. Politicians lead a hazardous
existence, but they are a race apart, as we shall see. At
first glance, the geography all but blots out the people
with its raw physical impact. But in due time these sombreroed men, these blue-shawled women, these grave,
quiet children advance by resistless pressure into the
foreground, more to be wondered at than Popocatepetl
itself.

Not only were the Spaniards loath to climb mountains,
but they had the woods hewn down. In Aztec days, great
forests of larch, oak, cypress and fir covered large areas
of the plateau. This meant more water and less heat, dust
and barrenness than now obtain. The valley of Mexico
City was called Anahuac, "near the water," and two
great lakes filled it. The capital of the Aztecs was built
like Venice. Now there is but one shallow and receding
sea.

Over this plateau land, all over Yucatan and Guatemala, at many points in the tierra caliente, we find today

not only a wealth of minerals and natural resources, but an incredible wealth of ruins predating the Spanish conquest, some of an antiquity almost Egyptian. In Yucatan alone, more than 100 city sites have been discovered, with perhaps an equal number still hidden in the jungle. In all Mexico, some 4,000 archeological ruins are known, a greater number than in the whole Greek world.

I stood on the top of a mountain in Guerrero, while Mr. William Spratling pointed out to me a remote castellated ridge, on the crest of which he had located seven pyramids, unknown to archeologists. Any traveller exploring the back country has a reasonably good chance of stumbling on a lost city or a buried pyramid. One early gets the habit of watching for un-Baedekered ruins from train, car or saddle, and perhaps one tenth of the likely mounds are authentic. Argument is frequent and heated as to whether the geometric formation on yonder mountain crest was made by God or man.

ANCIENT MAN

Down this wedge-shaped plateau, under the cypress and the larch trees, in the shadow of towering volcanoes, once came men, uncounted thousands of years ago. Some say they came across the islands of the Bering Sea from Asia. Some say they came over the Pacific in canoes from Polynesia. Some say they came from Europe via Greenland. Others are confident that they were the product of evolution in the Western Hemisphere, and point to human bones mingled with those of Paleozoic animals which flourished perhaps 500,000 years ago. The former theory has the widest acceptance, but I incline to the more catholic view. Why not admit *homo sapiens* into the Americas from all of these routes?

[23]

If we adopt this theory, we conjecture a very primitive indigenous race living in both North and South America. (Ancient bones have been found in the upper reaches of the Amazon.) Invaders come in Stone Age times from both Asia and Europe (via Greenland) and mingle with them—probably a series of invasions. From time to time sea-going canoes are wrecked, or land, on the western coast of South America, the point of departure being some island in the South Seas. From all these sources, acting over thousands upon thousands of years, was filled the biological pot which Leif Ericsson and, later, Columbus were to find. That many Indians have an Asiatic look about them is not to be gainsaid.

I am inclined to cast my vote, furthermore, with those who, like Dr. Franz Blom, hold that American culture in its more advanced phases was a purely American phenomenon. It took nothing from Egypt, nothing from China, nothing from Angkor. Granting the invasions, they came before Old World civilizations had developed, or from races out of contact with them. Peru, Mexico and the rest hammered out their own destiny from their own environment. Diffusion took place within the Americas, but hardly from the old world, unless we go back to stone hatchets and wooden dugouts. Any bright morning, however, this patriotic theory may be overturned. A stone Asiatic elephant that is obviously and conclusively not a macaw or tapir may be found on a newly excavated temple, thus proving beyond peradventure cultural diffusion from Asia. Until that definitive discovery is made, I shall continue to ascribe Mexico to Mexicans and not to Egyptians, Chinamen or Polynesians.

Men came into the valleys of Mexico, and there for thousands of years they lived, as wild tribes live, a hunting, nomadic, communistic life. They moved "following their watering places, where salt could be found." Then some native Burbank discovered maize. A "civilization," meaning, as the word connotes, a condition of affairs where men live in cities, is impossible without a stable food supply which can be counted on year after year. Thus civilization is based not only on men but on plants, and to a lesser degree on domesticated animals. If we knew, says J. B. S. Haldane, the history of wheat, or of the dog, we should know a great deal more about the origin of civilization than we do now. Generally speaking, three factors are necessary to the rise of city dwelling: (1) a cultivated plant giving high yields of storable food, (2) a plant or animal source of fibres for cloth making, (3) an animal to carry loads and to pull carts and ploughs.

With the discovery or introduction of maize in Mexico, the most essential factor in the economic groundwork of civilization was established. The fibres of the maguey on the plateau and the *henequen* cactus in Yucatan provided the second requisite. The third was never developed. The Peruvians had llamas, but the Mexicans had only their own sturdy backs. In a mountainous country, an animal to draw the plough is not so essential as on a level plain beside a river, but it may be even more essential to carry burdens over rocky roads. Certainly the Mexicans were seriously hampered by the lack of a beast of burden. Even now, on market day, the motor roads near Mexico City have twice as many loaded pedestrians as pack animals, and twice as many pack animals as vehicles. The man often carries a hundred pounds. The woman, in addition to her inevitable baby, may be toting a very substantial load. It is not uncommon, even in Mexico City, to see an Indian trotting along under an enormous trunk.

[25]

THE GREAT CIVILIZATIONS

Over the wedge-shaped plateau, particularly in the southern tip, cornfields, milpas, began to sprout. The ripe ears were gathered and stored in some such vase-like corncribs as we still see in Tepoztlan. Men no longer needed to give all their time to the search for food. Specialization of tasks became possible; leisure, art, thought became possible. Scholars discuss three major and a number of minor branches of this maize-engendered culture in Mexico. There is a good deal of acrimonious dispute as to which came first, the influence of each on the others, and whether the trinity was really one or really two. In brief, the story of Mexican civilization, like the story of the original population of the Americas, is still in the stage of conflicting theories, and will require many patient years of searching to unravel. Happily a number of able scientists are on the ground, and perhaps in the next decade they will come by agreement, armistice, or war of elimination to an historical chronology with the main interrelations made plain.

The three chief branches now discussed are the cultures of the Mayas, the Toltecs, and the Aztecs. The first may have been the most ancient of the three, and it may not. Maudslay says yes; other scholars say no. Certainly some highly developed people was on the Mexican plateau more than 2,000 years ago. It gave way to invaders from the north, commonly referred to as Toltecs, who took over the culture they found and came in contact with the Mayas, now indisputably to the south in Guatemala. In due time down from the north swept invaders again; and these hill billies, we know, were the Aztecs, the ultimate exponents of maize civilization before the arrival of Cortez.

Certain facts seem reasonably well established; certain dates have even been worked out. On August 6, in the year 613 B.C., the time record of the Mayas was begun. This is their year zero; it is exact and definite, founded, as Spinden has shown, on calculations from lunar and solar eclipses. In order to have started accurate astronomical time on that date, he and Blom believe—and we may take their word for it—that the Mayas began studying the stars no later than 2000 B.C. It would take as long as that to work out a calendar. Probably this research went on in Guatemala, but the late Dr. A. P. Maudslay thought that it was on the plateau, and that the Mayas built the great pyramids at Teotihuacan. Manuel Gamio, the archeologist most familiar with the scene, believes that 500 B.C. was the high point of the culture which built these pyramids, but others put it 1,000 years later. These are the two pyramids which loom like hills as one comes up from Vera Cruz. At first it is incredible that such masses are man-made.

About the time that Christ was born, the first Maya empire was founded in Guatemala, and all scholars agree that its great period was between 450 and 600 A.D. The architecture, sculpture and painting of the Central American ruins are the most sophisticated, balanced and beautiful yet found. The dates provide food for a philosophical aside. While America was at its zenith, Europe was floundering in the darkest era of the Dark Ages. Rome had been sacked and Charlemagne was yet to come. Angkor in Indo-China was yet to come. Is it unreasonable to suppose that, during these 150 years, the Mayas were the most civilized people on the planet?

Early in the seventh century the Mayas migrated from Guatemala to Yucatan, to build the cities of Chichen Itza, Uxmal and scores of others. The migration was due to war or to maize, perhaps to both. The agricultural methods used then (and now) depleted the soil with considerable rapidity. When the corn area around a given city was exhausted, there was nothing for it but to emigrate and build a new city upon virgin land. Stone was more readily worked than seed and soil. We know, positively that Chichen was twice deserted and twice reoccupied, with the jungle growing lush and wild for some 200 years between occupations.

Around 800 A.D. the Toltecs were on the Mexican plateau, with a capital at Tula—provided you believe in the Toltecs at all. Certainly some advanced people, probably from the north, was living in this region. In 1064 Tula was destroyed. In 1191 the Mayas in Yucatan, now going into a second decline, were conquered, according to Spinden, by a great prince from the plateau named Quetzalcoatl. We shall hear more of him—in fact we shall hear of him officiating as Santa Claus at Mexico City's official Christmas party in 1930.

In 1091 the year zero in the Aztec calendar was established, and in 1325 Tenochtitlan, or Mexico City, was founded. The latter is another date on which all scholars agree. It defines the time of the Aztec descent from the north. The story that the city was built where an eagle was sighted with a snake in its grip—the predicted ghostly combination—is not so well authenticated, but it is a romantic legend. From then on to the Spanish conquest, a period of some 200 years, we have a reasonably clear historical record, with the names and dates of the Aztec princes, ending with Montezuma and Cuauhtemoc.

The unravelling of the archeological net will be an absorbing matter, which all Americans should follow with patriotic pride. As I read the evidence already gath-

BOSTON PUBLIC LIBRARY

Diego Rivera 1931

ered, however, it becomes reasonably apparent that from a large and general point of view there was only one basic culture in Mexico and Central America, in which the Mayas, the Toltecs, the Aztecs, the Tarascans, the Zapotecs and various other nations shared, and took their turn at dominance. Through all these peoples ran a fundamental pattern, with maize, maguey, sun and rain worship at the bottom of it. Today as one goes about Mexico this basic unity—these milpas, this philosophy of life—still persists, despite a thousand colourful differences from village to village, and from state to state.

We might make a rough comparison with the world of the Greeks. The Mayas we might brand as the Athenians, the Aztecs as Macedonians, the Toltecs as Spartans. The point is that they were included in a culture which was greater than any of its parts. Unlike the Greeks, however, the early Americans had no common language. At the time of the conquest there were more than 150 dialects in Mexico. Today fifty-two Indian idioms are still spoken. The Mayas achieved the peak of the whole culture, higher even than that of Peru, in Central America in 600 A.D., 900 years before the Spaniards came. The Aztecs did not appear upon the scene until after 1000 A.D.; they were the dominant people when Cortez landed. These seem to be the outstanding historical facts.

Besides the little pyramid at Tepoztlan, I have seen the ruins at Uxmal and Chichen Itza in Yucatan, at Lake Patzcuaro in Michoacan, at Teotihuacan, Tenayuca, Xochicalco, Cuernavaca, all near Mexico City, and at Mitla and Monte Alban in Oaxaca. Teotihuacan is easily the most stupendous, but Chichen Itza most stirs the intellect and the emotions. The builders of Teotihuacan would have stared dumbly, vastly impressed, at

the Empire State building in New York. The architects
of Chichen Itza would have been moved, one suspects, to
questions and a gathering criticism. "What," they might
ask, "is the function of this structure? And why is it
spaced so that it cannot be seen?" The voluble answers
would somehow fail to convince. Their own city lies in
silent ruins, with no one to explain it; every year many
architects of the present go there to study its proportions
and its incomparable decoration.

CHICHEN ITZA

We take a little Yucatecan train on a narrow-gauge
track, with a wood-burning engine sporting a Civil War
smokestack like an inverted umbrella. Four hours and
140 kilometers from Merida, the city of windmills, east
across the low, thorny, flower-draped jungle, brings us to
Dzitas, a charming Maya village of oval huts, whitewashed and palm-roofed, set in immaculately clean compounds. From here a Ford truck bumps us twelve miles
deeper into the bush, until suddenly the cream- and
orange-streaked pyramid of Chichen looms over the
trees.

We enter a great cleared meadow. Immediately in
front is the seven-terraced pyramid, with a flight of
ninety-one steps running up each of the four sides to the
square sculptured temple which crowns the top. The
Greeks, you remember, bulged their columns at the
centre to obviate the optical illusion of concavity which
straight lines give. The Mayas, with the same end in
view, made the width of the stairway greater at the top
than at the bottom by some two feet, thus giving the eye
the illusion of parallel lines from base to temple. Four
flights of ninety-one steps, furthermore, total 364, which

with the platform at the top give 365, to fit the calendar year. The orientation is to the points of the compass.

To our left is the ball court. The Mayas played a game like basketball in a walled enclosure some 300 feet long. Instead of a horizontal basket, they used a vertical one, to receive the huge rubber ball, struck with the hip. One massive carved stone ring is still in place, the hole nearly two feet across. On the walls at either end are little pavilions, one a judges' stand, the other presumably for the more exalted of the fans. The emperor himself watched the games from a special temple, placed with just the right asymmetry toward the nearer corner, one of the most beautiful buildings in the world. A frieze of marching tigers in stone bas-relief surmounts the top. The emperor's seat is between two huge dragons' heads (the plumed serpent again), and in the vaulted back are carved medallions in ruddy brown.

Between pyramid and ball court, an opening through the jungle leads to the Sacred Well. Once it was a paved road, with little temples on either side. A third of a mile brings one to the great round *cenote,* and the seventy-foot drop down perpendicular fern-draped walls to the deep green water. Here a virgin launched herself into the air when a serious drought threatened, a living sacrifice to the god of rain. Here the pious threw in their gold and jewels. In recent years divers in helmets have descended and reclaimed some of the treasure. (But sportsmen are forbidden to dive for pleasure since Richard Halliburton profaned the spot before the watchful lens of his photographer.)

A little off the Sacred Way is the Temple of the Warriors, white and shining in its restoration by the Carnegie scientists, and the Hall of the Thousand Columns. The temple walls are richly carved, and through an opening near the top one may descend into a locked vault filled with paintings in relief and fresco. Mutilated as they are, they give a hint of the glorious colour which once covered all the temples of Chichen. The Thousand Columns reduce to not quite 300 according to my count, but it is supposed that they extended around a vast quadrangle. The varieties of column—round, square, carved, plastered, painted—show where successive generations rebuilt and improved. They give us a key to the abandonments and reoccupations of the site.

On our right—we have returned to the entrance of the broad meadow—is the low white house of the Mexican Government excavation station, and the white oval huts of a modern Maya village. Here nobody speaks English and only one native, Spanish. The Carnegie Foundation has its quarters down a jungle road near the earliest ruins—"old Chichen," as distinguished from the innovations of the year 1000.

Two sides of the main pyramid have been reclaimed, together with the temple at the top. The other two sides, both terraces and steps, are a rocky slide. We start up the ninety-one steps on the west. The going is goatlike but negotiable. Reaching the summit we turn around, and all sense of negotiability vanishes. We have come up at an angle of sixty degrees. The merest stumble in descending would plunge the climber to the plain below. Some visitors go down backwards, some zigzag gingerly to right and to left. Only the Indians walk straight down, even as their forebears, in rich robes and tall feather headdresses, descended in splendid procession. The steps at Uxmal are even dizzier. A chain has been laid along them, and once at the top, I should have hesitated a long time before descending without its aid. Obviously these pyramids were built by mountain people. No indigenous plainsman would rear such soaring angles. Yet here on this flat peninsula of Yucatan are these severely mathematical tests for rock-climbers. Failing all other evidence, one would naturally conclude that their builders had come down from the cliffs and precipices of Mexico or Guatemala.

From the top of the pyramid the grey-green jungle stretches outward like a sea. On the horizon to the west, one tiny notch is identified as probably the pyramid of another buried city. In the foreground, south and east, are other buildings—the domed House of the Astronomers, with its tortuous spiral stairs; the High Priest's House, the Nunnery, the Temple of the Dark Writing— as if they were not all temples of dark writing, their checkered glyphs undeciphered. From the House of the High Priest to the Nuns' House runs a stone passageway underground. This is not so indelicate as it sounds, even when you add that the tunnel was lined with skeletons. Probably no nuns lived there. Poets of an indifferent genius have given most of these buildings their names, and I, for one, resent them. They should be named in the Maya tradition, not in the Victorian.

Old Chichen, beyond the sometime henequen *hacienda* where the Carnegie diggers make their headquarters, is more massive, more ruined, and somewhat more phallic than the later buildings. The whole area of the ruins at Chichen comprehends several square miles. Dozens of jungle-covered mounds conceal temples as yet unexcavated. And these are only the public buildings, for the dwelling houses of common folk have disappeared. Perhaps 100,000 people once called this city home.

I find it difficult to resurrect the colour and splendour of Chichen in its prime. The imagination balks or sinks into a muzzy sentimentality, spurious and stale. What

[35]

registers most freshly is the picture suggested by the modern Indian excavators, wielding their bush-knives and setting stones in the restoration of the main pyramid. The brown skins, the white aprons, the bare feet, the primitive engineering, the manual precision—in a flash I see other Indians, similarly dressed, similarly deft, working here 1,200 years ago. The pomp and panoply fade before the incredible labour of clearing this writhing jungle, planting corn for untold thousands, and step by step, stone by stone, with lever, roller and chisel, quarrying the embedded limestone, carving whole acres of its surface, rearing these white terraces and towers to a matchless symmetry and grace.

The builders of Chichen come into focus, brown men in apron skirts, directed by master craftsmen with lined, wise faces. The rulers in their rainbow carnivals I cannot see.

CHAPTER III

MAIZE CIVILIZATION

On the slender economic foundation of maize and the cactus plant, the early Mexicans and their neighbours reared the extraordinary superstructure of their engineering, their astronomy, their religions and their architecture. No other race that I can call to mind allowed so wide a disparity between the simple bread with which they fed their bodies and the arts by which they nourished their souls. Perhaps there is some inherent inverse ratio in human psychology. Even today, Mexican Indians have only a rudimentary development of the so-called instinct of acquisition, and a very sophisticated development of artistic appreciation as reflected in their craftsmanship. *"Qué bonito,"* "how beautiful," is the sunset, the cathedral tower, the pot of flowers, the lacquer gourd. It is a word on everybody's tongue. In ancient times, according to Mary Austin, when a man discovered a deposit of gold or topaz he invited the neighbours to come and help themselves. The same stream flows clear in the "damned wantlessness" of the Indian, the despair of high-pressure salesmanship.

The maize culture on which this civilization grew included not only the tribes of Mexico, Guatemala and Yucatan, but the Cocles in Panama, the Manabis and Chitchas of Ecuador and Colombia, the pre-Incas and Incas of Peru. The span of time comprehended was close to 5,000 years. All these peoples had certain common traits. They were primarily agricultural, growing, besides maize, beans, squashes, melons, nuts, cacao and many fruits. Although they were smaller men than ourselves, all were remarkable for their work in stone. In Peru are found the largest cut stones ever hewn by human beings, up to 200 tons in size.

All were great engineers, building roads, bridges, aqueducts, irrigation works, as well as huge pyramids, temples and forts. Many of the latter were as sturdy and well designed as European fortresses at the time of the conquest. All used bows, blowguns, darts, swords and the throwing stick. All were good astronomers and mathematicians. All employed gold, silver and copper and worked them exquisitely. From South America come gold beads fabricated so finely that only a microscope can discover the design. (Perhaps the ancients used microscopes of crystal.) All were skilled woodworkers. In Chichen one sees great lintels of *zapote* wood, beautifully carved, and solid after 1,000 years of rain and ruin.

All wove textiles of fibre or wool or hair, some of them so fine that no modern machine loom can duplicate them. All were good herbalists, learned in primitive medicine. I asked the guide at Chichen if there were snakes about.

"Plenty," he replied, "many of them poisonous."

"What do you do when you are bitten?"

"The Carnegie people have serum. But the Indians have their own antidote which they make from an herb in the forest."

"And they never die?"

"No, they never die. The art has come down to them through the centuries."

All these civilizations domesticated fowls—turkeys,

ducks, geese and pheasants. All show marked similarity in their household utensils. All were sun worshippers, and all show the influence of the plumed serpent. All maintained an elaborate priesthood, and many practised the rite of human sacrifice, though in widely varying degree. Finally, none valued precious metals as we do. Silver, gold and platinum were esteemed mainly for their ductility and ornamental qualities. The greed of the Spaniards was incomprehensible to the people of these civilizations.

Let us look a little more specifically at the achievements of the Mexican branch. A classified list is perhaps in order.

ENGINEERING

Mexico City was supplied by a double aqueduct of stone, the massive structure running to Chapultepec. Another aqueduct at Texcoco, a sister city, connected three reservoirs on two levels and was several miles long. Extensive irrigation works were found at Cholula (where a Spanish church now rests on top of an Aztec pyramid), and of this city Cortez reported that "not a palm's breadth was left uncultivated." Irrigation works were extensive throughout the plateau. Three magnificent stone causeways, linked by bridges and drawbridges, led to Mexico City over its encircling lakes. Each was broad enough for twelve of Cortez' horses to march abreast. Mining was an advanced art among the Aztecs and they were capable of driving tunnels through mountain rock. The durability of the cement made by the Mayas has never been equalled.

The city fathers of Tlaxcala—an independent nation northeast of Popocatepetl—decided to add to the town's defences by closing a gap in the surrounding mountains.

They proceeded to build a wall of uncemented stone twenty feet thick, nine feet high and six miles long. A certain calendar stone weighing fifty tons was dragged from quarry to destination, a distance of twenty miles, over hills and across swamps. It broke through a bridge, was rescued, and continued on its way. With no tractors, donkey engines, oxen or horses, this is no inconsiderable feat of transport. Rollers and ropes were the only mechanisms involved. For purposes of flood control, a dam ten miles long, perforated with sluice gates, was built by Montezuma I.

From Chichen a paved road starts at the Astronomers' House and runs to the sea, 100 miles and more. In fact Yucatan was netted with roads, of "larger and better construction than the famous Roman roads of Europe." The Aztec hegemony maintained an elaborate system of rapid communication. Relays of messengers ran at top speed from posthouse to posthouse. The colour of their dress indicated to the public the kind of news they carried. When Cortez landed they had the news in Mexico City—250 miles away—within a few hours.

I have said that this far-flung maize culture was peculiarly distinguished by its stonework. Cut stones in vast numbers and often of huge size are found from the Rio Grande to Chile. Some of them are of the very hardest and least malleable varieties of rock. Yet on millions of them are inscribed deep and often exquisite carvings. How were the stones cut and the bas-reliefs made? Copper is too soft to use as a tool; gold and silver are too soft. No iron implements have been found. It has been concluded accordingly that the work was done with stone tools, many samples of which remain. But Dr. Verrill tells us a puzzling story in this connection. Like any other sensible man, he wondered how it was possible to cut

Diego Rivera 1931

BOSTON
PUBLIC
LIBRARY

the blocks, in the quantities found, with stone implements only. He decided to test the matter. In his excavation work in Panama, he drew a simple scroll design upon a piece of fairly soft stone found in the ruins and put four competent Indian masons to work with the old stone tools. At the end of a week they had broken all the implements and hardly scratched the surface! How to circumvent the implications of this laboratory test I do not know. Verrill believes that steel tools must have been employed—tools now rusted beyond discovery and identification. Metallurgists bear him out. If not steel, what was it that cut these stones? Volcanic glass and abrasives? This is one of the mysteries of maize culture. There are many more.

ARCHITECTURE

If a civilization is measured by its architecture, as some philosophers hold, that of Mexico ranks very high. I happened to come upon a distinguished New York architect as he looked for the first time at the frieze of serpents' heads on one of the temples of Teotihuacan. He was practically incoherent. "It's the finest thing I have ever seen anywhere; great God, it's the finest thing in the world." . . . This was higher praise than I could give it, but I am not an architect with an eye to technical subtleties. The pyramid of the sun, which stands close by, is approximately 750 feet square and 216 feet high, and forms part of the sacred city which in the great days of Teotihuacan was four miles long, two miles broad, and practically one solid block of architectural monuments. The court of the citadel is 160,000 square meters in area, and oriented to the compass. As I looked at its lines of masonry, clean and straight as on a drawing board, I could not believe, and I do not yet believe, that they could have been achieved without instruments of precision.

In the city of Mexico were 60,000 houses; in Cholula, 40,000. The great temple of Mexico had 600 altars in one enclosure; and a courtyard pavement so polished that the horses of Cortez could hardly stand thereon. The mile-long walls were covered with sculptured, braided serpents. Upon the court was built a pyramid 300 feet square and 300 feet high, by the conquistadors' measurements, rising in six terraces with 340 steps—thrice as lofty as the pyramid at Chichen Itza. Upon its summit rose two towers, each fifty-six feet high, and between them a great statue of the war god. Here sacred fires tended by virgins were kept perpetually burning.

The houses of the city were made of red *tezontle* (a soft lava rock), quadrangular in shape, with a central court and a porticoed walk. Mexico had nothing to learn from Spain in this sound design for sunny countries. The finest of the old colonial palaces in Mexico City are made of the same red stone. Poorer people lived in smaller houses of stone and unbaked brick. The palace of the administration included an armory, a granary, aviaries and a zoo. The palace at Texcoco measured 978 by 1,234 yards, counting the walled court. It contained 300 royal apartments, built of porphyry, alabaster and stucco, and finished inside with rare woods.

Maya architecture in Yucatan and Guatemala was not so grandiose as Aztec, nor so monolithic in effect as Teotihuacan, but it was more delicate and beautiful. It ran to elaborate sculpture in stucco, and included careful town-planning with an artificial acropolis as the foundation of the main temples and palaces. A kind of arch and vault—narrow, with capstone—were employed. The material was limestone rather than lava rock, plastered with a stucco of burned lime and oyster shells, painted in brilliant colours. Traces of red, blue and green are still to be seen. The early sculpture showed some realism, but this gave way later to the grotesque. In design it is held superior to Egyptian or Assyrian in foreshortening and composition. Hieroglyphics were frequently used with striking effect, indeed Spinden believes that here the Mayas made their supreme decorative contribution. "The Mayan temple of Palenque in Chiapas"—to quote Verrill —"is perhaps the finest example of prehistoric architecture in the entire world."

Finally, to entangle all our historical sequences, the largest building (not pyramid) in Mexico, 800 by 250 feet, with ruined walls still fifty feet high, is found in none of the districts we have been concerned with, but at Casas Grandes, away north in Chihuahua, a border state. It is thought to be pre-Teotihuacan, and so perhaps 3,000 years old.

ASTRONOMY AND SCIENCE

In astronomy the American mind reached its climax, and the Mayas were its high priests. Starting, as we have seen, with observations of the heavens some 4,000 years ago, the Maya calendar was developed to a point where it was possible to distinguish without duplication any given day in 370,000 years! This was far in advance of European astronomy; more accurate than anything so-called western civilization achieved until very recent times. Time was measured in *katuns,* twenty-year cycles, and records were kept by the priests, perhaps on chains of beads or shells. Blom recently found priests in Guatemala counting in secret the ancient calendar with red seeds.

Elsewhere I have held with some show of reason that modern science, and its offspring the machine age, would never have come to birth without the cipher, that symbol of nothingness which the Moors brought to Europe about 1000 A.D., and which they got from the Hindus. If you will try to divide 3,678 by 219 in Roman numerals you will immediately see the point. The Hindus originated this invaluable mathematical abstraction, without which no skyscraper could be built, not earlier than 600 A.D. But the Mayas had discovered it centuries before and applied it not to a decimal system, nine numbers and a zero, but to a vigesimal system, nineteen numbers and a zero. Their base line was twenty rather than ten, and so included toes as well as fingers. A cardinal step towards the development of higher mathematics, quantitative science, and—who knows?—a mechanical age, had thus been taken. Of physics and geometry the Mayas had a sound working knowledge, and they were marvellous draftsmen.

The Aztecs borrowed the Maya principles but never achieved such mathematical elegance. Their solar calendar, however, was more accurate than that of the Spaniards. They were found in full knowledge of the year of Venus, eclipses, solstices, equinoxes, and such phenomena. Their interpretation, however, did not equal their observation. They worked from a fifty-two-year cycle, initiated with great ceremony when the Pleiades came riding over a certain hill near Popocatepetl. To paraphrase Prescott:

The nation waited in suspense, growing more depressed as the days grew shorter, and on the arrival of the five unlucky days [intercalation to equalize the calendar, at the end of the fifty-second year] abandoned themselves to despair, breaking their household idols and furniture, tearing up their clothes, letting all their fires go out. On the evening of the last day a procession of priests, assuming the dress and ornaments of their god, moved from the capital towards the mountain. On reaching its summit, the procession paused—till midnight; when, as the constellation of the Pleiades approached the zenith, the new fire was kindled by the friction of sticks placed in the breast of a sacrificial victim. The flame was communicated to his funeral pyre, and as the light streamed towards heaven, shouts of joy and triumph burst forth from the countless multitudes who covered the hills, the terraces of the temples, and the house tops. Couriers, with torches lighted at the blazing beacon, rapidly bore them over every part of the country, giving assurance that a new cycle had commenced its march and that the gods had decided not to bring the world to an end. The following thirteen days were given up to one magnificent fiesta, dancing, games, pageants and the refurnishing of movables lately destroyed.

The last celebration before the conquest was early in Montezuma's reign, in 1507. In the present year (1931) the Pleiades climb that hill again, and though no such marvellous and dramatic pageant will greet their eyes, I should not be surprised if in one or two remote outposts the drums would sound. Anything can happen in Mexico. Incidentally, this wiping out of all personal property every fifty-two years and starting fresh strikes me as a most invigorating idea. Such an epoch, terminating, say, in 1879, with black walnut, red plush, ball tassels, china shepherdesses, crayon portraits in gilt frames, bustles, pot hats and whatnots on the propitiating pyre, would have provided a spectacle almost as rewarding as the midnight ceremony itself.

LANGUAGE AND LITERATURE

Aztec was a highly inflected language, with more deferentials, Frederick Starr says, than Japanese. There was no alphabet, but the hieroglyphic stage of recording had been reached. It can be read today by a few experts. The Aztec man of letters, like the Egyptian, was both author and artist, painting his story on skins, cotton, silk-gum and paper made from the fibres of maguey. The book was then folded like a screen between tablets. The profession of historian was subdivided between the chronicler of events, and the chronologist. Messrs. Fay and Barnes will be glad to hear that the falsifying of history was a capital offence. At Texcoco was a great library which held the old Toltec (or pre-Aztec) records, including, according to Prescott, an account of the migration from Asia (which is as it may be). Certainly it included manuscripts of priceless historical and human importance. The good bishop, Zumarraga, the first to be installed after the conquest, heaped them all upon a great pyre and destroyed them, to the glory of God. Only twenty-three Aztec manuscripts, or codices, survive, comprehending history, mythology, court records, prayers and poems.

The Maya language was more complex than the Aztec, and had advanced nearer to an alphabet. A few phonetic symbols for syllables had been achieved. This made it easier for Mayas to write, but harder for us to decipher. We can read Aztec, but not, as yet, Maya, except their dates. One major difficulty is that only three Maya books are left. Father Landa, not to be outdone by his bishop, secured immortality by burning the Maya library in Yucatan. He admitted that it contained great quantities of heathen matter on medicine, astronomy, chronology, geology, and the history not only of the Mayas but of other nations. The burning of the library at Alexandria was a minor calamity compared to the devout labours of Landa and Zumarraga. Duplicate material was available in other parts of the Greek world for much which the flames consumed at the mouth of the Nile. In Mexico the slate was wiped clean; the careful records are gone forever. The world will always be the poorer for the work of those two days.

HEALTH AND HYGIENE

The Aztecs had perfected an admirable system of medicine, based on their knowledge of herbs. They utilized hundreds of plants, including digitalis for heart disease, quinine, cascara. From anatomical studies of sacrificed victims, they worked out a reasonably complete nomenclature for the human skeleton, muscular and nervous systems. The Mayas were skilled in treating diseases of the eye. The Tarahumares trepanned skulls in such a way that the patient lived on at least three years. Aztec hospitals and asylums for veteran soldiers were the admiration of the Spaniards. They employed the sensible, if harsh, procedure of exposing those with probably incurable diseases, well supplied with food, to recover or die. They appear to have been a very clean people, particularly in respect to their streets and public buildings. The conquerors noted 1,000 street cleaners in Mexico City.

HANDICRAFTS

Organized into guilds, their craftsmanship reached extraordinary levels. Spanish silversmiths and metal workers acknowledged that they had met their masters. Exquisite jewellery, pottery to rival that of the archaic Greek (it is still being made in one or two remote villages), textiles of cotton, fur and feathers, expert dyeing (from the Aztecs we get cochineal), gorgeous lacquer work, straw matting and weaving, stone and wood carving were among the major crafts. The Aztecs were particularly skilled in mosaic. One shield, still preserved, contains 15,000 pieces of inlaid turquoise, designed to represent human figures. They also carved crystal exquisitely. Friable obsidian, that most refractory of stones, they carved and worked into ornaments, mirrors, swords and daggers.

The Mayas worked less in metals than the Aztecs, as ores were scarcer in their country, but the pieces which have come to light are wholly admirable. They used copper bells as currency, while the Aztecs—in large transactions, at least—used quills of gold dust. (No records, strangely enough, of monetary systems or of weights and measures have been found.) Manual skill was held in great esteem by both nations; every child was taught to be expert at a trade. It is improbable that this went under the name of "vocational education," with slab-sided brick buildings, and carpenters' benches row on row. No. It came as naturally as learning to walk and speak. Certainly this is the way Mexican craftsmen are educated today, and it was probably even more an indigenous part of the growing-up process then. Education was lived, not imposed from without. But priests lectured the children of the upper classes on morality and good manners.

SOCIAL INSTITUTIONS

Monogamy was the rule save for a few exalted dignitaries who had several wives. The position of women was far superior to that of Spain—then and now. It amounted virtually to equality, even up to the office of priest. Divorces were granted by a special court.

Among the Aztecs, land was socially owned but remained in the custody of a given family, from father to son, as long as it was cultivated. If the family died out, or failed to cultivate, it reverted to the clan for redistribution. Certain national lands were set aside and worked, the crop taken in lieu of taxes and tithes by government, Church, or army as the case might be. There were a few large estates belonging to nobles and worked with bound serfs—but very few. This incipient system of the hacienda the Spaniards were to develop to huge dimensions in due time. Moving boundary marks on land was, like forging history, a capital offence.

Slavery was practised, but in a mild form. A man could not be born a slave; he became one chiefly by being taken prisoner of war. Slaves could own property, including sub-slaves. The merchant class, Mr. Filene and Mr. Wanamaker will be delighted to know, was held in high esteem. They served as explorer-ambassadors, on the time-honoured assumption that the flag follows trade. They travelled with a large bodyguard and great equipment. Once, in a diplomatic impasse, a company of merchants stood a four years' siege, before the army and the flag effected their rescue. The Chamber of Commerce of the day was called the "council of finance," and then, as now, was frequently consulted by the administration. Gregory Mason goes so far as to call certain Maya cities manufacturing towns, the products of whose potteries, rope and textile factories were carried far and wide.

At this point our cumulative story of largely admirable achievement goes into reverse, and we must record a horrid and degrading practice. The rite of human sacrifice was infrequently practised prior to about 1300 A.D. The Mayas were not given to it in their great days, nor the pre-Aztecs so far as we know. A virgin was occasionally sacrificed in the Sacred Well at Chichen Itza, but only when a great drought or other national calamity threatened. The habit seems to have come into favour with the appearance of the Aztecs on the plateau, and after a century or two of sacrificing a few victims on very great occasions, began to grow, shortly before the Spanish landed, to incredible proportions. It became a reigning fad, as insidious as the radio, and almost as destructive of life as the automobile. No god could be consulted on the weather, the chances of victory, the prince's health; hardly a religious ceremony could take place, without butchering a poor innocent—sometimes a whole brigade of them—in the most revolting fashion. There was little if any torturing, death was immediate, but it was horrible. Every year the Aztec and Tlaxcalan armies joined in a gigantic freshman-sophomore rush, the sole purpose of which was to drag off sacrificial victims. Aztec armies purposely refrained from killing their enemies in battle, preferring to take them prisoners and lead them to the sacrificial altar. There they were laid as on an operating table, their breasts cut open by knives of obsidian, and the heart torn out; while the priests, mad with a variety of conditioned sadism, shouted their omens and portents, plastering themselves with blood. Sometimes the execution was followed by a ritual cannibalism. According to the early Spanish chronicles the annual tribute amounted to 20,000 victims. This figure, however, must be regarded with the utmost suspicion, as the early chroniclers were mostly churchmen, and the Church had reason for wide dissemination of atrocity stories. It sought to stamp out the Aztec religion and substitute Christianity. The greater the case against the heathen cult, the more freedom it had to use any means to the desired end, and the weaker the criticism thereof. This was the period, too, of the Inquisition, when offsetting butcheries were particularly welcome. If we cut the figure in half, to 10,000 victims a year, I suspect that we have a generous allowance. Like other fads, it might have passed, if for no other reason than lack of victims, but it was at its zenith when the Spaniards came.

Frazer in *The Golden Bough* says that the Aztecs' system of sacrifices, which he calls "the most monstrous on record," was magical rather than religious; that is, it was a crude substitute for science and designed entirely to bring about practical results. They thought that the sun, giver of life and energy, needed to have his own renewed with an infusion of human blood. The maize, too, needed victims to strengthen its growth, so they "sacrificed human beings at all the various stages in the growth of the maize, the age of the victims corresponding to the age of the corn." Every September priests chose a pretty slave-girl of twelve or thirteen to represent the maize goddess Chicomecohuatl, and after doing her reverence with ceremonial offerings, sacrificed her and sprinkled her blood on the goddess's idol and on the harvest offerings, clearly as insurance for next year's crop. "No more striking illustration could be given," comments Frazer upon the whole system, "of the disastrous consequences that may flow in practice from a purely speculative error."

Finally let us consider the organization of government. About the Mayas we know little, save that a list of kings or princes has been established. For the Aztecs the record is comparatively voluminous. As we turn to it, we encounter a profound misunderstanding which has twisted the thought of every schoolchild, indeed of nearly every one who has read or heard of "Montezuma's Empire." As a matter of fact, Montezuma was not an emperor and he had no empire. The confusion arises because the Spaniards, steeped in the terms and forms of European feudal monarchy, could neither understand nor properly explain the Aztec system. Montezuma was obviously the head of the state, he lived in splendour, he must be at least a king; while if he were called emperor it would make the conquest all the more magnificent. It was about as sensible as if a Cortez, four centuries later, invaded Washington, and finding a plump gentleman in control, promptly called him the "Great Emperor Hoover."

The Aztecs were a nation numbering several millions, who lived in and about the region where Mexico City stands. In the course of the 200 years following the founding of their capital in 1325, they had conquered a territory vastly greater than the home state Over this territory they held hegemony, enforcing a fairly onerous tribute in kind, and continual wars and reprisals to secure slaves and captives for sacrifice. Bandelier calls it a loose confederacy of democratic Indian nations—which may err on the other side, but is certainly far nearer the truth than to designate the arrangement as an empire.

The Aztec nation, as well as presumably a number of its allies, was founded on a unit called the *calpulli,* in Spanish, *barrio* or clan-district. (There are seven such barrios still clearly marked in Tepoztlan.) To the barrio belonged the lands referred to earlier, lent to citizens, never owned. It proves again, this feudal-communistic cell, what anthropologists have so often proved before, that man is primarily a social animal. Conceptions of private property in land and natural resources, of the duty of acquisitiveness, are reasonably alien to *homo sapiens.* Group security, incorporating individual security, is the basic desideratum.

The barrio had a special emblem, and normally contributed to the army one fighting unit of from 200 to 400 men. It had its own protecting god—which in Spanish days was readily convertible into a *santo*—its own place of worship, and its own council house. It was essentially a democratic unit governed by folk-moot, the body of the whole. (I am following Waterman and Bandelier.) A war leader was elected to instruct the young men in arms, and captain the company in battle. He was called *achcacauhtin,* or elder brother. An executive civil officer was also elected by the clan. He supervised the land boundaries and distribution, was storekeeper of maize, and presumably acted as judge in property disputes. Thirdly a *tlatoani* or "speaker" was elected, who was the clan deputy or congressman in the higher councils of the nation.

Five clans composed a phratry, primarily a military organization, with an elected colonel or general at the head; and four phratries constituted the tribe or nation. Obviously the Aztec nation must have been composed of a number of such tribes, for with a unit of only 400 fighting men to a clan, the total population of the tribe of twenty clans could not have run much above 50,000, and there were 60,000 houses, sheltering at least 300,000 persons, in Mexico City alone. The Aztec nation, whatever its size, was ruled not by a despot, but by a national council, composed of the clan speakers. This was the most important body in the Aztec system. It met once every Mexican month of twenty days, and in crises it might meet daily. Together with the elders of the nation, women and men, the council elected the war chief, the titular head of the nation. This group elected Montezuma, and when he became a hostage within the Spanish lines, deposed him, and elected Cuitlahuac in his place.

His office was not hereditary, but the war chief had to be chosen from among the members of one noble family. He had no power to declare war; this was vested with the council of speakers. (In passing through this armed camp, it is interesting to note that previous to the rebuilding of Chichen Itza, about 900 A.D., and including the great period in Guatemala, we can find no hint of war or military manœuvres in Maya art or architecture. As pacifists, apparently, they reached the zenith of Amerindian culture.)

A step below the head of the nation stood an officer almost equally important, and though he was a man, he bore the extraordinary name of the Snake Woman. He was second in command of the armies and also the gatherer and keeper of tribute—a sort of military treasurer. Why snakes should be so intimately associated with revenue officers is a mystery which we shall leave to the Indians. He seems to have had no religious functions whatever. The president or war chief, the Snake Woman, and the phratry generals were the only persons in the nation permitted to tie the hair with red leather.

Three hundred years before Thomas Jefferson! No wonder the Spaniards failed to make head or tail of this unheard-of arrangement. (One hundred years after him, their colonial descendants still flounder in the alien fetters of republican constitutions.) But to an Anglo-Saxon it is perfectly clear that the Aztec civilization was an experiment in democracy, and a reasonably successful one, the only major exceptions being the principle of communistic landholding, at the bottom, and the election of president from among the members of one family, at the top. The latter might be termed "prince" but hardly emperor. It is only fair to say, however, that under Montezuma the Aztecs were drifting towards empire. Like the

elected consuls of Rome, some Julius Cæsar would probably have seized the imperial purple, and relegated the
council to an obliging body of yes men, and that shortly.
Whether the rank and file would have tolerated it is
another matter. The Aztecs were a sturdy and independent folk. Montezuma had certainly arrogated to
himself more power, more pomp and more obsequious
attention than his predecessors had dreamed of. He even
fancied himself a god. But he was at bottom a weak
and vacillating fellow, and quite possibly would have
been deposed when his arrogance became unendurable,
with or without the help of Cortez.

The curtain rings up for the greatest of all American
tragedies. A civilization which in the fifteenth century
Means holds, conservatively I think, to be "hardly inferior to Europe in the middle of the thirteenth century,"
is to be erased from the map of history. In astronomy it
was far in advance of Europe; in architectural ornament
it was as great as the world ever has seen or will see; in
its conception of the rights of the individual it stood
manifestly above the feudal conceptions of the old
world, so far indeed that the Spaniards could not understand its political philosophy; in its minor arts of weaving, metal working, jewellery, pottery, it challenged the
best which the Eastern Hemisphere had to offer; its
knowledge of plants and medicinal herbs was profound;
it honoured women, it loved flowers, and the writers
of untrue books of history it put to death.

The curtain rings up, for over the sea to the east there
comes a fleet of tiny sails. . . .

CHAPTER IV

THE SIX HUNDRED

ON the tenth of February, 1519, 100 years before the *Mayflower* sighted the dunes of Provincetown, eleven small ships stood out from the harbour of Havana and bent their course due west. The slender resources of the island of Cuba had been all but exhausted to fill their decks and holds. Aboard the vessels were 633 men, of whom 100 were seamen and the rest soldier adventurers; sixteen horses—then almost worth their weight in gold in Cuba; thirty-two crossbows, thirteen muskets—the ancient type which were fired from stands like small cannon —and four falconets. The alleged purpose of the armada, as broadcast by Velasquez, the governor of Cuba, was to found a Christian colony in the great mainland to the west which two earlier scouting expeditions had located and roughly charted. Its real purpose was to find, and hopefully encircle, the source of that gold which the earlier expeditions had definitely determined the natives possessed.

Ever since I can remember I have been puzzled by the conquest of Mexico. How could 600 white men, seventeen firearms, and sixteen horses liquidate, practically overnight as history counts time, a nation of courageous warriors and mighty builders, with a total population running into millions? We shall sketch briefly the story of the conquest, and try to unravel the mystery as we go.

In command of the fleet was Hernando Cortez, a

gentleman of whom little was known. He was then thirty-four years old, and had been steadily running himself into debt trying to work "a grant of Indians" in Santiago. Velasquez had rescued him from obscurity and put him in charge of the expedition primarily in the hope of having a pliant agent who would not be too punctilious when it came to the division of spoils. The logical candidate, Juan de Grijalva, who led the second scouting trip to Yucatan, a brave man and well loved by his soldiers, was passed by in favour of the bankrupt Cortez. Velasquez was to find that he had caught a tartar, and history to carve a generous niche for another immortal.

The choice was not quite so inept as it initially appeared to the citizens of Cuba and the soldiers of the fleet. Fifteen years before, when the nineteen-year-old boy first set foot in the new world, he had already hitched his wagon to a star. "I came to get gold, not to till the soil like a peasant." And later in a burst of confidence he told an Aztec chieftain in Vera Cruz: "The Spaniards are troubled with a disease of the heart for which gold is a specific remedy." Velasquez could not have picked a man better adjusted, philosophically, to the real, as against the alleged, purposes of the expedition. Nor was our hero blind to an effective bit of publicity. He ordered two standards to be made, worked in gold with the royal arms and a cross on each side, and underneath a legend which read: "Comrades, let us follow the sign of the holy Cross with true faith, and through it we shall conquer."

The Captain General was a fine figure of a man. "He began to adorn himself and be more careful of his appearance, and he wore a plume of feathers with a medal, and a gold chain, and a velvet cloak trimmed with knots of gold; in fact he looked like a gallant and courageous Captain." In a later portrait we see a square, resolute face, a long aggressive nose, bushy beard, and large fine Spanish eyes, with a touch of sadness in them. The times and the man were joined. Cortez may not be remembered without anguish, but he will always be remembered.

Aboard the fleet in the capacity of a petty officer was another gentleman to whom history will remain profoundly in debt. Without the memoirs of Bernal Diaz del Castillo, we should lose at once a great part of our documentary knowledge of the conquest, how it progressed from day to day, and one of the most dramatic tales ever got between the two covers of a book. I know of nothing to compare with it, save possibly the Antarctic diaries of Captain Scott. Either Diaz took notes during the campaigns, or he had a memory like those geniuses who play thirty games of chess at once, or he was a thundering liar—probably all three. But if half he tells is true—and I suspect the ratio is higher than this—the story is sufficiently tremendous. I suspect it is mainly true because of the authentic human touches which appear on nearly every page. He seldom fails to give us the details of what he had to eat, the quality of the forage and camping quarters, the peculiar merits and demerits of Indian maidens, whom he found amiable but not over comely, and the exact exchange value in Spanish currency of all gifts, findings, partitions and ceremonial presentations of articles containing gold or silver. Even as the boyish remarks of Cortez shed light on the conquest, so does the expert accountancy of Diaz. Both men were carved from the same Castilian granite, infinitely courageous and infinitely greedy. I shall use the memoirs of Diaz constantly in the pages to come. If the reader wants to add a grain of salt he is welcome to, though I have already put in a shaker full, as well as checking his more incredible statements with the accounts of other historians.

The end of the peninsula of Yucatan was sighted about the first of March, following a stopover in western Cuba, and landing parties were put ashore. The natives were unfriendly and gold in negotiable quantities was not to be found. All along its northern coast, the peninsula was raided with indifferent success. Here lived the Mayas, who, as we shall see, put up the sturdiest defence of all the native armies. One pitched battle was fought near Ceutla in Tabasco, in which a detachment of Spanish infantry was all but overwhelmed before Cortez and the cavalry came to the rescue. The gunfire the Indians had withstood, despite its terrible punishment, but the horses were too much for them. Terror of the supernatural came into play, and thinking that "the horse and its rider were all one animal," they turned and fled. Thus a page from Greek mythology saved the Spaniards, and was destined to save them again and again.

Perhaps even more valuable than the victory of the centaur was the acquisition in Maya territory of Doña Marina. It was a sorry day for Mexico when this able Indian girl was traded in, together with four diadems, some gold lizards and ducks, and two masks of gold, to appease the invaders after the battle of Ceutla. Presented at first to Don Alonzo Hernandez Puertocarrero, one of the fleet captains, she became in the end the mistress of Cortez, and worth a whole squadron of horses to the Spanish cause. She was both chief interpreter and vice diplomat to the invading army.

In the early raids he began to give evidence of his command of the idiom. Could the masters of Hollywood, I wonder, better this little publicity demonstration? A delegation of Tabascan chiefs, anxious to make peace, signified their intention of waiting upon the Captain General. He set the hour and also the stage. He ordered the biggest cannon to be loaded with a large ball and a good charge of powder. He ordered a mare to be picketed where the delegation would stand when it arrived, and a stallion to be held in readiness. When the visitors came, and nervous they were, he lectured them through an interpreter on their derelictions, the power of the great king Carlos of Spain whose agent he was, and the highly unreliable temperaments of his cannon, guns and horses. (The Indians thought the guns shot themselves off.) The latter, he said, had been seriously upset by the recent violence, and were likely to vent their wrath in all directions at any moment. He gave a secret signal and a match was touched to the cannon. "It went off with a thunderclap and the ball went buzzing over the hills, and as it was midday and very still, it made a great noise, and the *caciques* [chiefs] were terrified on hearing it." Another signal and the stallion was brought where he could scent the mare, and he "began to paw the ground and neigh and become wild with excitement, looking all the time towards the Indians whence the scent of the mare had come, and the caciques thought he was roaring at them and they were terrified anew."

In brief it was a difficult day on native nerves, and the beginning of a wave of terror and awe, rolling steadily and growing as it rolled, towards Montezuma and the capital. Were these indeed the *teules,* the white-faced gods who, as it was foretold, had come to rule the land from oversea? Was this Quetzalcoatl himself? Destroyer or messiah—the psychology of the defence stumbled between these alternatives. Later when Montezuma dispatched his camera men to the front—skilled painters who set down on parchment every detail of the Spaniards' accoutrements—Cortez dressed his troops, his cavalry and his cannon anew, and for their benefit presented another super-cinema opening. The paintings were rushed back by fleet runners over the mountains, to the bewilderment of the Aztec chief of staff.

Yucatan was good ground for propaganda, but altogether too prickly a coast to conquer. The fleet sailed west again until the great snowy cone of Orizaba hove into view, and a series of high white dunes and the germs of a harbour (there are almost no natural harbours on the Gulf coast of Mexico) arrested its attention. Here the expedition disembarked not far from what is now called Vera Cruz.

The mosquitoes, then as now, were terrible. (But the defence is better today. Above every hotel bed one finds a great shower bath of netting.) The little army pitched camp on top of the dunes and swore and slapped and sweltered for many days. The landing was on Holy Thursday, April 21, 1519, and the march to the capital did not begin until August. Nearby a town was built— a town which, with fitting justice, the pirates of the Spanish Main periodically captured and looted for the next 200 years; a town as wicked as Port Said and as pestilential as a sewer. Here Cortez came into direct contact with Montezuma through his accredited ambassadors.

The head of the Aztec commonwealth at this juncture decided to placate rather than attack the invaders. His methods were fittingly imperial. He sent a great cacique "who in face, feature, and appearance bore a strong likeness to our Captain Cortez"—the camera men had done their work well—together with one hundred Indian bearers. After kissing the earth, fumigating Cortez with *copal* incense from braziers of pottery, and delivering many courteous speeches of welcome, the delegation proceeded to the business of the day, and spread on the ground what any archeologist today—and I think I myself—would give eye-teeth to see.

"The first article presented was a wheel like a sun, as big as a cart wheel, with many sorts of pictures on it, the whole of fine gold, and a wonderful thing to behold, which those who afterwards weighed it said was worth more than ten thousand dollars." (Here we have the authentic Diaz touch.) There followed an even greater wheel of pure silver, intricately carved and symbolizing the moon. Then a helmet of grains of gold as they came from the mine—a fatal gift. The company gathered around with glittering eyes. "This helmet was worth more to us than if it contained twenty thousand dollars, because it showed us that there were good mines there." Then twenty golden ducks, beautifully worked, and images in gold, "very natural looking," of dogs, tigers, lions and monkeys; ten necklaces of exquisite workmanship; twelve arrows and a bow with its string, two rod-like staffs of justice five palms long—all in beautiful hollow work of fine gold. There were crests of gold, plumes of rich green feathers, silver crests and fans; a deer copied in hollow gold, and thirty loads of "beautiful cotton cloth worked with many patterns and decorated with many-coloured feathers; and many other things that I cannot remember."

To which Cortez gave measure for measure in flowery speeches, but all the tangible property the ambassadors took back to Montezuma—if indeed they carried it so far—was a gilded glass cup of Florentine ware engraved with trees, and three holland shirts—a trading ratio

Diego Rivera. 1931

BOSTON PUBLIC LIBRARY

which, by and large, Spain and Mexico were to retain for 300 years.

A fiction was established of the most extravagant friendship between the Spanish monarch through his agent, the Captain General, on the one side, and Montezuma on the other. Their regard for each other's persons, characters and achievements was astronomical. Meanwhile each busily plotted and schemed the surest way to assassination and annihilation. Indeed they might have been the chancelleries of a pair of modern European powers. But Cortez was the shrewder man. He knew precisely what he wanted. Montezuma could not make up his mind, and alternately threatened and abased himself. A resolute prince could have thrown the Spaniards into the Gulf of Mexico in an hour's time—centaurs, temperamental self-exploding cannon, and all. It would have cost something in manpower but it could have been done.

The negotiations dragged on. Cortez was determined to be invited to visit the capital. Montezuma was charmed to receive him today, and regretful tomorrow. The army slapped mosquitoes, "both long-legged ones and small ones which are called *xexenes* which are worse than the large ones, and we could get no sleep on account of them"; and foraged not too successfully for food. Thirty-five died from sickness and malnutrition. The rank and file grumbled and presently demanded a return to Cuba. Nobody save Cortez seems to have had the slightest illusions about the suicidal attempt to march with a few hundred men through an unknown country, filled with mountainous chasms and thousands of well-armed enemies. But the Captain General was indomitable. Whatever his motives, his sheer grit in this intolerable situation was superb. And he made one transcendent discovery. A delegation of Totonacs came into the Spanish camp one day when Montezuma's people were absent. From them Cortez learned that Mexico was not united, that there were nations who hated the Aztecs and their taxgatherers.

With this information in hand, it did not take him long to act. He gave secret orders to a few dependable men, and while the little army looked on in horror, its ships went up in flames! All but one small vessel. That settled the retreat to Cuba; it was forward or perish. He seized the Aztec taxgatherers in the nearby territory of the Totonacs, and thereby bound that tribe to him in deadly fear of what the Aztecs would do in retaliation. Then he released the assessors and sent them back to Mexico, laying the whole blame on the Totonacs—thereby checkmating Montezuma. He proceeded to gather a native army of porters and second-line warriors from among the tributary states, left the sick and weak-hearted at Vera Cruz as an apology for a base, and on the 16th day of August, with 400 odd Spaniards, a dozen horses, and some thousands of Indian allies, started for the capital. The negotiations were over. Invitation or no invitation, he proposed to look Montezuma in the face. Lindbergh, starting across the ocean for France, was taking no greater risk

He made his way across the steamy jungles of the coastal plain with little opposition save that of nature. Then the army began to climb; and the allies sweated under the load of the cannon. To the crest of the plateau was nearly 8,000 vertical feet of heaving, serrated cliff and chasm, but fortunately the native trails lay open and undefended. A few warriors, a few boulders could have held those canyon passes literally forever. Neither horse nor cannon could have deployed against them. Once on the crest, Cortez headed for the country of the Tlaxcalans, a numerous, sturdy, and independent people, allies of his native troops. They had no use for Aztecs, and by the same token it presently appeared that they had no use for Spaniards. Diplomacy almost immediately collapsed, and the 400, temporarily deserted by their allies from the coast, found themselves in the most desperate circumstances which perhaps the whole conquest has to record. The Tlaxcalans descended upon them like locusts on an orchard. Only the Castilian phalanx prevented instant annihilation. There were many skirmishes and three pitched battles. Let Diaz tell the story of one of them:

All the plain was swarming with warriors and we stood four hundred men in number, and of those many sick and wounded. And we know for certain that this time our foe came with the determination to leave none of us alive excepting those who would be sacrificed to their idols.

How they began to charge on us! What a hail of stones sped from their slings! As for their bowmen, the javelins lay like corn on the threshing floor; all of them barbed and fire-hardened, which would pierce any armour and would reach the vitals where there is no protection; the men with swords and shields and other arms larger than swords, such as broadswords and lances, how they pressed on us and with what mighty shouts and yells they charged upon us! The steady bearing of our artillery, musketeers, and crossbowmen was indeed a help to us, and we did the enemy much damage. . . . The horsemen were so skilful and bore themselves so valiantly that, after God who protected us, they were our bulwark. . . . One thing only saved our lives, and that was that the enemy were so numerous and so crowded one on another that the shots wrought havoc among them . . .

They gave me two wounds, one in the head with a stone, and one in the thigh with an arrow; but this did not prevent me from fighting, and keeping watch, and helping our soldiers, and all the soldiers who were wounded did the same; for few of us remained unwounded.

Then we returned to our camp, well contented, and giving thanks to God. We buried the dead in one of those houses which the Indians had built underground, so that the enemy should not see that we were mortals, but should believe that, as they said, we were *Teules*. Then we doctored all the wounded, with the fat of an Indian. It was cold comfort to be even without salt or oil with which to cure the wounded. There was another want from which we suffered, and it was a severe one—and that was clothes with which to cover ourselves, for such a cold wind came from the snow mountains, that it made us shiver, for our lances and muskets and crossbows made a poor covering.

The Tlaxcalans who lived under the shadow of Malinche were not to be won by honeyed words, but they had the fighters' respect for men strong enough to defeat them. According to some accounts, internal dissension lost them the decisive battle. However that may be, in the end they elected to join Cortez, and became the fulcrum of the invaluable native support in his subsequent campaigns. (It was the Tlaxcalans, you will remember, who had the annual rush with the Aztecs for dragging off sacrificial victims.)

Reinforced by a strong detachment of these allies, Cortez continued his march. His next objective was Cholula. Here he took no chances with native sentiment, and after promises of a peaceful parley he butchered in the citadel 2,000 disarmed warriors. The Cholulans were close allies of the Aztecs, but not technically members of that nation. He crossed the towering pass between Popocatepetl and the White Woman—one of his captains climbed the smoking volcano and peered into its crater of writhing sulphur—came down into the broad valley in which Mexico City stands, and at the gates of the metropolis met Montezuma, even as he had sworn to, face to face.

If we could conceive the novelty and wonder of that descent and meeting! How it makes all other epics of exploration shrink and fade. Uncharted islands, unscaled

peaks, the icy wastes of polar seas, tombs of pharaohs
long dead, are little things compared with the first vision
of a living race, building mightier monuments than
Europe had ever dared, passing and repassing in this
fair city which they had raised. To come upon the forgotten dead is indeed adventure; but to come upon the
unknown living, forging a great civilization, is an experience which perhaps only two expeditions in all history
have known—those of Pizarro and Cortez. It will never
be equalled again upon this planet. Only when half-frozen
men step from their aeropile upon the crust of Mars,
may such a moment come again.

Gazing on such wonderful sights, we did not know what to
say, or whether what appeared before us was real. On one side,
on the land, there were great cities, and in the lake ever so many
more, and in the causeway were many bridges at intervals, and
in front of us stood the great City of Mexico, and we—we did
not number four hundred soldiers! . . .
And when we entered the city, the appearance of the palaces
in which they lodged us! How spacious and well built they were,
of beautiful stone work and cedar wood, and the wood of other
sweet-scented trees, with great rooms and courts. . . . We went
to the orchard and garden, which was such a wonderful thing to
see and walk in, that I was never tired of looking at the diversity
of the trees, and noting the scent which each one had, and the
paths full of roses and flowers, and the pond of fresh water. Great
canoes were able to pass into the garden from the lake outside
so that there was no need for their occupants to land. And all
was cemented and very splendid with many kinds of stone monuments with pictures on them. Then the birds of many kinds
which came into the garden. I say again that I stood looking at
it and thought that never in the world would there be discovered
such lands as these. Of all these wonders that I then beheld, today
all is overthrown and lost, nothing is standing.

An old soldier, with the scar of an Indian sword on
his throat, writing his memoirs in his eightieth year, re-

members a garden, the sweet-scented trees, and the birds
that came there. . . . Remembers, and almost regrets
that he and his comrades went into that garden and cut
it down.

Now the tale becomes so involved that we shall have
to leave it to the historians, giving here only a bare outline. After exchanging more presents—at the usual ratio
—and prodigious parleying, Cortez and his followers
were invited into the city and lodged in one of the great
government palaces. Here they were kept virtually
prisoners. The Aztec captains would have rushed and
slaughtered them at once, but Montezuma held back:
"weighted down by superstition, and rendered powerless
by a timid and vacillating character, the autocrat felt
himself fatally conquered before beginning the struggle."
One day in a careless moment he let himself be seized by
seven Spanish soldiers, of whom Diaz was one, and made
hostage. This was a stroke as decisive as it was obvious.
Now the Aztecs did not dare attack lest their prince be
murdered. The poor man swore fealty to the king of
Spain, and, what was more to the point, connived to
hand over to Cortez some 700,000 gold dollars. (It is
interesting to note that in the subsequent division, each
common soldier received only about one hundred dollars.
Some of them "fell ill from brooding and grief," but our
good Diaz did not mourn. As special sentry over Montezuma, he was so helpful and respectful that the prince
declared him a special dividend of "gold and mantles,"
and a beautiful Indian girl.)

The deadlock dragged along. The Aztecs held the
Spaniards captive, and the Spaniards held the Aztec
prince. In March, 1520, Panfilo de Narvaez arrived at
Vera Cruz with sixteen ships, 1,400 soldiers, ninety cross-

bowmen, seventy musketeers, and eighty horses. He had
come from Cuba to depose Cortez for grossly exceeding
his orders. Cortez, leaving Montezuma in the care of a
small garrison captained by Alvarado, managed to get
out of the city and went down to meet the fleet, taking
all the gold he could stagger under. Once out of Aztec
territory, he travelled with comparative safety, for the
country was rising against Montezuma. At Vera Cruz
the police force—then as now—was ready to discuss the
question reasonably in the light of adequate cash consideration. It deserted *en masse* to Cortez, leaving Narvaez
the captain of his own soul, perhaps, but of nothing else.
With this handsome addition to his army, Cortez
marched up to Mexico again, and got into his beleaguered
stronghold, only to find an even more critical situation.
The garrison under Alvarado had been repeatedly attacked. Food was running low. Native respect for Montezuma was all but gone. A new prince, Cuitlahuac, had
been appointed by the Aztec council, and a wholesale
assault upon the Spaniards was imminent. Suddenly the
deadlock broke. In the midst of a skirmish, Montezuma,
who had been asked by the Spaniards to mount a battle-
ment and speak to his people, was killed by a shower of
stones; killed, the Spaniards insisted, by the Aztecs themselves.

This was the end. The Spaniards must leave, and that
with the utmost dispatch. On the dreadful *"Noche
Triste"* some 2,000 men sought to hack their way out of
the city, but between the vigour of the Aztec assault and
the amount of gold each man strove to bear away on his
person, only a battered fraction of the force left the
metropolis alive. One is still shown the spot called "Alvarado's Leap" where the fleeing captain jumped his
horse over a yawning ditch. The faithful Tlaxcalans re-

ceived the bloody and impoverished survivors and nursed their wounds. It was touch and go, furthermore, whether they were to be comforted or annihilated. (By way of gratitude the expeditionary force presented the nation with smallpox, and the king of Tlaxcala died of it. So did Montezuma's brother and successor, Cuitlahuac, after four months in office.)

Cortez sent to Cuba for more reinforcements. The governor, now convinced that it was the Captain General or nobody, sent them. A great army of native troops, Tlaxcalans and others, was assembled. The country about Mexico City was invested and put to fire and sword. Food supplies and drinking water were cut off. The Aztec nation, stripped of its allies, now began to fight for its life on its native soil. On the 21st of May, 1521, the siege proper was begun. It lasted eighty-five days. Sea battles were fought on the great lakes; the causeways ran with blood.

Not for one moment did the Mexicans show signs of discouragement, notwithstanding the scarcity of fresh water and provisions, the superiority of the arms of the Spaniards, and the immense number of their native allies. Each day as it came was for them as the first day of the strife, so great was the determination and the strength with which they appeared on the field of battle, and moreover they never ceased fighting from dawn to dusk. When the greater number of them had already perished, the few who still remained stoically resisted thirst, hunger, weariness and pestilence in the defense of their country, and even then refused, with indomitable fortitude, the proposals of peace which Cortez repeatedly made to them. In this manner only did they die.

Somehow it puts me in mind of the Alamo.

The city fell on the 13th of August, 1521, and a great civilization passed into history. But it was not until 1541, twenty years later, that the Mayas of Yucatan were subdued. Repeatedly they defeated the Spanish armies, driving every white man into the sea. The Zapotecs to the south put up an equally stubborn defence; while high in the mountains and deep in the jungles lived tribes who were never conquered, and have not been conquered to this day.

In all Mexico today there is no statue to Cortez. But in the Paseo de la Reforma, one of the great avenues of the capital, stands a lofty and impressive monument to Cuauhtemoc, the leader of the defending forces in the siege, and the last of the Aztec princes.

With the essential facts before us, the mystery of the conquest begins to clear. Cortez and his original 600 did not subdue Mexico. They never had one respectable fight with the Aztecs. They fought the Mayas in Tabasco, and beat them in one scrimmage, but promptly left them. They fought the Tlaxcalans to a standstill, and made this nation their lasting allies. They marched into Aztec territory proper—the valley of Mexico City—nominally as Montezuma's guests; the way before them was strewn with flowers. With the prince as hostage they were safe for a time from attack. But when he was stoned to death, the Spaniards, though reinforced by the 1,500 men of Narvaez, were ejected from the city overnight, and the greater part of them killed. This was the first real trial of strength between the two forces. Up to then diplomacy had been the rule, tempered by a few skirmishes. If Montezuma had been a man instead of a weakling, and if his office had not been held in such veneration that, like the President of the United States, he could do no wrong, Cortez would have needed thousands of musketeers and hundreds of horses to conquer the country unaided.

Unaided. This brings us to a second major reason for the downfall. The Aztecs held a large part of Mexico in subjugation, as we have seen. From the tributary nations they collected taxes in precious metals and in kind, and young men and women in war and as a punishment on every pretext, for sacrifice on their altars. As the cult of the blood sacrifice grew, potential revolt increased. The Spaniards acted as a spearhead to lead perhaps the original Mexican Revolution. They came at the psychological moment. The priests had foretold the return of Quetzalcoatl, the blond god. Into this prophecy the Spaniards, with their white faces, their horses and their falconets "breathing thunder and lightning," fitted admirably. The coincidence both paralyzed Montezuma and encouraged the tributary states to take gods as leaders of their revolt.

Cortez, in his own accounts, uses the following phrases in respect to the formidableness of his native military support: "numberless people," "an infinite number," "which could not be counted," "more than one hundred and fifty thousand men." After the reform of his battered battalion following the "Noche Triste" and the arrival of reinforcements from Cuba, native troops came swarming into his camp. It is safe to say that the total force far outnumbered the Aztec army penned in its own watery territory. At one juncture Diaz and a detachment went swinging around to Tepoztlan and Cuernavaca in an encircling movement. In this not too equal encounter, Cortez won, and would have been an indifferent commander had he not.

In brief, while the march of the 600 is one of the world's odysseys, an analysis of the relevant facts makes the conquest as a whole an understandable achievement. Cortez, as the saying goes, had all the breaks. No amount of luck, however, can lessen our appreciation of his courage in burning his ships, and daring that march inland, with its appalling dangers and its unknown end.

We salute the Captain General; but great courage and great conquests, while they make history, do not necessarily make the generality of mankind any happier. All too often they plunge the race backward in its slow ascent. Consider Alexander, Napoleon, von Hindenburg. Let us see if we can strike a balance between the human gains and losses which followed this exhibition of resolute heroism.

To begin with, we must emphasize again that the conquest of Mexico was a gold rush with no more thought of settlement than had the invaders of the Yukon in '98, although settlement ultimately proved necessary to stabilize the business of exporting valuables. Here we find the cardinal difference between the taking of New Spain and the taking of the territory to the north which was to become the United States. In the latter Europeans came primarily to live, in the former to loot. Cortez travelled to the new world to seek his fortune. But his steadfast plan was to take that fortune back to Spain, and there lead the roistering life of a *caballero*.

It remains an open question furthermore whether Spain conquered Mexico or Mexico conquered Spain. Economists and historians have held, and I think with justice, that the flow of gold into the Iberian peninsula, and the habits which the ruling classes drifted into as a result of it, formed one of the cardinal reasons for the decay of the Spanish Empire. Even more significant to our story is that Mexico, like China, tended to absorb its invaders. As we shall see, Tepoztlan today is more Aztec than Spanish. Here we find another sharp difference from the United States. The North American Indians were to all intents and purposes obliterated. Hardly a vestige of their culture remains except in such words as "moccasin," "canoe," "tobacco," and costumes at fancy dress balls.

The outstanding gain of the conquest, humanly considered, was the liquidation of the blood sacrifice. The practice might or might not have proved a temporary phenomenon—the Mayas and pre-Aztecs were not addicted to it—but the fact remains that it was gaining under Montezuma, and its abrupt termination, even at the immediate cost of many lives, can only be construed as a blessing to all concerned.

From Spain the Mexicans derived a number of useful material improvements, notably the horse, mule, donkey as beasts of burden; new foods in the form of wheat, rice, domesticated fruits; while a unified language, with a phonetic alphabet, may have been a greater contribution than wheat and horses. Finally, the wealth of Mexico certainly added to the power and prestige of Spain for a time, however much of a boomerang it proved in the end. It contributed much to the pageantry of civilization in sixteenth century Europe.

Of the specific losses, to my mind the most poignant of all—and it is a purely hypothetical one—is that the conquest terminated a great experiment. Nobody knows to what heights indigenous American civilization might have climbed with its splendid beginnings, and nobody will ever know. Mexican culture continued and still continues, but it is the body only, decapitated by the conquest.

Meanwhile the tangible losses to the Mexicans were very great. Hundreds of thousands died in the wars and uprisings and epidemics attending the inauguration of the Spanish rule—probably more than the blood sacrifice had ever taken. The whole race was thrown into peonage, where it could not escape to the mountains, and thousands were needlessly lost in the mines, haciendas, and building operations of their Spanish masters. Craftsmanship of a high order persisted, and still persists, but the exquisite artistry of the old period, the masks of turquoise, the great golden wheel of the sun with its bas-reliefs, such things are gone forever.

And finally, it is infinitely mournful to contemplate four centuries and more of cringing abjection in a land where once civilized men walked free, fearless and masters of their destiny. I wish with Bernal Diaz that he and his kind had never stepped into that garden on Lake Texcoco, beside the white palaces, where the trees gave forth each its own sweet odour, the roses bloomed, and the birds sang.

CHAPTER V

THE DECLINE OF MEXICAN CIVILIZATION. I

THE capital city of the Aztecs fell in 1521. Porfirio Diaz, dictator of Mexico, fell in 1910. Between these two dates lie almost four centuries, and as I read the records, a slow and steady decline in civilization. This opinion will meet indignant denials in various quarters. The pious will object that during the period Christianity was substituted for the worship of the sun and the plumed serpent. The Spaniard will object that his civilized culture replaced that of Montezuma. The admirers of constitutional democracy will object that Mexico threw off the yoke of Spain in 1821 and shortly after introduced ballot boxes, two houses of Parliament, and a president in frock coat and tall silk hat, all complete. Finally, the American colony in Mexico, and not a few business men at home and abroad, will object that the administration of Porfirio Diaz, with its safeguards for foreign persons and property, was as near Utopia as it is possible for investing aliens to get on this unreliable planet. As one goes about Mexico today, two decades after Diaz took the first available liner for Europe, never to return, one has only to mention his name to affluent Americans and old family Mexicans to receive a reaction as automatic as the knee jerk. "Don Porfirio! There was a man. The best thing that ever happened to Mexico. Ah, if we but had him back!"

Yet in the face of these hostile ranks I maintain that

civilization rolled steadily downhill in Mexico for 400 years, and that the close of the Diaz regime was its lowest point. Not many pages back I defined civilization quite simply as city living. Here I must be allowed to add to the original definition a modicum of well-being on the part of the underlying population.

Christianity was not substituted for paganism. The religion of the Indians was diluted with dashes of Roman Catholicism, here weaker, there stronger; but the wayfaring Mexican Indian is neither pagan nor Christian, but a mixture of both as we shall see. He dropped the blood sacrifice, which was an excellent thing to do, but he gained spiritual confusion. His ancient certainties were uprooted, and he was too stubborn, or too wary, to accept the new certainties imported from Jerusalem and Rome.

Whether sixteenth century Spain exhibited a higher type of culture than Montezuma's Mexico is arguable, but beside the point. Granted that Spain was on the whole superior, it distinctly does not follow that that culture was introduced into Mexico to supersede Aztec and Maya cultures. Like the church doctrines, scraps and patches of it were introduced, but only in single communities, one might almost say in manor houses. The Indians would have none of the Castilian pattern, or very little of it, and as we shall reiterate throughout this book, it is the Indian and not the white that makes Mexico, that *is* Mexico. North of the Rio Grande, the whites elbowed the Indian steadily westward, and Europeans bearing European culture flowed freely into the vacuum. Not more than 300,000 Spaniards ever settled in Mexico, forming only an eddy in a deep constant river of ten or more million Indians. I doubt if any Mexican city with the exception of the capital was ever as Spanish as, say, New York in its early days was Dutch. The Spanish influence, such as it was, undoubtedly added some valuable things to Mexican life, but it also made very grave subtractions. No. If Cortez and his captains had slaughtered the entire Indian population with the thoroughness exhibited in the city of Cholula, and thereafter Spaniards of all classes had colonized an uninhabited country, we might—possibly—have held that the new civilization was an improvement on the old. But the facts make no such conclusion tenable.

A great deal is made, both by foreign historians and by Mexicans themselves, of the revolution of 1810. It is compared not unfavourably with the glorious days of the American Revolution. The tyranny of Spain—like the tyranny of England—was cast off. Father Hidalgo —like George Washington—went through the days that tried men's souls to establish independence, freedom and democracy. Father Hidalgo was undoubtedly a great man, but alas there was no soil into which freedom and democracy could be sown. Independence from Spain was won, paper constitutions were set up, but again the Indian population negatived the programme. It had no tradition of individualism, of property holding in the western sense, of ballot boxes, of free speech. The Indians had retained a certain amount of democracy in their villages from Aztec times, but they had no conception of it in national terms. The world ended with the mountains which encircled their pueblo. (And still does.) All that happened, accordingly, was an exchange of Spanish rulers and exploiters for native creole rulers and exploiters. The viceroy gave way to the "president," and which was the greater rogue it would be difficult to determine. To the political historian Mexican independence is a major fact, but to the economist and sociologist it appears a minor phenomenon, setting in motion no forces tending either to mitigate the evils of the feudalism established by the Spaniards or genuinely to raise the level of Mexican civilization. The curve was downward to Hidalgo, and continued downward for another century.

Finally as to Diaz. The man was an excellent administrator; he made the country safe both for foreign bankers and for tourists. He had a programme for Mexico and I think he was sincere in putting it into effect. But it was the wrong kind of programme. He tried to Westernize Mexico, to introduce the machine and industrialism. To this end he gave foreign concessionaires every encouragement, and the Indian population—who went to work for the aliens—every discouragement. The peon was driven to a point below that ever witnessed in the Spanish regime. He was stripped of his communal lands; stripped of his human dignity. The proof of the unsoundness of the Diaz regime lies in the completeness of its collapse. Nothing enduring had been built into the national fabric. A few whiffs of gunpowder, a few speeches about land and justice, and programme and system liquidated like a cracked egg.

A toboggan slide for 400 years. But at last, if I am not mistaken, the bottom of the run has been reached and the course starts up. It started up in 1917. In that year Mexico turned from prostrating herself before white men from all points of the compass, and regarded her own brown men, their imperishable traditions, their authentic artistic gifts, their gentleness and essential dignity. And this, if you please, is the best thing which has happened to Mexico since the Mayas built their shining cities.

Let us try, in a few brief pages, to catch at least a hint of the flavour of these slowly sinking centuries. The record, while discouraging to the social philosopher, is replete with colour for the artist.

THE INCOMPLETENESS OF THE CONQUEST

Mexico City has fallen. The great temple is torn down. Montezuma's successor is most villainously tortured to disclose the treasures of his people. The Spanish enemies of Cortez recede before his colossal *fait accompli,* and the king of Spain appoints him Governor General, with grants of land in Mexico as vast as European nations. From the conquered city, files of men in armour, supported by armies of Tlaxcalans and other allies, wind their laborious way north, south, west, over mountains and down barrancas, to consolidate the conquest. As one looks from a train window at shattering cliffs guarded with great green sentries of organ cactus, one wonders how they ever made their way at all. Perhaps the trails were better then. The Aztecs kept them up. One by one the plateau peoples were subdued, their temples overthrown, their leaders killed, the surplus products of their lands taken by the adventurers and the clerics who followed the looting armies. Some surrendered voluntarily; others died fighting; others held out against the invaders for decades.

Upon the plateaus lived a sedentary population, schooled for centuries in maize civilization. They could be dealt with, and sooner or later conquered. "They continued," says Tannenbaum, "their stagnant agricultural life with such changes in land holding, crops, tools, methods of cultivation as were introduced by the Spaniards." But the mountain peoples were another matter. They moved suddenly, they were experts at ambush, they travelled light and fought desperately. When the ridges

[84]

began to rise too steeply, the Spanish domination ended. Most of the mountain tribes were never conquered, although most of them, in due time, came down into the valleys to trade, and to absorb something of the invader's culture. Some races, like the Pumas and the Apaches, practically disappeared. Others kept rigidly to themselves. A missionary speaking of the Kikapus in Coahuila (a border state) says:

It is pre-Cortezan America. They are a proud race and have conserved ninety-five per cent of their costumes, ideas, religion, government, spirit of warfare—which they now take out in hunting. They hate the white man. They use bows and arrows and look upon schooling as a means to learn evil.

The Huichol is another haughty people. "Never for a moment will they allow any race superior to theirs. Even when far from home, they hold themselves as though they had never known a master." The governor of the territory of Quintana Roo—on the Yucatan peninsula—is to all intents and purposes a figurehead. The Maya Indians possess the region and obey only their caciques. Speaking of them, a Mexico City paper said editorially as late as 1927, "We are concerned with an important part of Mexico which it is necessary to reconquer."

The Tarahumare Indian rarely keeps horses and never pigs. Pigs are held to be Spaniards in disguise. The Cora Indians plant maize once a year, sowing with the first rains. They do not occupy themselves with work after that but pass the time in celebrating feasts, and have for their main distraction dancing with their idols. (Reported in 1922.) These Indians will come down from the mountains from time to time to work for the haciendas, and barter in the markets, or even go into the mines for

[85]

a short period. But they always return to their mountain villages, shunning the white man, and preserving their own language, songs and religion.

I saw an island in Lake Cuitzeo in Michoacan where, we are told on good authority, a tribe of Tarascans speak no word of Spanish, allow no white man to approach, and keep their ancient customs uncorrupted. On the slopes of the dead volcano of Malinche, named for that brown mistress of Cortez who did so much to betray her own people—and whose ghost, it is alleged, repented—there lives a tribe of Tlaxcalans who also permit no white man to approach. The Mexican Exploration Club must take a roundabout route to the top of this rugged giant, despite the fact that it stands close by the large city of Puebla. Who knows if these people inherit their revulsion from some branch which seceded when Tlaxcala helped Cortez take Mexico?

There are authenticated instances of tribes which embraced—or were forced to accept—Christianity, which later reverted to the worship of their idols. In Oaxaca I penetrated to a mountain village, nominally Catholic, near which on the Day of the Dead, November 1, 1930, was found the fresh blood of a sacrificed turkey, candles, tobacco and other offerings in front of a sculptured monolith. In Oaxaca, furthermore, the valley people wear wide straw sombreros with designs in red and green worked upon them; the mountain people wear little black peaked hats, like gnomes in fairy stories. One can never hope to understand Mexico unless he fully realizes how incomplete the work of the Spaniards was. They left great gaps in the map—chiefly where the contour lines make rich, brown smudges—which acted as reservoirs to perpetuate the ancient way of life. Even on the plateau and in flat Yucatan, "we were conquered physically but our cultural life persisted. We retained our language, costumes, type of house, food, songs, dances, social relations." Which all runs current with our expedition to Tepoztlan.

THE HACIENDA

Two hours on horseback from Mexico City brings one to the fine old hacienda of San G——, raising wheat, cattle and pulque. It is quite possible to go over a bumpy road in a car, but more in keeping with the spirit of colonial times to ride across the vast dry fields which surround the capital, Popo and the White Lady shimmering to the east, along the banks of irrigation ditches, up and down the steep sides of dry barrancas, and so at an easy gallop up the mile-long avenue of eucalyptus which forms the entrance to the estate. As we canter along—the hour is near sunset—we pass the workers coming in from the fields. There are a score of Indians in white pyjamas with wide straw sombreros, and twice as many mules. Each man is driving a pair yoked to an iron plough. It is ancient and battered, but incontrovertibly metal. This, then, is an enterprising hacienda, in a land where the great majority of ploughs are made of wood. Underneath the blade as it scrapes along the ground is a broad leaf of maguey to save its edge and make it slide more easily.

We pass old stone walls and water channels of moss-green masonry. Eucalyptus trees, towering 100 feet or more, form a green arch above our heads. We enter a gate guarded by huge, stone towers and find ourselves in a large compound encircled by high walls of incredible thickness. To a motor car or to pedestrians the foreman might be surly, but the man on horseback is welcome. He gives us an *adios*—that Mexican good-bye which also means how do you do and God bless you, answers our questions with the utmost friendliness, and waves us the freedom of the establishment. On the left is a large, deep pool with a touch of green scum, but attractive in its border of· trees and flowers. This is the general reservoir of the estate. Behind it is the arched portico of the manor house in pink stone. It is shuttered; the family is away. Between the pool and the mansion is a garden, rank with flowers. It has tried to be a formal garden, but nature has been too much for it. The flowers lean against the white wall of the little hacienda church.

To the right of the compound are the barns, and a glimpse of other compounds through massive arches. There is hardly a splinter of wood to be seen; everything is of stone, tile or adobe brick. We note a tall stone silo and beside it a little creamery, operated by a steam engine well nigh as ancient as the ploughs. This is the only mechanism to be seen on the place. We trot through the courtyard to the workers' houses. They form a small village. The little lanes are alive with babies, pigs, chickens, turkeys, dogs. The babies regard us with round, serious eyes, the pigs grunt slowly out from underfoot, the mongrels snap at our horses' hoofs. The huts are of adobe brick, their window sills bright with flowers. I note with amazement that each hut has a small, square chimney—the first chimneys I have ever seen in a Mexican village. Smoke, curling from under the tiles, reassures me, however. The chimney is not working, or has been deliberately stopped up, and smoke from the charcoal cooking brazier is following its normal course—out of the eaves or out of the door. (Charcoal, however, does not produce much smoke.)

Perhaps after *mañana*, which means tomorrow, which means everything that had better not be done now, there is no word more common in Mexico than hacienda. Riding across the country whether by railroad, motor or horse, one's notice is constantly drawn to broad fields culminating in the façade of a great stone structure. Sometimes it looks like a stockade, sometimes like a palace, sometimes like a monastery. Sometimes it is resplendent, sometimes in utter ruin. It is so and so's hacienda—or it *was* so and so's hacienda. In the cities, this man and that man is pointed out. "He has a huge pulque hacienda in Hidalgo. . . . That little dark chap over there owns a string of haciendas in Jalisco." The curio shops, the Thieves' Market deal in old iron, furniture, bric-a-brac retrieved, stolen or pawned from haciendas located at all points of the compass. Visiting foreigners dream of the ideal hacienda which may be purchased cheaply and made inordinately productive. There is hardly, if I may say so, a politician in Mexico who has not his eye upon a neat hacienda to which he may some day retire. In many cases the hand has already supplanted the eye. As for the Indians, they are divided between the desire to have an hacienda functioning nearby about which they may orient their economic effort, and to split up the lands of adjacent haciendas and add them to those of their own village. On the whole the latter urge predominates.

Repeatedly in these pages we refer to free village and hacienda village. The former is dominated by primitive communism and the agricultural methods of the old civilizations; the latter by a landlord, and a heavier infiltration of Spanish crops and methods. The former tends to lie in mountain valleys, the latter on the plateaus. Both are populated by Indians, and many ancient *mores* survive in hacienda village as well as free. Both are deplorably inefficient in the light of scientific agriculture,

but the free village at least maintains a balanced economy, promoting its survival over centuries, where the
hacienda may collapse from over-specialization and con-
sequent soil destruction, or from loss of market. Free
villagers often come down to work on the hacienda when
ploughing or harvest labour is in demand, but when the
stint is over they return to their own fields and homes.

To my mind the hacienda was the major contribution
of Spain to the organic life of Mexico. Where it func-
tioned strongly, it twisted the Indian pattern more violently than any other imported institution. The Church
twisted souls, but the hacienda affected bread and butter
—or better, corn and beans; it went straight to economic
roots. An hacienda was—and still is to a degree—a giant
farm, under the absolute domination of an individual
with powers often running back to royal grant, and a
largely self-sustaining economic unit. It is feudalism plus.
Along with the grant of land went a grant of Indians.
The inhabitants of one or more villages were assigned
to work the farm of the patentee. Gradually they lost
their status as citizens of the Aztec confederacy, and became to all intents and purposes serfs of the landowner.
As such they co-operated to make a little self-enclosed
world. As farm labourers or herders they worked the
lands and produced their own food; as carpenters, masons, blacksmiths, potters, weavers, they erected the
buildings, kept them in repair, and fabricated practically
all necessary tools and utensils; as servants they kept the
owner—the *hacendado*—and his family from ever doing
a stroke of useful work; as consumers they were forced
to purchase their salt and trinkets, brandy and cotton
cloth at the company store, and were kept by monstrous
bookkeeping safely in debt thereto from generation to
generation. These debts made them in effect bound serfs;

Diego Rivera 1931

BOSTON PUBLIC LIBRARY

so far as possible paid in kind rather than money. To round out the picture, one seldom sees a sizable hacienda without its private church. Noble and clergy co-operated to keep the Indian in his place.

On the typical hacienda were found:

An administrator
Mayordomos, or superintendents of local ranches
A priest, clerks, and in rare cases, a schoolteacher
Foremen and cattle herders
Resident indentured workers
Resident crop sharers
Resident renters
Temporary renters and crop sharers
Seasonal harvest gangs (Indians down from mountain villages)
A police force and prison
A magistrate
Handicraft workers—smiths, carpenters, masons, etc.
Household servants
And once in a blue moon—an hacendado

By and large the agricultural methods employed, whether the chief crop was corn, maguey, henequen, wheat, sugar, coffee, fruits, or cattle, were marvellously inefficient. We have already noted how water and fertility were restricted by a wholesale levelling of the pre-conquest forests. Some authorities hold, with considerable show of evidence, that despite the animals, tools and methods brought in by the Spaniards, output per man *declined* as compared with Aztec production. We remember that Cortez found the valley of Cholula so rich "that not a hand's breadth was left uncultivated."

[93]

The hacendado made his chief home in Mexico City, Merida, the city of Oaxaca, or even Europe; left the farm in charge of an administrator, paid a few regal visits to the estate—or estates—and demanded only one thing: a salable surplus crop large enough to keep him and his dependents in the style to which they were accustomed. This demand operated to kill all initiative in the direction of improved methods and processes. The overseer's job was to produce a crop large enough to prevent the local Indians from starving, thus conserving the labour supply, and to keep the señor in velvet, wine and French mistresses.

The hacienda system produced a static economy which never changed, never progressed, took no chances, eluded most of its taxes, drove to a single objective— the master's cash crop. It effectively prevented the development of a middle class, and muffled with a vast apathy all attempts of Mexicans to exercise their minds.

Inefficiency was further increased by the economic policy of Spain in respect to her colonies. Products both raw and manufactured which she herself produced were, in many cases, proscribed in Mexico. Thus the most effective crop or process for a given soil or area often could not be utilized. It was the fixed policy of the mother country to drain her colonies of wealth. Imposts, duties, fees, monopolies, charges, commissions, royalties, tributes, licenses were laid on every person and every article of sale. Gruening cites unlimited evidence to show how these were enforced. The royal monopolies included salt, tobacco, quicksilver, gunpowder, playing cards, cock fighting, indulgences, lotteries, the sale of titles and offices, and, if you please, snow and ice from Popocatepetl! The king of Spain took an average of $7,000,000 a year from Mexico. In 1804 this amounted to two thirds of all the royal revenue. Colonists were forbidden to trade with foreigners, even with other Spanish colonies. Everything must clear through the mother country, resulting in such fantastic transactions as the following:

1. Raw materials were shipped from Mexico to Spain.
2. Spain shipped them to other European countries where they were made into manufactured articles.
3. As such they were imported back to Spain.
4. Spain then shipped them to Mexico—duly loaded with freights, duties, imposts, commissions and profits.

A barrel of wine worth six pesos in Spain cost forty-eight pesos in Mexico City. Consider calmly the economy if Mexico had been permitted to manufacture her own wine and kindred articles. The growing of olives, grapes, flax, hemp, silk, saffron was prohibited. In 1557 a Mexican, de Medina, discovered the quicksilver process for refining silver—a really great industrial innovation. Spain immediately appropriated the process, and literally prevented Mexico from refining her own silver with her own mercury, by throttling the supply. Inventors, men with ideas, sought kindlier shores.

In due time the hacienda spread throughout Mexico. On the plateau it became the dominant economic system. The big estate was not unknown in Aztec days, but it amounted to little compared with the free village and its communal land. Now the free villages were forced farther and farther up the mountains, the haciendas rolling snugly over most of the fertile, reasonably level territory. The plateau peoples went by the millions into peonage. Back over the centuries comes the Indian cry as the institution gained: *"Ni tlaca"*—"We are also human."

Occasionally they were bought and sold as slaves, but normally this was unnecessary. With debts and penalties they were bound to the hacienda just as efficiently as though legally chattels. Some holdings were so huge that their owners never saw, or could even locate, their boundaries. In 400 years the grants to Cortez, still held by his descendants, had swollen to one city, fifteen towns, 157 villages, eighty-nine haciendas, 119 *ranchos,* and five *estancias,* embracing altogether 150,000 people. As late as 1925, Prince Pignatelli of Italy came to Mexico to protest against the breaking up of the hacienda Atlacomulco in the state of Morelos. He descended from Cortez through the Dukes of Monteleone. For nearly four centuries income from that hacienda had been going to absentee owners in Italy. Alvarado, Cortez' captain, who executed one of the most brutal massacres of the whole conquest, was rewarded with Xochimilco, its floating gardens and 30,000 people. A favourite of the king was given the entire state of Guanajuato. By 1572, some 500 huge grants accounted for most of the plateau and fertile lands of Mexico. Later the Church was to make vast inroads into these properties, until, by 1850, it owned a good half of all landed property in the nation. Diaz accelerated the hacienda system. He gave over 30,000,000 acres to seven owners in Chihuahua; 5,000,000 acres to two owners in Coahuila; 12,000,000 acres to a single woman. In Morelos, thirty-two people owned the entire state.

An hacendado, reviewing his workmen as they went to their huts for the night, noted that each carried a bit of wood from the considerable forest on the domain. He remarked in clear tones to the friend who stood beside him that it would be a good idea to tax the men five *centavos* a log, and use the proceeds to buy farm equipment. One straight old Indian dropped his log at his master's feet and marched on without a word.

Here is the valley of Teotihuacan. Before the conquest it was in a flourishing state of civilization. It contained the great pyramids of the moon and of the sun, with their stupendous architecture, sculpture and painting. It produced pottery, textiles, industrial implements, exquisite jade, obsidian jewellery, feather cloths, a fantastic and beautiful mythology, and splendid rituals. Its glory had declined when the Spaniards came, but it was still a rich agricultural and industrial district. The haciendas spread over its face, but a number of free villages were spared. Its real calvary came with Diaz. In 1917, Dr. Manuel Gamio made an intensive study of the valley, and published his findings in three large volumes. He investigated every phase of its economic, social and artistic life. And this is what he found (remember it was before the land distribution of the real revolution) :

Arable land, 25,935 acres.

Population, 8,330—5,657 Indians; 2,137 mestizos —mostly following the Indian way of life; 536 whites.

Average acreage—three per individual. More than adequate to provide comfortably for every man, woman and child.

But 7,907 persons owned no land whatsoever. Four hundred and six persons owned 2,594 acres of poor land. Seven persons, living in Mexico City, owned 23,-341 acres, or all the rest of the arable land, amounting to a cool 90 per cent. Their crops were sold in the capital, thirty miles away, leaving the resident population with the choice of starving or going to work on the haciendas at fifty to seventy-five centavos (twenty-five to thirty-seven cents) a day.

The result: overwork, undernourishment, villainous housing, an infant mortality rate at fifty-six per cent, no medical service in the valley save native herb doctors, illiteracy at sixty-six per cent. Nearly all the old arts and crafts had evaporated, or woefully degenerated. In the school he started, Dr. Gamio had to teach the Indians all over again the ancient and beautiful pottery designs.

The valley of Teotihuacan, in the shadow of the capital, is an extreme case. But it shows the trend. Latifundia have cursed Mexico even as they did Rome. For centuries, fewer than 10,000 families have dominated the country. Tannenbaum found, in 1921, 12,782 properties of more than 2,500 acres and thus legitimate haciendas, embracing some sixty per cent of all Mexico's land not owned by the government. They held in fief 50,000 villages and not far from 4,000,000 persons. Northern states like Coahuila had ninety-four per cent of their area in haciendas. In 1921, furthermore, the tide had begun to turn. The peak of the hacienda system was in 1910, the year that Diaz was overthrown.

Ten thousand principalities ruled by the man on horseback; 10,000 little self-sufficing economic empires as primitive and backward in their technical methods as in their sociology—such was the principal gift of Spain to Mexico; a gift made even more poignant by Don Porfirio. But we must remember that through all these dreadful centuries, up on the mountains the free village, accounting for half the population, still stubbornly held its own.

CHAPTER VI

THE DECLINE OF MEXICAN CIVILIZATION. II

THE CHURCH

OVER the Mexican border in Guatemala, in Maya-Quiche territory, Franz Blom and Oliver La Farge not long ago discovered a church, theoretically Catholic, in charge of twenty men. These men were in fact priests of the old Maya cult, keeping the ancient calendar with red seeds, and starting the new year count in the spring. They met in a secret cave, and here initiated new members.

This is probably an extreme case of pagan survival, but it serves to accent the strange and anomalous position of the Catholic Church in Mexico. At Taxco, where Borda built his baroque but lovely cathedral, I saw the famous tiger dance. It was performed in the courtyard of a hillside chapel by a group of Indians arrayed in masks and special costumes, to the music of drum and pipe played simultaneously by a single musician. For hours the pipe wove its primitive tune, the drum thumped its stirring, monotonous rhythm, and the dancers, surrounded by a dense ring of enchanted Indians, stamped out the long and involved story of the tiger hunt. (By tigers Mexicans mean jaguars; there are of course no genuine wild tigers in the Western Hemisphere.) At its conclusion, dancers and spectators filed into the chapel and listened to a priest perform mass, while little boys in the towers turned the great bells over and over. The mass finished, everybody repaired to the churchyard again, ate and drank at little booths which had sprung up like mushrooms, discharged fireworks, listened to the village band, gambled with grains of corn on pictures, and watched itinerant acrobats perform on bars and wires strung to the church wall itself. I tried with no success to picture such a scene in front of any Catholic church I had ever seen. Aztec dance, Roman mass, itinerant circus, all enacted in the same holy precincts, and in a fairly sophisticated town as Mexican towns go.

In Tepoztlan the victories of the ancient god are celebrated by a dance in the churchyard. At Guadalupe—and nearly every big fiesta—the ferris wheel is stationed squarely in front of the church, as close to the building as possible. In Oaxaca I saw the solemn procession of the banners and lanterns of Our Lady of the Soledad inaugurated by two old Indians with pipe and drum, while the marchers themselves sang a weird, primitive chant which sent chills up one's spine. Nor was the procession from gate to church door concluded before two gentlemen appeared in the courtyard, clothed completely in fireworks, and proceeded to fight the most luridly comic battle imaginable. They leaped into the air like game cocks, the rockets, pinwheels, bombs and Roman candles attached to their persons exploding in all directions. The combatants were protected by an asbestos undergarment, but the delighted spectators were not so fortunate.

Cornfields need divine protection in a maize civilization. The chances of finding an idol as against a cross guaranteeing that protection are, considering all of Mexico, perhaps about equal. In Michoacan the idol is away ahead. Even when the cross is used, it may be sur-

rounded by offerings of rum, *cocoposole,* candles, incense
or a freshly killed chicken. Idols are called *"santos"* by
the Indians today. A saint or a god, what is the difference? There is a headless idol on a hill in Chiapas. In
front of it are clay bowls with burned *copal,* candlesticks,
coloured paper, and festoons of pine needles. At Chakal-
chib is an ancient pyramid surmounted by a cross. Religious ceremonies are conducted here, but not by a
Christian priest. At Mitla not only is the principal church
built upon a half-ruined pyramid, but a higher pyramid
is crowned with an unattended shrine containing three
crosses and many incense-burners for the dead; the name
Mitla means "city of the dead." Gruening reproduces a
photograph of an idol, presumably of the Aztec rain god,
in a cloister of a church at Milpa Alta, within twenty
miles of Mexico City. Flowers are always growing in
this cloister and in no other. Idols have been found
buried under crosses, used as corner-stones of churches,
hidden in bouquets of flowers for priests to bless. In
Cuilapan I saw a magnificent great church and convent
partially destroyed by earthquake. In the wall above the
crumbling altar, two stones have recently been inserted.
Upon them are carved dates in the old Zapotec calendar.

Dr. Manuel Gamio, studying this phenomenon in the
shadow of the great pyramids at Teotihuacan, goes so
far as to make a clean division between "pagan-Catholic"
and "Roman Catholic" congregations. Personally I feel
that the two streams are so hopelessly intermingled that
classification is impossible. Where idol stops and the
trinity begins is beyond exact determination. Anita Brenner's book, *Idols behind Altars,* is full of more evidence
of the confusion.

The Church baptized every Indian, not too far up the
mountains to be reached, between the Isthmus and the

Rio Grande. In 1537, Indians, by a specific bull of the pope, were declared to be human beings with souls, susceptible to conversion. Hardy and perspiring fathers toiled over mountain passes, tearing down temples, holding mass baptisms (15,000 in one day in Xochimilco), building churches and monasteries. Presently they claimed some 9,000,000 converts, a number, Prescott remarks, "probably exceeding the population of the country." But the holy water—like vaccination serum in certain blood streams—simply did not take. The Indian would accept the Church only on his own terms, while the Church, it must be admitted, made compromise after compromise to bring him into the fold. Did the Aztecs worship their gods with religious dances? The dances were supplied with Christian scenarios and symbols, while the steps and music remained unchanged. Did they fast for forty days before the fiestas to their rain god and their god of war? They might go on fasting for forty days before Easter, which fortunately arrived near the beginning of the rainy season. Had they the habit of worshipping at certain sacred spots where they built their pyramids? The same sites remained sacred when churches were built on the ruined foundations. With these numerous concessions and fundamental parallels, it should not have surprised the holy fathers that the Indians, while accepting the Catholic saints as so many new gods, showed a disposition to keep their old ones even within the Christian calendar. For four centuries the Church has been trying to make good Christians of its Mexican congregations, and they remain stubbornly more than half pagan. This does not refer to the urban population or to the upper economic classes. It does refer emphatically to the village Indians, who are most of Mexico.

The Spaniards built—or better, directed the Indians

to build—some 10,000 churches, almost all of them of stone, constructed for the ages. Although some villages supported as many as thirty clergy, others never had a resident priest. Indians would trim the altars and keep the candles burning. Once in so often, perhaps on only one day in the year, an itinerant father would come over the mountains on mule-back to perform mass. For a time in 1927 and 1928, the revolutionary government forced priests from the churches altogether. Did they close? No indeed. The native altar-tenders conducted their business as usual; old Indian women dropped upon their knees before their favourite santo, the candles and ribbons gleamed, the incense smoked at fiesta time (the same copal gum that had honoured Quetzalcoatl); the "Moors and the Christians" danced their old dance, Christian symbolism overlaid on pagan, in the church courtyard.

Terry reports in 1845, after several revolutions had tried to break the power of the colonial Church, but before Juarez' reform laws finally succeeded in shaking it, 7,200 clericals in Mexico—2,000 nuns, 1,700 monks, 3,500 secular clergy. This is not a large number in a population of upwards of 7,000,000 at the time; say one to 1,000. Their wealth, however, was out of all proportion to their numbers. The nuns alone owned fifty-eight estates with a floating capital of 4,500,000 pesos. It has been estimated that in its great days the Church owned one-half of all landed wealth. It was the nation's chief banker, floating the loans which financed the haciendas, and lending to the government at five per cent. Its vast estates were farmed by the Indians in much the same manner as the haciendas were farmed. Indeed the two systems interlocked at every turn—feudal lord and Church—even as they did in the middle ages. Both were

[103]

rich, arrogant, materialistic; both conspired to keep the peon in subjection.

As for the colonial state, it was practically married to the Church. Ten of the thirty archbishops of Mexico ultimately became viceroys. The Church was responsible not to the pope, but to the king of Spain. It had its own courts; the government helped it collect tithes, enforce monastic vows, maintain censorship and the index expurgatorius. Vows of celibacy, however, were discreetly forgotten. In one remote village I was told of the visit of a bishop not so many years ago. Among his other duties, he baptized thirty children of the local priest by seven mothers.

"Neither Church nor state alone," says Gruening, "could have made the common sources of income . . . so productive." Carrying out its side of the bargain the Church excommunicated civil offenders—contrabandists, adulterators of pulque, and other such criminals. The Inquisition, while relatively mild in Mexico in respect to life, freely confiscated the property of well-to-do "heretics." Church power was at the disposal of the law as long as it saw eye to eye with the law. After independence, and particularly after its property rights were undermined, the Church turned anarchist. For 300 odd years the high clergy of Mexico enjoyed an exhilarating and profitable time, living like princes. The income of the archbishop, in Mexico City, was $130,000 a year. We have to look to old Russia to find a parallel. The underlying population in both countries defrayed the costs.

We note, for instance, the Codex of San Juan Teotihuacan, reproduced for us by Dr. Gamio. It is a document presented to the king of Spain in Aztec picture-writing, prepared by the Indians who were building the convent of Acolman. It depicts corpulent monks whipping and kicking Indians; bleeding Indians led yoked and shackled in long lines; Indians in the stocks; Indians exposed to tortures suggestive of the Inquisition; Indians not only coming from long distances to work without food or pay, but paying tribute as well, in hewn lumber, cut stones, foodstuffs. It is not a pretty picture, but one fears it was all too common as the walls of the 10,000 holy buildings rose. Dr. Gamio as a result of his studies is forced to conclude that, by and large, the Church was animated by a persistent commercial spirit which made it the national banker on the one hand, and set exorbitant rates for marriage services, baptisms, burials, saints' day collections, tithes and so forth, on the other. For its intake it failed to return anything substantial in the way of education, care of the sick and needy, genuine solace for the soul. That there were outstanding exceptions to this broad conclusion goes without saying. Willa Cather in *Death Comes to the Archbishop* has told the poignant story of one of them. The old records show scores of devoted men, trying to understand the Indians, learning their dialects, writing down their histories, organizing their handicrafts, teaching their children. But the basic policy of the Church, as an institution, lay in a more worldly direction.

One of Mexico's labour leaders, sprung from the loins of the recent revolution, was haranguing, under a sputtering torchlight, a vast gathering of Maya Indians in Yucatan. "In the name of God who is called love, you have been beaten, kicked, wounded, killed; in the name of Jesus, the humble, you have been oppressed, enslaved, robbed of your houses and your lands; in the name of Mary the mother of God your wives have been dishonoured, your sisters and your daughters have been raped. But now in the name of the *devil* [the revolution] you have your houses, you have your lands, you have your families. . . ." As one man the multitude forgot its catechism and responded: *"Viva el diablo! Viva el diablo!"*

Today the Church owns no property in Mexico. The government has taken title to the 10,000 edifices and their lands. The commercial spirit has been scotched, though marriage fees are still too high for most Indians to pay—more than five times the cost of building a cottage. With the problem of corruption largely solved, some attention may be paid to a less dramatic question, the effect of church teaching on public health. It is amusing to us to think of pasting a plaster which the priest has blessed on the chest to cure a cough, but multiply it by thousands and one begins to understand why pneumonia and tuberculosis take a heavy toll in Mexico. It is quaint to see in the market little silver images called "miracles," representing arms and legs, heads and hearts, to be hung on a saint's image so that the saint will cure these ailing members. But when you see four walls of a church solidly plated with such *milagros*—I estimated 50,000 in the Chapel of the Divino Rostro in Mexico City—it means that many thousands of sick people have been encouraged by their priests to substitute these pathetic offerings for common medical care It is not uncommon for priests to disparage the efforts of doctors, and suggest instead a pilgrimage to some distant shrine. At Patzcuaro I saw invalids walking on their knees to the church of the Virgin of the *Salubridad*—Our Lady of Health.

Meanwhile to this day priests and Indians still carry on their ancient compromise of idols flanking altars, perhaps the strangest and the most colourful religion in the world.

THE DECLINE OF MEXICAN CIVILIZATION

THE LEGACY OF SPAIN

In the 300 years of Spanish domination, sixty-one viceroys were appointed by the king. Scholars have listed
some thirteen of them as decent men. It was the era of
the man on horseback, of a feudalism more absolute
than that of the middle ages in Europe. Hacienda,
mine, and Church drained Mexico of her wealth and
gave little in the way of tangible service in return. Economic initiative being blocked by the mother country,
enterprising Mexicans found the only outlet to wealth
and success in office holding. It was indeed the sole career.
A sheriffship might cost 120,000 pesos, but its perquisites
made good the capital outlay in a remarkably short time.
Judgeships were traded in as briskly as in modern Tammany Hall. The tradition was laid down that only saps
work; a gentleman obtains his living by peculation if he
has no Indians to exploit directly. It is this tradition,
stamped in, generation after generation, which curses
Mexican political life today, a cultural lag which the
windy speeches and the violent deeds of the revolution
have not effaced. The economic policy of Spain in respect
to her colonies is thus chiefly responsible for the deplorable standards of integrity found in current statesman-
ship.

Three hundred years of slow decline in civilization.
But the record is not all black. If it was a period of stag-
nation and decay it was also one of comparative peace.
As the observing traveller goes about Mexico it is only
too evident that the tales of unmitigated horror, exploitation, brutality, charged by some historians to viceroy, hacendado and priest, must be heavily discounted,
when considering the country as a whole. If they had
been half as rigorous as painted, the Indians would have

[107]

been wiped out; their culture, like that of their cousins north of the Rio Grande, obliterated. But as a matter of cold fact, I repeat that Mexico is an Indian country, its pre-conquest traditions surviving with unbelievable vitality. Many of the *mores* were profoundly modified, but the Spaniards, for all their horrendous deeds in this locality and that, did not, or could not, eradicate the Indian way of life. Look at Tepoztlan; look at thousands of other towns and villages today. The Church as we have seen compromised right and left with the plumed serpent. Even the hacendados, if their annual surplus was forthcoming, were mostly too lazy to interfere seriously with the traditions of their subservient villages, especially the play traditions. Says Wallace Thompson, analyzing *The Mexican Mind* for American employers, with considerable impatience and an occasional flash of understanding: "The Indians . . . desire nothing so much as to be left alone. . . . Spain discovered early that the easiest way to rule the Indians was to leave the communes to themselves, and to allow their only contact to be with the paternal Church and the paternal landlord. The viceroys early adopted this easiest way, with effects of which we are only today reaping the full fruits. . . . The feudal age was dead in Europe when Columbus sailed. . . . But feudalism was revived in Latin America, and that far less because of Spanish cupidity than because of the immovable mountain of Indian tradition and the inertia of Indian psychology."

Straight down from the Mayas and Aztecs, accordingly, comes a flood of colour: dances, costumes, music, pottery, weaving, masks, toys, flower-culture; colour which sings and vibrates all over modern Mexico. Conquerors who let such a rainbow through were not wholly vicious.

Again, we must admit that however impressive were the pyramids, temples and towers which the Spaniards pulled down, they made at least partial restitution in decorating the country with an extraordinarily impressive architecture of their own design. The Indians built it, but Spain laid out the pattern. Mexico would lose a great fraction of its charm without these crumbling cathedrals, these arched and patioed palaces, these stout hacienda walls, these tiled domes raised against the profiles of glittering volcanoes. I for one would exchange them all for a quarter of the monuments of the old civilization restored and shining on their oriented hill tops, but the new (not so new as our own early American architecture) is a far from unworthy substitute.

We have noted how from the fusion of idol and cross came a new religion. The conclusion can be pushed further to cover nearly every phase of Mexican life, save where high mountains and deep jungles cut off the Spanish influence altogether. What we have in Mexico today is a culture neither Indian nor Spanish. Four hundred years of interaction have created a synthesis, a mosaic which is Mexico herself. She has modified Castilian Spanish to her own softer tongue, even as the Yankee has modified the king's English. She has worked out her own diet, her own piquant cookery; she has combined church and market into her own inimitable fiesta; she has adapted Spanish ballads to the guitar-threaded *corrido*, full of news and satire. The culture is drenched with Aztec survivals and with Spanish importations, but a chemical reaction has taken place; a totally new compound is in the making.

Finally, it is not altogether unreasonable to suppose that Mexico, one of the last stands of the handicraft age, bears a large share of responsibility for the coming of the machine. It was the gold and silver of her mines which in the seventeenth and eighteenth centuries created fluid capital in Europe. Out of that capital, thrifty merchants set aside their profits, the early factories were built, Watt began his tinkering, and the industrial revolution was born. Without the metal of Mexico, the machine age might have been indefinitely postponed.

OUT OF THE FRYING PAN

One morning in the year 1810 the bells of the parish church in the little town of Dolores began to toll. The Indians flocked to the call of a man they respected and loved, Father Hidalgo, the parish priest. He had established or, better, recalled the arts of pottery, leather-work, and weaving in the village. In defiance of the crown, he had encouraged silk and wine culture. He had declared his allegiance to the Indian Virgin of Guadalupe, that most miraculous of all the Virgins of Mexico, disclosed to a peon, and enshrined on the site of a pyramid to Tonantzin, mother of the Aztec gods. Best of all, he was in open rebellion against the Spanish domination which often lay so heavy upon his Indians. He was in rebellion against the practices of his own Church. White-haired and earnest he faced his congregation:

My children, this day comes to us a new dispensation. Are you ready to receive it? Will you be free? Will you make the effort to recover from the hated Spaniards the lands stolen from your forefathers three hundred years ago?

This was the "cry from Dolores," the Patrick Henry speech that inaugurated the revolt from Spain. It was delivered by one of the gentlest men who ever lived.

The independence of Mexico became inevitable, according to Gruening, when Napoleon crossed the Pyrenees in 1808. We can well believe him. It was the signal for the dissolution of the Spanish Empire. Men of the breed of Cortez and Cervantes had ceased to inhabit the Iberian peninsula. Its vitality was gone, sapped in part by that very gold which Cortez set sail to find. Montezuma at last was revenged.

Three distinct classes were to be found in Mexico in 1810:

(1) The small ruling class of Spaniards, called by the natives *gachupines,* a word which means "wearers of spurs."

(2) The White Mexicans, or creoles. They were of Spanish blood, but born in the country had a Mexican rather than a Spanish point of view. They could hardly be called patriots, however, except in a highly personal sense. They wanted the prerogatives of the gachupines. Their numbers were relatively few.

(3) The underlying population, Indian and mestizo; the third estate for whom Father Hidalgo spoke. They numbered perhaps 5,000,000, a greater population than that found in the revolting American colonies in 1776.

At this time Mexico was in area the fourth largest country in the world, surpassed only by Brazil, Russia and China. Under Hidalgo the Indians rose, other leaders, notably Morelos and Guerrero (for whom adjoining states are now named) joining with them. The land of peace became a land of blood. Step by step for the next ten years the gachupines were driven from stronghold to stronghold, until finally only the prison fortress of San Juan de Ulloa in the harbour of Vera Cruz remained to them.

So far so good. At this point the revolution took a turn to the right which was to defeat the inspired dream of Father Hidalgo for 100 years. (The good man was executed shortly after the first uprising.) The creoles captured the movement, and forced the third estate back into its place. The first champion was a precious rascal named Iturbide. He promptly proclaimed himself emperor in 1821, with Napoleonic trimmings. He was shot and succeeded by a beautiful paper constitution, based on a combination of French and American models. General Antonio Lopez de Santa Anna took exclusive charge of this instrument for thirty years. When not president himself he usually managed to pick his presidents. Despite the loss of Texas and the humiliation of the war with the United States in 1846, he dominated Mexico for a generation, wooden leg and all. Hacienda and Church remained substantially unchanged. The creoles took over the work of exploitation from the gachupines: different and no better masters for identical institutions of hacienda, mine, Church. In some respects they were distinctly worse. As a last resort from local bedevilment the Indians could, during the colonial period, appeal to the crown. Sometimes the crown actually interposed in their behalf. A number of royal clemencies are on record, both as to lands and as to persons. Now they had nobody to appeal to; the supreme court had been abolished.

Matters went from bad to worse until 1857, when a Zapotec Indian appeared to take up the task which Father Hidalgo had laid down. His name was Benito Juarez, and it is perhaps the greatest name in Mexican history. His statue stands in scores of plazas, and he has been compared not unfavourably by historians to his contemporary, Abraham Lincoln. Juarez, as president, actually undermined the financial power of the Church, and inaugurated a series of energetic reforms designed to aid the Indian. His enemies multiplied; his friends were largely inarticulate. In 1859, the value of Church real estate, not including buildings, was estimated at $125,000,000. This Juarez tried to restore to the nation by ordering it sold at a fair return to the clerics.

While the United States, immersed in the Civil War, was too busy to enforce the Monroe Doctrine, the infuriated Church and hacendados succeeded in inducing Maximilian of Austria, supported by the troops of France, to invade Mexico. I climbed a mountain road above the town of Orizaba which the French Zouaves built in one night, dragging their cannon up to shell the city. Juarez' forces won one considerable battle near Puebla, giving occasion for every other street in Mexico to be called the Cinco de Mayo (Fifth of May), but the French returned to the attack and placed Maximilian and the indefatigable Carlotta in Chapultepec Castle, emperor and empress of Mexico. The amiable pair lasted until the Civil War was over, the carpetbaggers began to drift south, and the United States had leisure to recall the exact wording of the Monroe Doctrine. The Zouaves tumbled over each other to reach Vera Cruz, Carlotta went to throw herself at the feet of the pope begging assistance, and poor befuddled Maximilian was promptly tried and executed, his chief contribution to Mexican life being an inundation of quite ghastly Empire and Victorian furnishings, which still clutter the houses of the well-to-do. It was a romantic and, on the whole, an unimportant interlude.

THE INDUSTRIAL INVASION OF DON PORFIRIO

One of the generals who helped execute Maximilian was Porfirio Diaz, a young and ambitious mestizo born in Oaxaca, not far from the birthplace of Juarez. He bided his time while Juarez came back to the presidency. When the liberator died—strangely enough in his bed—Diaz overthrew his successor and, like Santa Anna, became dictator of Mexico for a generation. Statistically this was altogether the most progressive period in Mexican history. Humanly, as I have hinted, it probably marked the lowest point to which the third estate had ever fallen. But let us give Don Porfirio his due.

In the thirty-five years, from 1875 to 1910, during which Diaz ruled Mexico, railroad lines increased from 691 kilometers to 24,717. The production of silver rose from 523,000 kilos to 2,417,000, and of gold from 1,636 to 41,400 kilos. The total value of exports and imports increased almost tenfold. Internal customs duties—that bane of feudalism—were abolished. The gold standard was introduced. Banditry was suppressed, and Mexico became one of the safest countries for tourist traffic in the world. The budget was balanced; obligations on account of foreign loans were paid on the nail. Free schools were established in many communities—an unheard-of innovation. The great drainage canal begun in the seventeenth century was pushed to completion, freeing Mexico City from the plague of floods—"easily the most spectacular modern engineering feat from the Roosevelt Dam to the Panama Canal." Ports were developed with breakwaters, lighthouses and modern loading equipment. Public buildings were erected by the score, each more flamboyantly rococo than the last. Cast iron bandstands were to be found in every village plaza—and still are. Statues,

BOSTON PUBLIC LIBRARY

memorial columns, winged victories, shot skyward. Mexico City was converted from a quaint colonial town to a leading metropolis numbering close to 1,000,000 people.

It would be almost impossible to cite any commercial or financial index that did not show an advance during the Diaz regime. In 1910, Mexico easily led all Spanish America, in the opinion of foreign bankers. A few months later, seemingly without warning, Porfirio Diaz, an old man but still sturdy, was fleeing for his life, the political edifice that he had reared so patiently and apparently so well collapsing in utter chaos behind him. Wall Street scratched its head, dumbfounded. The statisticians and the professors of economics, looking at their thirty-five-year graphs, like so many Popocatepetls, doubtless declared that prosperity was not dead but sleeping, and that Mexico could not be sold short. But all the king's horses and all the king's men could not put Humpty-Dumpty back on his wall. Indeed there has been nothing more surprising in this century than the collapse of Diaz and his system, unless it be the collapse of American prosperity in 1929.

Systems, either in Mexico or in the United States, do not collapse without a reason. After twenty years it is fairly clear why the Diaz formula, despite its soaring statistics and its substantial material contributions to Mexican life, was headed for disaster. Indeed the reason is prettily demonstrated in the architecture of the period. Study the buildings of the Diaz epoch. What do they look like; what do they represent? They look like Versailles in a state of nervous collapse, and they represent an attempt to make a third-rate Europe out of Mexico. Not one of them is grounded in the country's soil—that rich soil blended from Aztec and Spanish elements. In short, the Diaz policy turned its back on the Mexican inheritance and faced an alien culture; welcomed foreign capital, foreign industrialism, foreign immigration, foreign art. The machine was to be embraced; Mexico was to be modernized, commercialized, cosmopolitanized, made property conscious, brought up to date.

That Diaz was reasonably honest I, for one, do not doubt. That he had tremendous gifts as a leader and administrator, nobody can doubt. The trouble lay in his policy. It was wrong for two cardinal reasons. He tried to set up Western Civilization in the midst of a land stubbornly devoted to handicraft economy; and far worse, he tried to do it by head-on rather than flank attack. He would force Mexico to accept the West; he set himself to break down and stamp out the Indian way of life. His career furnishes us with a sublime example of how *not* to introduce the machine.

The haciendas in the Diaz period were not broken up, they grew more swollen and bloated than ever before. Huge foreign concessions were granted, together with levies of peons to work them, until a full quarter of the country was in the hands of aliens, who came, like Cortez, seeking only a quick return. Whole areas were depopulated *en masse* and forced into slavery. One of the most heart-rending odysseys I know is the march of the Yaqui Indians from the haciendas of Yucatan back across all Mexico to their beloved northern mountains. They had been sold into slavery at sixty-five dollars a head; they had been chained, whipped, branded, in a low, hot land utterly alien to their peaks and precipices. They broke their chains and left that land, passing over one of the most dangerous and God-forsaken swamp areas on earth. The survivors had tramped and fought for 2,000 miles when they reached their villages in Sonora.

Wages in the new factories were kept at starvation levels, and working conditions were unspeakable. Food prices rose, while hacienda owners put up tariffs against cheap American grains. The standard of living of the third estate went down. The free villages were further stripped of their lands, which were added to those of the haciendas —much after the fashion of the Enclosure Acts in eighteenth century England. Debt bondage reached its apex. J. Russell Smith tells of an American hacendado who kept a ledger account with each peon, and instructed his bookkeeper to add the date, 1899, to the debit column every time he turned a page! The Indian, in the name of the survival of the fittest—this was the age when Darwin was most grossly misinterpreted—was treated as a biological inferior, marked for ultimate extinction and replacement by foreign immigration.

Worst of all, to my mind, Diaz ruthlessly sought to break down the conception of communal property and community responsibility which the villages had inherited; to replace the spirit of co-operation with unrestrained and greedy individualism. He tried to make each villager stake off his own land, trade in it, buy and sell it, irrespective of the needs and desires of the community about him. Individualism in this sense was—and thank God still is—incomprehensible to the Indian. He was willing to sell "his" land for a peso or a drink of *tequila,* simply because alienation was unthinkable. Unscrupulous land speculators, the rurales at their heels, took full advantage of this rooted philosophy. Thus the villager was defrauded at once spiritually and materially.

In the United States today, the bankruptcy of the farmer is on every tongue. How shall he be saved? Many of the most conservative statesmen and bankers, as well as informed economists, are agreed that co-operative societies furnish the only ultimate solution. Very good.

[119]

But American farmers by and large find it exceedingly difficult to co-operate. They have been steeped in the tradition of every man for himself. They will not hold to agreements for restricting crop acreage. It will take years, decades, to unlearn these habits, and form the new ones which alone may rescue them economically. Yet here were thousands of Mexican villages ripe and ready for co-operation. It was the only way they knew how to live. They had been taking it in with their mothers' milk for 1,000 years. And Diaz tried to shatter it; to force them painfully to unlearn that which they must some day inevitably learn again if agriculture is to go forward in Mexico. Fortunately he did not succeed.

No. Rural Mexico seethed as it realized the plunder of its lands, its precious ejidos—and that meant most of Mexico. The new industrial worker was miserable in his factory, his mine, his plantation—and that meant the rest of Mexico. A handful of politicians, generals, hacendados, priests, and concessionaires were doing very nicely, thank you, and when was the new 5,000,000 peso marble opera house to open?

It never opened. Still-born, it rears its crazy bulk at the end of the Alameda in the capital city. The only real revolution Mexico ever had began when she swung on her heel and faced inward to her own brown people. At that moment the decline of Mexican civilization came to an end.

1808. Napoleon crosses the Pyrenees.

1810. Miguel Hidalgo, a parish priest, inaugurates the revolt from Spain. He is shot in 1811, but the revolt continues.

1822. Agustin de Iturbide proclaims himself emperor of Mexico. The last viceroy returns to Spain.

1823. General Antonio Lopez de Santa Anna proclaims a republic, ousts Iturbide, and becomes virtual dictator of Mexico for a generation.

1836. Mexico loses Texas to the cry of "Remember the Alamo!"

1846. War with the United States, and further territorial losses.

1858. Benito Juarez becomes president. He starts forthwith to nationalize the property of the Church. Piteous cries from priest, hacendado, and concessionaire.

1861. Juarez suspends payment on foreign loans. France, England, and Spain occupy Vera Cruz.

1862. The French troops of Napoleon III invade Mexico—the United States being too busy with the Civil War to make effective protest. On May 5th the Mexicans win a great battle, but the French reorganize and continue their march.

1864. Maximilian Hapsburg of Austria proclaimed emperor of Mexico.

1867. Following vigorous notes from the United States, Maximilian's French troops are withdrawn. The emperor lured to Queretaro and shot. Juarez reinstated.

1871. Diaz starts abortive revolt against Juarez.

1872. Juarez dies.

1877. Diaz overthrows Juarez' successor and annexes the presidential chair. With the exception of the period from 1880 to 1884, he keeps it warm for thirty-three years. Business and trade statistics reach dizzy heights.

1911. Diaz overthrown by Francisco Madero.

1913. Victoriano Huerta, a Diaz man, overthrows Madero and has him murdered. Venustiano Carranza rises against Huerta, and is joined by Pancho Villa and Alvaro Obregon.

1915. Carranza recognized by United States as *de facto* president of Mexico.
1917. Famous new Constitution is adopted. Mexico faces definitely inward to her own people.
1920. Carranza defeated by Adolfo de la Huerta (not to be confused with Victoriano Huerta) and Obregon elected president.
1924. Plutarco Elias Calles succeeds Obregon as president.
1926. Church riots, as protest against government anti-clerical policy.
1928. Obregon reelected president; assassinated.
1931. Calles, though no longer president, still the strong man of Mexico. All revolutions against him have been crushed. Statistics are climbing again, but not on the Diaz pattern. The Indian is recognized (by all but certain gun-toters) as the background and wellspring of Mexican life.

NOTE: I include political mileposts from 1910 onward to bring the record down to date. A more intensive examination of this period will be forthcoming in a later chapter, where we shall attempt to get modern politics into focus.

CHAPTER VII

MACHINELESS MEN—THEIR FOOD
AND DRINK

WE return to Tepoztlan as a symbol of the Mexico of today. Here lies our dominant interest. And we have to keep a steady head. On the one hand the inquiring traveller carries with him the usual complement of American prejudices, conditioning him to find dirt, squalor, inefficiency, banditry, laziness, political peculation and instability to the exclusion of all else. On the other hand he is bound to spend long evenings in the company of compatriots who have gone virtually native, listening as they remove cover after cover from the surface of Mexico until he stares dizzily into a bottomless pit of mysteries, atavisms, sorceries and primitive profundities. . . . *Beyond that mountain lies a village. . . . Sometimes you can hear the drums. . . . On the Day of the Dead. . . . Descended from a conquistador and the last prince. . . . Down this street lives an Aztec sorceress. . . . You saw these herb charms in the market?* . . . *They are making vases in that valley exactly as they did 1,000 years ago, but you can't buy them. . . . Tombs of three Zapotec kings. If the department would only excavate here. . . . He tried to find out the secret, and has never been heard of since. . . . Being* simpatico *is not enough, you have to establish* confianza. *. . . Still mining the gold they hid from Cortez. . . . Three men have tried to dig it up and all three have died. . . .*

No white man has ever been there, but an old Indian has promised to take me. . . .

Between this Scylla and Charybdis the traveller must steer, on guard against crude Nordic reflexes, and against sheer sentimental mysticism. Personally I found it not over-difficult to subdue my bathtub and Listerine complexes, but exceedingly difficult to neutralize the powers of the air. There *is* a mystery about Mexico; there is something in the atmosphere incredibly old and not a little fearsome, heightened, doubtless, by the raw violence of the scenery. Some of the weird stories are grossly exaggerated and some are literally true. I have, however, not gone native and do not propose to. Mexico, like any other considerable area of the planet, is here, drab and dirty, there, colourful and mysterious. Only the drabness is not quite so dreary, and the mystery more encircling and pungent. While the colour is more vivid than in any land I know.

Which brings me—I do not quite know why unless it be a violent attempt to be practical—to the definition of a "Mexican." It is a matter which perplexes every observant traveller, and had best be clarified forthwith. There are five distinct connotations of the word:

1. All citizens of the nation.
2. All citizens other than those living in Yucatan. The latter, from their flat plain, look down on "Mexicans."
3. All Aztecs. Cortez and Bernal Diaz call "Mexicans" the people whose capital they razed. The Tlaxcalans, Zapotecs, Tarascans and other nations were always identified as such. The distinction lingers today. Indians speaking Aztec dialects—such as the residents of Tepoztlan—and

[124]

    people dwelling generally within the old Aztec boundaries, are occasionally called Mexicans, marking them off from other areas in the republic.

4. All citizens of Mexico City. Travellers soon learn to say "I'm going up to Mexico," meaning specifically the capital.

5. All well-to-do citizens, or citizens formerly well-to-do, with white blood, as against the Indians.

This is all very confusing; particularly as nobody seems to know where the word "Mexico" comes from. The most likely clue is a derivation from an Aztec god of war, a ferocious gentleman named Mexitli. In Tepoztlan the matter is admirably taken care of. The more educated, with a dash of white—or two or three—are called *"los correctos"*; the rank and file *"los tontos,"* the simple. Perhaps the distinction which holds most currency at the present time, though appallingly undemocratic, is "Mexican" and "Indian"; the former applying to the educated, particularly the townsfolk with white blood, the latter to the villagers. I think, however, that I shall speak for the age that is dawning, and call all citizens Mexicans, even as I term a southern negro with one mule, a Dakota farmer, Mr. A. Drexel Biddle, and myself, Americans.

Our business in Tepoztlan is lodged in three portfolios. We want to know how a community of machineless men carries on; how a handicraft culture actually functions; how it compares with an American community, the best documented being Middletown. We want to know the extent of the legacy from the Aztecs; how much of the pre-Columbian civilization survives. Finally we shall inquire into the specific inroads of the machine age to date, and speculate as to the future course of that invasion. While, due to the indefatigable researches of Mr. Redfield, we know more facts about Tepoztlan than about any other native community of the free village type, and it becomes our symbol, we shall not confine ourselves to this locality. The experience of other regions will be drawn upon as the analysis develops.

THE SETTING

Tepoztlan, you recall, is a town of 4,000 people, sixty miles south of Mexico City, in a mountain valley embracing a few square miles of arable land, about 6,000 feet above the sea. Not fifty citizens show plainly their white blood; the town is thus overwhelmingly Indian and everybody speaks *Nahuatl* (Aztec) as well as a varying amount and quality of Spanish. It was a town when Cortez landed, and the same seven barrios, or wards, with their peculiar organization, are still actively functioning. Very few Spaniards ever came to settle in Tepoztlan, and thus the outside influence, such as it is, has been derived chiefly from natives journeying to Mexico City and returning with new ideas. Of the present population, all but fifty of the men were born in the valley. The town is primarily to live in, trade in, play in; one goes outside to the fields or forests to work. Under the Aztec system, village lands were held by the whole community, with specific fields allotted to each family, inalienable so long as properly cultivated. Today the families of Tepoztlan continue to cling to these ancestral fields, although they now have legal title and in theory can buy and sell. The less fertile areas and the mountain slopes are still held communally, and called *ejidos*.

Indian pueblos and Castilian villages 400 years ago

had much in common—and doubtless still have. It was accordingly not difficult to introduce certain Spanish ways upon Aztec soil. Indeed all handicraft cultures of a relatively high level have much in common, and tend to a kindred pattern. The same rhythms of agriculture, trade, worship, play, the same inexorable limitations of environment are in operation. Mexican villages remind me constantly of Russian villages—the rows of huts, the enormous colourful church, the market produce spread in the dust. We must beware accordingly of conceiving Tepoztlan as an Aztec pueblo. It is a fusion of Aztec and Castilian, with a dash of modern. The resulting compound can only be called Mexican. Aztec civilization, as we have seen, was decapitated by the conquest. The brain ceased functioning; the body still lives.

The first municipal government was established about 1820, at the time of independence from Spain. Previous thereto the Aztec cacique system was in operation, and, despite the aforementioned government, continued in operation until recently. A cacique is a chief, a head man with a life term dependent on good behaviour, or behaviour adequate to prevent his overthrow. He is judge and land distributor. I was invited to go and see the "king of Tepoztlan," who now lives in Xochimilco. If time had allowed, I might have found the mystic reins of invisible government—or I might not. Today the local political unit embraces Tepoztlan and seven adjacent hamlets. (Not to be confused with the seven barrios.) There is a municipal council consisting of a *presidente* and eight assistants, a secretary and a judge. The latter hears local complaints—some of them—and when overwhelmed by technical points, transmits them to the court at Cuernavaca, the capital of the state of Morelos. The theory is that these dignitaries are elected by the free

[127]

suffrage of the town. Actually they are appointed from Cuernavaca, or were in 1927.

This sad collapse of democracy is not, however, so ominous as it sounds. The theoretically elected, practically appointed municipal government has no serious business whatsoever. Above all it has no revenue. Occasionally it makes a left-handed drive for local taxes with the most dismal success. Actual pesos are forthcoming only when the state tax collectors arrive, gun on hip, remaining "only long enough to exploit and defraud the natives."

The presidente presides; the council sits—and sits. Actual work is done communally, as it has always been done. If a street is to be repaired, washing stones replaced, the water supply remodelled, citizens toll themselves off to do it—apparently automatically. It is not always done promptly, but it is done. To keep the village functioning is as necessary a part of one's daily work as to keep one's household functioning. The two are inseparable. This is what village communism means. It is surrounded with no body of theory; it is a set of rooted habits. The new "government" comes in each January first, accompanied by a lonely rocket or two and complete public indifference. Its only real function is to preside and assist with the fiesta schedule. When all is said and done it is "a form of play." Thus the working of the sublime principles of Jeffersonian democracy in Tepoztlan. In more remote villages, perhaps in the majority of Mexican villages, we do not find even the pretence of elected officials. The cacique still rules, or in his absence, citizens draw on their ageless communal habits. At the other end of the scale, a great metropolis like Mexico City with 1,000,000 population has a very highly organized municipal government. The chief of the Federal District is one of the great *politicos* of the republic. The responsiveness of this government to democratic control, however, is not on a scale to create enthusiasm in the breast of Mr. Frederick C. Howe or the National Municipal League.

The street layout of Tepoztlan is pre-conquest. The division of families in seven barrios, each with its chapel and santo, is derived directly from the Aztec calpulli, or kinship group, with its local god, religious structure, military organization, judge and public buildings. Even the old names survive. There is the barrio of the "toads," of the "ants," of the "lizards," of the "maguey worms" (the latter a Mexican comestible). These names are held aptly to describe the people of the barrios. The "ants" are so called because there are so many of them—it is the largest barrio in town—they run over the ground in all directions and get into all manner of trouble. The "toads" swell with their own importance. When the saint day of the barrio of Santo Domingo on January 12 approaches it will be said: *"Ye acitihuitz ilhuitl cacame—* Now comes the fiesta of the toads." The "lizards" are quick and light-minded, they like to sing at night on the street corners. The *"cacomixtles"* live under the rocks like the creature whose name they bear. Of the highest barrio in town, with huts below beetling precipices, the designation is sound.

Time is measured by sun and climate, not by clocks. If you ask a Tepoztecan, shortly after high noon, what time a given fiesta dance will start, he is likely to reply: "It will take place right now at about three or five o'clock." This is as definite to him as it is infuriating to one who, like the author, was reared in sight of the Waltham Watch factory. Mexicans, even as Russians, have no mechanical time sense. "Mañana," tomorrow, stretches from 12:01 A.M. through the weeks and months to infinity. It is far more difficult and painful for a westerner to rid himself of his clock habits than of his appendix. But once the operation is over and the wound healed, there is much to be said for right now at about three or five o'clock. There is much to be said for consigning unpleasant business to an endless mañana. It was Mark Twain, if I remember rightly, who held all his incoming letters for six months, and was amazed and delighted at the small percentage which then required answer. The clock is perhaps the most tyrannical engine ever invented. To live beyond its lash is an experience in liberty which comes to few citizens of the machine age.

Arriving in Yucatan in the late fall of 1930, I found local hacienda owners and business men in the depths of despair. The price of henequen fibre was scraping an all-time bottom; production had been suspended for two months; the trade of the peninsula was at a standstill. The overwhelming majority of the residents of Yucatan are Maya Indians.

"This," I said, "is terrible. Unemployment spreading, starvation in the villages. Is the Red Cross active; have you appointed suitable relief committees? In the United States we have many millions of unemployed, and two relief committees to every man." This with a certain pardonable pride. I was met with a blank stare.

"Unemployment, starvation, Red Cross? What do you mean, señor? Times are very bad. Nobody has any money, but everybody has enough to eat."

"But how about the poor Indians?"

"The Indians? There is nothing the matter with the Indians. They have their corn and their beans. Nothing ever hurts them. But trade with us is a calamity. . . ."

Out in the bush, I verified this astonishing generalization. The world-wide depression affected a few bankers and business men in Merida, the capital; a clerk or two was out of a job; but the third estate did not even know there was a depression. The villages were largely self-sustaining. Even the peons who work on the henequen ranches have their own milpas. Corn, beans, squash, eggs, chickens, turkeys, wild game, chocolate, is the village menu. Nobody is ever seriously hungry; famines are unknown. Stomach-ache is the ranking disease.

Tepoztlan is 1,000 miles from Yucatan, with utterly different topography, but the same ability to eat obtains. With Mr. Redfield's aid let us examine the sources and organization of its provisioning. Every family in town, with one or two exceptions, has its milpa. During the harvest season the carpenter leaves his bench, the merchant his counter, the *arriero* his mule, and all make their way to the cornfields. The ripe ears are piled in great heaps in the house yard, and a year's food supply for the family is stored in a circular corncrib. Any surplus may be exchanged or sold. Every woman in Tepoztlan knows how to take the kernels, pound them in a stone *metate,* add a little lime water, slap the meal out in her hands to thin, round cakes, cook them over a charcoal brazier, and produce *tortillas*—the national dish of the old civilizations; the national dish of Mexico today. (They taste as flat as they look at first, but one grows to like them.) She knows how to roll the tortilla, like a French pancake, around a bit of meat and sauce for *enchiladas,* or surround the meat with cornmeal, slip it into a corn husk and so produce the *tamale,* famous in Mexico as the hot dog in America, and far more nourishing.

Wherever one goes, from capital to remotest hut, the pat pat of women's hands fashioning tortillas is con-

[131]

stantly in one's ears. It is impossible to conceive Mexico
without maize. Remove it, and the country would shrink,
weaken, aye, dissolve, before our eyes. Substituting an
even more nourishing staple would do no good, for it is
the tradition and the habits of the maize which make
Mexico what it is. Nor should we of the North forget
how Indian corn kept the first New Englanders alive.
Mary Austin tells of a baby food made by Indian recipe
of "boiling cornmeal many hours, straining it, making hickory nut cream, and combining them in given
proportions. On this the little Puritan babies were
raised."

Mexican food is not so lurid as generally painted. I
have been for weeks in the back country living altogether
on the local diet without ever scorching my throat—and
it is easily scorched. The *mole* is a red-hot Aztec sauce,
chocolate brown in colour. I tasted it first in a cool grotto,
but even there it brought the tears starting to my eyes.
Thereafter I avoided moles. One can go through a fortnight of regular *table d'hôtes,* and never connect with
a single overspiced dish. Fire-eaters can order them, but
they are not continually in evidence.

On the whole I like Mexican food. Like French cooking, it is always tasty. It is innocent of pie—to me, though
a New Englander, a great blessing. The soups are de-
licious; the eggs are always fresh (as cold storage is unknown) and admirably cooked; the rich brown *frijoles*
(beans) are good; the crisp rolled bread is good—despite its lack of butter; an astonishing variety of exotic
fruits is generally available, as well as bananas, oranges,
and a kind of green lime, failing which one has never
tasted a real cocktail. Drug store counter addicts suffer
frightfully in Mexico, but a cosmopolitan palate has no
cause for alarm. The major weaknesses are coffee and

meat. The former is roasted until it burns, and to cap the indignity is often served cold from a bottle, hot milk being added to produce *café-au-lait*. Meats are generally tough and forbidding. Chicken and turkey, however, are normally good and very common. In some places food is thickly lubricated with oil and lard, but hotels generally desist from this practice.

In connection with the food supply of Tepoztlan we find the following agencies:

A steam flour mill, small and ill patronized, because of the prejudice which holds it something of a disgrace for the housewife to take her corn to the mill rather than to her own metate; tortillas are not so succulent when made from mill meal. This is, of course, sentimental nonsense, and costs the good women of Tepoztlan untold hours of heavy, monotonous work. In a Yucatan village I found a little corn grinder run by the remains of a model T Ford. Every woman in town came down with her basket of yellow kernels, and sat entranced as they were reduced to meal in sixty seconds rather than six hours.

Two corn factors, who take the selling of the surplus crop in charge.

Three butchers—and a ghastly display they produce.

Six bakers, for wheat is also obtainable in the valley. Their specialty will be sweet bread.

Dairy men for the little milk that is used.

A soft drink bottling works with two employees.

Five storekeepers, selling some canned foodstuffs purchased in Mexico City.

The market. On Wednesday and Sunday mornings, some hundred vendors take up their positions in the plaza near the old white and rose cathedral. Most of them come from Tepoztlan and its seven encircling hamlets, but a few are from villages beyond the home valley. Each pays a small "floor tax" for his right to squat on the ground and spread his—or her—wares on a bench or on the soil. Above him he may rear a sail of cloth and wooden sticks to keep off the sun, adjustable from east to west. Each takes the same position from week to week, from generation to generation. The vendors come by villages and sit by villages. In Aztec times all adult men were required to attend market, which occurred every fifth day. It was a compulsory holiday with festival and games. The feeling still persists. The five-day interval has been broken by the Christian calendar (the Aztecs had a twenty-day month), compulsion is internal rather than external, the copper axes, the fine paper which Tepoztlan used to make are gone, together with a nobler quality of handicraft altogether; but all the town still comes down to the plaza on market day, a festival spirit in the air.

Not only goods are exchanged, but equally important, news. Stop an Indian on a mountain trail, market-bound with a load of pottery on his back, and offer to buy the lot at his own price. Nine times out of ten he will refuse to sell at any figure. To part with his pots would deprive him of excuse to go to market. Money is but heavy metal; the plaza is colour and news and life.

In many village markets, exchange by barter still obtains. In Tepoztlan, the cartwheel pesos, the tiny silver ten centavo pieces, the coppers in assorted sizes—particularly the coppers—will be the usual medium. No paper money is ever seen, and very little gold. Indeed the traveller in Mexico must revise all his money habits. He must secure a canvas bag and carry around a dead weight of silver pesos sufficient to sink him to the bottom of the

[134]

Diego Rivera.
1931

saltiest sea. Paper money is unpassable, and his travellers' checks are regarded with suspicion in the provinces. If happily he can cash them, he must be prepared to sacrifice a stiff percentage of the going exchange between dollar and peso. I came to find that worry as to ways and means of transporting cash far exceeded worry as to its safety from theft. Outside the cities, Mexicans are a scrupulously honest people. Aztecs, you remember, valued silver and gold primarily for their ductility. At a wayside station in Michoacan, I gave a newsboy what I thought was a nickel five-centavo piece. He took it and departed for another customer. The train began to move. I heard a yell outside the window. It was the newsboy running beside the track, holding up fifteen centavos change in coppers. . . . Yes, I told him to keep it. No, he had no racket. I had given him too much money, and he was simply giving it back. But if there is a similar urchin in Mexico City, he belongs in the National Museum.

The great bulk of the goods on sale in the Tepoztlan market is either produced in the valley or brought in by vendors from the neighbouring valleys which constitute an economic region. In order to gauge the extent of local self-sufficiency, let us classify the foodstuffs and their point of origin.

From the town itself

Maize	Limes and lemons	Milk
Beans	Melons	Honey
Chick peas	Beef	Coffee
Squash	Game	Spices
Tomatoes	Turkeys	Wild yeast
Wild vegetables	Chickens	Herb tea
Wild fruits	Eggs	Bread
Bananas	Pork	Pastry
Oranges	Lard	Soft drinks

From the region

Rice	Lettuce	Brandy
Wheat	Potatoes	Pulque
Sugar	Onions	Beer
Chocolate	Beets	Salt
Carrots	Peanuts	

From the outside world

Canned foods⎫ for sale in the stores at high prices but not
Bottled foods⎭ heavily patronized.

The above tells us both what Tepoztlan eats, and why business depressions do not affect a handicraft culture. Cut off from the outside world, she would eat just as well as heretofore. In fact, better; the canned foods I saw on the store shelves looked old and unappetizing. At a pinch she can feed herself; but as is so often the case in Mexico, the self-contained unit is not the village so much as it is the *region*. Sample the goods on sale at the Sunday market. Plot on a map the villages from which they come, and you have the economic unit, all within a day's march on a burro trail. Within the unit, furthermore, it is customary to stagger the market days, so that each section of the area will have regular access to all the products of the area. Wednesday market at village A; Thursday market at village B, and so forth.

About half as far north of Mexico City as Tepoztlan lies south, is the valley of Teotihuacan. Here Dr. Gamio paints for us a very different picture. In 1917, of the 8,000 odd people in the valley, the great majority were utterly dependent on money wages for food. They worked for seven great haciendas, and raised only a small fraction of their own supplies. When hard times hit the haciendas—say world low prices for wheat—the Indians promptly suffered. Nearly all their food was imported into the valley. This makes it only too clear that economic specialization is possible in a handicraft culture. Fortunately, between the free village system and the self-supporting hacienda system—a more common type than the specialized haciendas of Teotihuacan—the majority of Mexicans are within calling distance of their food supply. The cities of course are fed by imports, often foreign imports. Most of the butter in Mexico City comes in tins from Kansas; in Yucatan it comes from Denmark. Of late years, urban areas in the heart of maize civilization have been importing corn from Africa.

Now let us glance at the extent of the Aztec tradition in the diet of Tepoztlan. A list is again the clearest method.

Aztec foods and food habits

Maize (tortillas and tamales)	Turkeys
Beans (frijoles)	Wild fruits, vegetables and
Squash	game
Tomatoes	Chocolate—beaten and frothed
Chilis	Native herb teas
Moles	Honey
Gruels	Pulque

Spanish importations

Cattle	Potatoes
Swine	Chick peas
Chickens and eggs	Certain fruits
Milk	Cinnamon
Sugar	Coffee
Rice	Beer
Wheat	Sugar alcohol drinks

With corn as the great staple, and meat a rarity, by far the larger share of Tepoztlan's diet is still set in the

Aztec mould. The contribution of Spain, however, is manifestly important. The machine to date has hardly scratched the surface, either in tools and devices for farming and processing, or in factory-made foodstuffs. Wooden ploughs and Aztec tools are still the prevailing agricultural instruments. Perhaps the chief contribution of the factory to the menu of Tepoztlan is bottled beer.

Middletown, on the other hand, would be lost without its tin cans, its bottles and its packaged goods. The kitchen shrinks visibly before the delicatessen and the chain grocery store. The town gave up feeding itself from its own soil fifty years ago—if it ever fed itself. It eats far more meat, sugar, candy and wheat than Tepoztlan. It engulfs oceans of ice cream soda, unknown in the southern community. Tepoztlan likes sweets, but tends to get them in the natural state, in fruit or by chewing sugar-cane. As a result its teeth would bring a resident dentist close to bankruptcy. Latterly Middletown, like all America, has been eating more vegetables, a move which Tepoztlan would do well to follow. Were it not for pulque, Mexican village diet would be seriously short of vitamins. Many regions do not drink pulque, and perhaps all fail to achieve a soundly balanced diet. Intestinal disorders rank very high in the list of Mexican diseases.

As one rides over the plateau about Mexico City, the maguey plants, like files of soldiers, march away to the foothills, and often over the foothills. This is the great pulque region. Here the hacendados keep themselves in the style to which they are accustomed, selling the milky fluid secreted by these great plants to town dwellers and villagers in regions where the maguey is not grown, like Tepoztlan. The only occasions when I have tasted pulque —or rather pre-pulque—were when, dismounting from a horse in the midst of a maguey field, I have removed the covering stone and dipped a cup of the liquid straight from the natural bowl cut in the plant's heart. This is the raw sap draining in from the fat, flat leaves to the measure of several quarts a day. It may run for months before the plant finally bleeds to death. It tastes like cocoanut water, only worse—insipid, sweetish, and muskily disagreeable.

The sap, when treated, readily ferments, and produces a dirty white liquid with a most forbidding smell, and about the same alcoholic content as beer. This is pulque proper. Distilled, it becomes *tequila* or *mescal*. The Aztecs were very fond of pulque—witness Tepoztecatl and his temple in its honour—and the tradition is unimpaired. Indian and mestizo often swill it in unimaginable quantities—ten, twelve, fifteen litres (quarts) a day. With this cargo aboard, one becomes markedly befuddled. For such two-handed hoisters, pulque is undoubtedly a curse and a campaign against it is in full swing. But the majority drink it more moderately. It is even fed to children. Far from doing them harm it now appears that they could hardly survive without it! Aztecs, and Mexicans after them, never ate enough fruit and vegetables to offset properly the high protein intake of corn and beans. Why did they persist so sturdily? Dr. Jose Zozaya, a brilliant young investigator who has been called Mexico's foremost scientist, tells me that the answer is pulque. It follows the law whereby all surviving primitive peoples, after long centuries of trial and error, balance their diet. The Chinese peasant has worked out the same law with rice and greens. To prohibit pulque means the breaking of this ancient and excellent balance. Despite its abuse, manifestly it should not be prohibited unless something of equivalent value is substituted. Beer has been advocated, but beer is equally intoxicating and not so rich in vitamins. More vegetables and fruits would right the balance, but it is hard to grow them in some areas, to say nothing of the lack of dramatic appeal. One cannot wind up a fiesta on cabbages. Perhaps it can be done in Indiana, but not in Mexico. It is a pretty problem, calculated to give the embattled Drys plenty of room for thought. But if we know our Drys, they will probably overleap it. Meanwhile the prevailing unsanitary and frequently disgusting methods of fermenting pulque should certainly be prohibited.

Alcohol is a mixed blessing—or evil—in Mexico as elsewhere on this reeling planet. It is abused by nature peoples as by the ultra-sophisticated—proving that Nature does not give her favoured children quite all their natures crave, and warning us not to become too lyrical as to their psychological satisfactions. First and last I saw a good many drunken Mexicans, but never a fighting drunkard or one who made it his business to annoy the passer-by. Mostly they mumbled and dropped into a stupour. The most serious case which came to my personal attention was an intoxicated mestizo driving a Buick at sixty miles an hour through the narrow streets of Cuernavaca. He barely missed a squadron of soldiers, and knocked down and painfully injured their officer. I suspect he will never drive another car as long as he lives. . . . But if a Prohibition law were enacted, there would be a revolution inside of half an hour.

A friend took her cook, an Indian woman from Taxco, to see the mummies, the pottery, and other artifacts excavated under a lava flow at San Angel near the capital. The cook was stolid until her eye lighted upon a grinding stone in the collection. She was enchanted with its shape, and implored the mistress to secure it for her kitchen. "The metate I've been looking for. Ah, if I only had it; such beautiful little tortillas I could make you!" That stone was used by some pre-Aztec woman, overwhelmed by volcanic eruption two thousand years or more ago. The maize tradition does not die.

CHAPTER VIII

MACHINELESS MEN—THEIR SHELTER, CLOTHING, HEALTH

FARMHOUSES strung along the turnpike are rare in Mexico, as in Russia. People live in compact villages, with their fields encircling them. The most that one sees in the open country are crude huts run up for temporary shelter during road making, charcoal burning, herding animals on far pastures. These villages vary greatly in size; Tannenbaum estimates the average population at 300. Tepoztlan with its 4,000 people is thus more town than village. On a steep pine hillside beside a roaring stream in Oaxaca, I found a miners' village of seventeen families, which is close to the minimum.

The material of which houses are built also varies widely, but follows one relentless law: It is local material. Every youth as a part of his education will learn how to work that material and build, if need be, his own house. So we find mud, adobe brick, rough stone, cut stone, rubble and occasionally wood on the plateau, and thatch, bamboo, native grass, wood, and mud in the tierra caliente. Roofs run to thatch in the latter and red tile in the former, but a long, lean sort of rough shingle is also much used.

Villages to the approaching eye thus change their colour from region to region. In Yucatan they are mostly white—basket work covered with mud and then immaculately whitewashed. In the jungle they may be green;

on the plateau a dusty grey or brown, brick red, cream colour. Sometimes one finds a pink village; or even a rainbow village with whites, blues, pinks, yellows. I remember one little town up a rocky gorge which my travelling companions laid entirely to a bottle of beer. They simply refused to admit its existence. I called the conductor to my defence. Yes, it was San Pedro. The señor had good eyes. It was made of the same rock which lined the gorge. Travellers rarely saw it, though it was only a mile away. There were five hundred people living there. It was as perfect a sample of protective coloration as an iguana on a stone wall, or a green caterpillar on a leaf.

Once inside the door, however, diversity gives way to uniformity. All over Mexico a single pattern animates house interiors of the common people. There is one room, a griddle, a metate for grinding corn, a huge water pot, brightly painted wooden bowls, a square tin oil can, assorted pottery, hammocks or straw mats (*petates*) to sleep upon—the former in the hot countries; a little shrine with tinsel and candles—now not so frequent as in the Diaz days; two dogs, three hens, four babies; a broom of rushes, and somewhere flowers. This is not quite so primitive as it sounds, in that the total household equipment includes various outbuildings set in a walled compound. In many regions, the wall will be of organ cactus, furnishing at once a comely design and all the practical utility of barbed wire fence. The outbuildings often include a storehouse for maize, small stables for livestock, a fowl house, sometimes a separate shed for cooking, and in various sections the old Aztec bathhouse.

Where topography permits, the village plan tends to be uniform throughout the nation. It holds for towns and cities as well. It consists of a central plaza, with the main church at one end, shade trees, bandstand, fountain or well, space for market. Around the plaza are grouped the *palacio municipal* or town hall, the whitewashed village school, a store or two, and the houses of "los correctos," lordly structures perhaps two stories high with balconies and actual windows of glass. Lanes of dirt or cobblestone run out from the plaza, usually in gridiron formation, and along them, pretty well bunched, will be the compounds and houses of the commoners, with the poorest on the outer fringe. Mr. Franklin P. Adams will be glad to learn that even in the meanest village, a hundred miles from nowhere, the lanes will be named—*"Calle Cinco de Mayo," "Calle Hidalgo"*— and a six-inch street number painted on the hut wall. We were informed that this is a recent development, and due more to the tax department than to the post office. To most of the dwellings in Mexico the postman never comes, and his offerings could not be read if he did come.

The poorest village will attempt a plaza, and often contains a vast pile of crumbling masonry which once was a great church. Pathetic are the attempts to come to terms with the iron law of depreciation. I have seen stone walls with beautiful old carving surmounted by a huge thatched roof. The stone arches had fallen in, and thatch was the best that local talent could substitute. The architectural ensemble was deliciously fantastic— like an eskimo hat on top of Bishop Manning. I have seen great buildings, shattered by earthquake, where only one tiny chapel has been salvaged for current religious needs. I have seen curtains of shingle laid across a huge nave, 100 feet wide and 100 feet high, to divide utter ruin from an area where mass may still be chanted.

Increasingly Mexico runs to the little white schoolhouse. Three years ago in the state of Oaxaca, fewer than 100 villages had federal schools; now (January, 1931) there are 417. When journeying across country on horseback one may secure a letter from the educational authorities giving permission to sleep on the schoolhouse floor. It is the most sanitary place in town. There may be no municipal building, no bandstand, no iron balconies, no store—but increasingly there will be a school. Again and again, as the little square white building with its red-tiled roof shone out from the prevalent village grey or brown, I was reminded of my own country. The outstanding piece of architecture in the American town is almost invariably the high school. Mexico, at a totally different economic level, is following the same trail.

The plaza buildings tend towards the Spanish colonial type, but the compounds are almost pure pre-conquest. In the larger towns, the plazas are often very beautiful. Witness Taxco, with the great cathedral towers, warm brown and heavily sculptured, looming above the wild fig trees, and the booths and rainbow market. Near the plaza we find the open court style of architecture—sometimes in the hands of one family; sometimes the court with its fountain and flowers serves a whole regiment of families. There is nothing more fascinating than to glance through iron grills into these *patios,* drenched in sunshine and lurid with colour.

Most poor families in Mexico City live in large courts like this called *vecindades*—neighbourhoods. Each family has its room, its shrine, its livestock and garden by the door. The plumbing is co-operative; sketchy as it may be, the law requires it. For health and sanitation these homes would compare unfavourably with a New York tenement, were they not so close to earth and sun.

By rights a vecindad should be sordid, but the birds, the flowers, the smiling babies, even the women slapping tortillas and washing in a dirty tank, make it gay instead.

Let me soberly set down from my notebook the points of the compass as observed from one spot in the lovely old city of Oaxaca. (The city was badly shaken by an earthquake an even month after my visit.) It is true that it was fiesta time, and thus more resplendent than usual. It is true that it stands—or stood—among the foremost exhibits of the republic. But it serves to show the kind of architecture into which the traveller is suddenly precipitated as he wanders about Mexico. The picture is taken from the upper steps of the Church of the Virgin of the Soledad, at noon on December 18, 1930. The sun is blazing and the thermometer stands at about eighty-five degrees.

To the South:

Stone steps lead down to a little park with fountain, shade trees, rows of red hibiscus flowers, and canvas-covered booths. The steps are lined with Indians in varied costumes, taking their midday siesta. Below the park more broad steps descend to a street with pink houses, and paper flags stretched from roof to red-tiled roof. Over the houses rise wooded hills, and above them the deep blue sky.

To the West:

The two towers of the Virgin's church rear their hundred feet of pale green stone, between them a façade of amber stone, richly carved, and bisected by a tall cedar. At right angles to the towers runs a smooth high wall of green masonry, pierced by an arch in white and rose. Over the wall, edged with jagged glass in every colour

[148]

(a common sight in Mexico) we catch a glimpse of the paved churchyard, where the "Apaches" are performing their five-hour dance, their green, white, and red plumes bobbing rhythmically up and down. The wall about them is lined with brown boys, white-pyjamaed, straw-sombreroed, and barefooted. To the right of the arch is an old pink parish house, with overhanging eaves and massive walls. The iron-worked balconies are full of flowers and wooden bird-cages. A soldier lounges in the archway, and above him shrubs, vines and flowers are growing from crevices in the masonry itself.

To the North:

We look up a steep street, charging a hillside in cobbled terraces beyond the capacity of a Ford tractor. The houses are low, massive, coloured white, pink and cream. A drainage gutter flows through the middle of the street, great flagstones for pedestrians beside it. Pennants in blue and white paper stream from roof to roof. The street divides about a little yellow chapel, trimmed with white, a great bronze bell swinging in its tower; and goes winding up in two lanes bordered with bougainvillea, and with sheaves of yellow-green sugar-cane piled against house walls, until the lanes lose themselves in a heavy grove.

To the East:

The wall of another green church, pierced with grilled, pink-fringed windows. Long stone gargoyles lean from the roof, and between them scrub cactus sprouts. There is a squat green tower, a lofty pink one, and between them stone windows over a wooden door, both sculptured. Electric light wires cross the palm-shadowed wall—they are never concealed in Mexico—and out of one round window, if you please, clicks a typewriter. To the left of the church is the open door of a large lemon-coloured house. We glimpse an interior court with a carved stone fountain, banana trees, multicoloured wash hung out to dry, dogs, cats, hens, babies, a goat, an old stone bench, washing stones, flowers and green squashes on the roof.

Practically the entire scene is Spain's legacy to Mexico, and it is no small gift.

Tepoztlan, as we saw in the first chapter, follows the standard village pattern. It has its plaza, shade trees, cathedral, bandstand, stores, municipal building, schoolhouse, balconied mansions, gridiron layout, street numbers, all complete. Let us classify the houses of its citizens who live in the seven barrios reaching back from the plaza.

THE AZTEC INFLUENCE

The same pre-conquest rectangular dwellings with walls of adobe, of rough stone in mud mortar, or of withes, wattles and cornstalk.

Thatch, or flat baked mud for many roofs.

Few windows, no glass, no chimneys.

Dirt floors.

Flowers everywhere.

The circular storehouse for corn on the cob, six feet high, of vertical cornstalks bound with rope.

The vasiform granary, mud plastered, for shelled corn.

The sweathouse, a rectangle of stone, five feet high, with two chambers. (Elsewhere it may be circular and made of mud.) In one steam is generated; into the other the candidate crawls, and, enveloped in steam, sweats,

and sweats. The object is more therapy than cleanliness.
One house in four has this Aztec *temazcal*.

The fowl house.

The hearth, clay griddle, grinding stone, and pot—the
domestic big four, literally unchanged from Aztec days.

Mortar and pestle.

Baskets, often in bright design.

The sleeping mat, or petate.

The cradle or small hammock for the baby.

Clay toys as ornaments.

Rush brooms, and a lovely rush fan to stir the fire.

THE SPANISH INFLUENCE

Red-tiled roofs on many houses.

The charcoal brazier, sometimes displacing the old
hearth and griddle.

Steel knives.

Kerosene flares, candles.

The household shrine.

Occasional newspaper pictures and postcards pinned
on walls.

In the houses of "los correctos": china dishes, glass,
metal pans, sideboards, beds, brick floors, iron grillwork,
plastered walls, hinged doors.

FROM BOTH AZTEC AND SPANISH

Pottery essentially Mexican.

Stools and benches.

Water tanks.

CONTRIBUTIONS FROM THE MACHINE AGE

Sewing-machines, in the houses (some of them) of "los tontos," as well as "los correctos."

Square tins, once containing alcohol or oil, now used for water or for flower pots, braziers, saddle-bags. I visited no part of Mexico where these tins were not in evidence.

A phonograph for "los correctos," and perhaps by this time, Heaven help us, a radio.

Of these furnishings, the majority, in both number and tonnage, come from the valley, or may be had in the plaza market by virtue of regional exchange. From the outside world arrive kerosene for the flares, bar iron and silver for local fabrication, and the furnishings for the houses of "los correctos." None of the outside shipments are in any quantity. The few local specialists who assist in this department include three carpenters, four masons, brick and tile makers, rope spinners, two iron workers, silversmiths, charcoal burners, woodcutters—all on part time.

It is clear from the above that the Aztec influence is very strong in Tepoztlan's housing, stronger relatively than in the case of its food. No such innovations as meat, hen's eggs, wheat, rice, sugar, coffee, have occurred in the equipment of the compound. And precisely as in the case of food, the great bulk of this equipment may be had either locally or in regional exchange. Only a minimum of necessities and a few luxuries for "los correctos" trickle in from the outside world. In this department, however, we find the major contribution of the machine age to Tepoztlan. Since the old looms were discontinued it has taken on considerable importance. The town would undoubtedly be handicapped without its sewing-machines.

All over rural Mexico, huts, houses and their furnishings follow strongly the pre-conquest tradition. In Yucatan, the old elliptical wattled huts still obtain. Inside are the same hammocks, griddles, pots, cabinets and grinding stones. In the valley of Teotihuacan 300 families live in caves, an equal number in crude huts made of maguey leaves, and the balance of the common people in *jacales,* one room stone or adobe houses, set in their compounds, guarded with hedges of organ cactus. Is it unreasonable to suppose that before the coming of the Spaniards none lived in caves or in flimsy huts of maguey?

Of the furnishings of "los correctos," the less said the better. The observation holds for all upper class Mexicans. Indeed the more wealthy they are the more appalling their taste. With exteriors in the gracious colonial pattern; with flowering patios, great high rooms beautifully dimensioned, charming ironwork balconies—the furnishings themselves remain inconceivably bad. They date more or less from Maximilian and Diaz, and are assembled from the worst products of late Empire French and Victorian English. They show how desperately this class of Mexicans sought to evade their own country. The lovely old Spanish pieces have gone to the Thieves' Market—or into foreign museums; the handicrafts of the Indians have never been admitted, and we are faced, if you please, with iron alligators whose tails writhe up to support a marble table top on which perch china shepherdesses, kewpie dolls, and collections of sea shells. This I saw in a village near Toluca.

Here is a bedroom, thirty feet square and twenty feet high, in a rich man's house in Yucatan. The ceiling is in pink and baby blue plaster, tortured with scroll work and rosebuds. The floor is of marble slabs. There is one colonial remnant—a fine carved armchair, encircled with three hideous gilt Empire chairs. A marble-topped table surmounted by a Neptune—apparently expiring. A carved pedestal, five feet high, for a non-existent bust. It can doubtless be spared. A wardrobe, ten feet high, of carved wood and mirrors, pure Victorian. One electric bulb hanging like a drooping lily out of an enormous brass chandelier beset with countless glass dangles. One bureau of jig-saw fretwork and brown marble. One jig-saw double bed with a twelve-foot canopy. One copy of a copy of a Murillo in a gilt frame six inches thick. . . . You receive, I trust, the general picture.

The houses of the well-to-do in Middletown are in violent contrast with those of Mexico. They are worse outside and better inside. Approaching them we are struck with a culture which has found neither dignity nor unity—early American jostles half-timbered English, mansard roof is cheek by jowl with Florentine villa. The houses themselves are often well enough, particularly those built in the last decade, but the total effect is an architectural vegetable soup, boiling the leftovers of centuries. In Mexico the solid colonial pattern lines the street; massive stone walls, overhanging tiled roof, grilled balcony, portal of old carved wood. The eye follows the just proportions, the clean lines, the blended colours, and is at peace.

Inside, however, American taste, for all its standardization, is vastly better. The black walnut, plush and marble have been all but eliminated, giving place to shaded lights, overstuffed davenports and cheery colour schemes. Even iron dogs upon the lawn are growing scarce. Indeed the only advantage of the Mexican interior—and this reflects particularly upon the American apartment house—is its feeling of unlimited space. Stuffy furniture loses something of its oppressive biliousness in a room that one can hardly see across. There are a few old Mexican palaces furnished in colonial Spanish and Indian handicrafts. Mr. Morrow has one in Cuernavaca. When so arranged, they are without exception the most delightful houses in the world.

The habitations of the commoners south and north of the Rio Grande disclose a contrast even more violent. The Indian village is compact, comely, unified. Often it melts into its background of forest and field. The poorer districts of the American town are screaming eyesores, whether back of the railroad tracks, or out in the newest suburban development. They assault the surrounding landscape; they shatter perspective; they insist truculently upon their own ugliness. Inside, their crayon portraits, ball tassels and insurance company calendars are only less bad than Mexican palacios because there are fewer of them. But the supreme contrast is a matter of tonnage. In the consumption of food the wayfaring Mexican eats as much in bulk, or more, than the wayfaring American. In the consumption of housing I would estimate that the American leads in a tonnage ratio of at least ten to one. His house is larger, more complicated, more interconnected with public utilities, and replete with far more stuff. One reason of course is the northern winter with its mandatory heating systems and tons of fuel. Another reason is that Indians have never been educated in the philosophy of acquisition. The rise of the Joneses leaves them cold. Their wantlessness is the despair of travelling salesmen. But I must admit, when all is said and done, that I should grow uncomfortable, being limited for any length of time to the ascetic furnishings of an Indian hut.

CLOTHING

Let us return to the courtyard of the Church of the Soledad in Oaxaca, and add a few native costumes to the architectural ensemble. The picture of walls and towers I tried earlier to give is incomplete without the living element.

A man with two nesting sombreros on his head, one felt, one straw; coarse shirt; white pyjama trousers, tight and rolled almost to the knees; bare feet; black, white and rose *sarape* on one shoulder; large rainbow-coloured hemp bag bulging with foodstuffs.

Woman with bouquet of onions on her head, large bouquets of ditto in her arms, baby slung in a blue reboso across her back, sound asleep.

Boy in blue shirt, white pants, brilliant orange sandals, selling lollypops in all colours, thrust like pins into a huge staff at least six feet high, surmounted by a rainbow whirligig, turning in the breeze. The effect is that of a gigantic, exotic bush.

Old woman in pink skirt, white blouse, blue reboso, barefoot, with enormous round basket on her head, ornamented with snakes and eagles in red and green. Smoking cigarette as she walks.

Charro (ranchman) in huge brown felt sombrero with flowers embroidered in gold, and black ribbons hanging down his back; yellow jacket, tight white trousers of whipcord, sandals of crossed leather thongs.

Family: two women, one man, one child about ten. They are manifestly from a remote mountain village. The women have yellow gourds upon their heads, and heavy long braids bound with strips of purple wool. Their blouses are of yellow linen with short sleeves. Jade earrings, pure pre-conquest. Tight skirts of tan homespun blankets, elaborately folded, caught up by a huge red leather belt, intricately worked. Their feet are bare. Their skins are dark mahogany and their self-possession is complete. They stride into the Church of the Soledad with no head covering save their yellow gourds—defying the stringent rule that women's heads must be veiled in church. The man is equally bizarre and self-possessed. He has a worked leather pouch around his neck, a wickerwork bag on his shoulder, short white breeches, a black peaked sombrero out of a Grimm's fairy tale, a wisp of beard on the point of his chin, magnificent eyes.

Woman in lemon-coloured skirt, pink blouse, nursing baby as she walks.

Man—white pyjamas, thong sandals, great black sombrero, scarlet and black sarape—a stunning total effect. I longed to have Rivera paint him.

Man with crownless hat brim, white shirt with holes revealing pink shirt beneath, clean pyjama legs badly fringed, brown knees showing through holes. Dusty bare feet.

Girl in white skirt, orange embroidery; white blouse, pink embroidery, blue reboso, barefooted, chewing large stalk of sugarcane.

Man—white pyjamas, sandals, green, red and black sarape, straw sombrero ornamented with red and green snakes, huge basket suspended by ropes over his shoulder.

Youth, in blue overall-cloth short jacket and trousers, tan shoes, curling straw sombrero.

Flapper—member of "los correctos"—olive skin, fine eyes, long lashes, black paint under eyes, eleven spit curls, long jet earrings, pink rayon frock very snug and very short, rayon stockings somewhat wrinkled on slightly misshapen legs (there is something wrong with mestizo ladies' legs), pumps with two-inch heels.

Man, violet shirt, white pyjama legs, with at least 500 cubic feet of fireworks on his back.

In Tepoztlan both Spaniard and machine have made wide inroads into the Aztec costume—particularly the latter. Fifty years ago the prevailing dress for women was a homespun skirt, white above the hips and black below, and a white triangle of similar homespun worn over the head like a poncho. This was the indigenous Indian garment. The number of women who wear it today is small and steadily diminishing. About the only Aztec item which survives strongly is the sandal. There are, however, a number of Mexican elements which represent a fusion of Aztec and Spanish, to wit:

The *sarape*. The bright-coloured blanket worn by men

of all plateau peoples, overcoat during the day, bed covering at night. It has a hole in the middle like a poncho. When tourists buy them, they sew up the holes, and use them for rugs, wall hangings and couch covers. The sarape is adapted from the Indian *tilmatli,* but it has become authentically Mexican.

The *reboso.* This too is typically Mexican. It is the shawl which Indian women wear over their heads to ward off the sun (they seldom use sombreros); to carry their babies in, normally slung over their stomachs; and to don modestly when entering church. It is allied to the Aztec *ayatl* for carrying babies and burdens. In some areas the ayatl, woven of maguey fibre, persists.

Beads and earrings. Derived from both old Mexico and Spain.

The *sombrero.* Perhaps the item which first comes into focus when one thinks of Mexico. The Toltecs and Tarascans, with their rainbow *panaches,* contributed something to it; Spain contributed something. One hardly ever sees a bareheaded male Mexican. The sombrero insures against sunstroke, sheds water like an umbrella in the rainy season; groceries may be—and are—carried in its brim; it can be used to fan a fire, and above all it gives dignity to the soul. Here is none of your derby or straw hat techniques—10,000,000 blank faces under 10,000,000 mass production hats of an ugliness which passes understanding. Sombreros are hand woven to begin with and thus no two are quite alike; and, if I may say so, hand worn to end with, no two at quite the same angle, indented in quite the same manner. I know of no single article of dress, save it be a royal golden crown, which can so satisfactorily bolster up the ego as the Mexican sombrero. (If we hatless fanatics ever make headway in the republic, spiritual disintegration is sure

Diego Rivera 1931

to result.) Fortunately the Mexican sun demands a head-dress. Even I, who have not purchased a straw hat for twenty years, was forced to buy a sombrero, or be overcome. Incidentally I never saw a bald Indian. This would seem to militate against the notion that inveterate hat-wearing diminishes hair.

The men of Tepoztlan wear shirt, blouse and trousers cut by their women-folk from bolts of white cotton cloth. This is where the importance of the sewing-machine is demonstrated. The general effect is that of pyjamas, although the blouse is shorter, the trousers crossed in front, and the total costume less *negligé* than what we term pyjamas in the north. Males are given to coloured vests and gaudy sashes on occasion. Sombrero, sandals and curved machete complete the usual attire. In addition a man may have an outfit of store clothes, sack suit, felt hat and factory shoes for use when he goes to the city. Men of "los correctos" will be found in European costume or in the tight trousers of the charro, rows of silver buttons down the side, like the keys of a flute.

Women wear white cotton underclothes, petticoat, overskirt of ankle length, full and gored, a collarless blouse tucked into the skirt, an apron, a sash, usually locally woven. Overskirts and blouses may run to vivid colours. For Sunday and fiesta a one-piece dress may be available. Earrings and necklaces appear. Bare feet are perfectly good form. Hair will be worn in long black braids, tied with bright ribbon. The bulk of this clothing is home made from store cotton. Children's clothing will tend to reproduce that of adults. It is not uncommon to see a barefooted mother in peasant dress leading by the hand a little boy in full store regalia—shoes, sack suit with diminutive long trousers, straw hat and black ribbon.

The only specialists in Tepoztlan catering to the above confections are the storekeepers, two shoemakers, and five barbers. Barbering is a great industry in Mexico. As the sanitation displayed is normally non-existent, we are again brought to a full stop in the matter of baldness. Common combs, common shears, common parasites, fail to affect these luxuriant shocks of straight black hair.

Every item on the clothing list is obtainable from the valley or from village exchange in the market, with these exceptions: cotton cloth, factory woven rebosos, figured handkerchiefs, bone buttons, store clothes. They are important exceptions. Without the bolts of cotton cloth it is safe to say that the present clothing regime of Tepoztlan would break down, but not immediately. Garments last many a long month in a Mexican village, and never go out of style. Once textiles were woven from a local fibre. The old looms are still to be seen, and at least one is occasionally put to work. Cut off from the outside world, Tepoztlan would doubtless revive them. But the period of re-education, one suspects, would be painful.

In Yucatan, the Maya women also wear white cotton cloth, but it is cut on the old henequen fibre pattern. Around the hem and the collar run strips of flowery embroidery, largely home sewn. The work is as beautiful as it is colourful—some of it fit for the museum—while the whole effect is more unique, indigenous and pleasing than the costume worn by women of Tepoztlan and the plateau. It gives us a hint of what pre-conquest women really looked like. In the valley of Teotihuacan, clothing, like food, has ceased to be a local industry. Much of it is bought ready made from Mexico City—fearful stuff from the slop shops. And sandals are made from old automobile tires. . . .

Middletown of course has a vastly more extensive and costly wardrobe than Tepoztlan, but I doubt if it gets full value for its money. Its men are far less appropriately and picturesquely attired; indeed the costume of the male in the machine age is a scandal and a disgrace. His smokestack suits, his horrible derby, his mandatory coat in summer, render the poor wretch as uncomfortable at certain seasons as he is unappetizing at all seasons. Only in some of his sport costumes can he be said to look like a human being. One would no more think of painting him in his normal regalia than of lithographing a gas range. Nine Mexican men out of ten make one itch for brush and palette.

Not so much can be said for the Mexican woman. She tends towards the European dress of fifty years ago. On the whole I think the girl of Middletown today is more becomingly, as well as more expensively, attired. The south has three advantages, however: a bold use of bright colours which sun and atmosphere sanction; bare feet or sandals which give one the carriage of a queen; complete indifference to changes in style. These are not inconsiderable virtues when all is said and done, particularly when one computes comparative costs. Where an American working girl may spend $200 a year on clothes—usually more if she works in an office—a Mexican village girl will not spend ten dollars, plus her own labour as dressmaker. For her outlay she does pretty well. There has however been a sad retreat from pre-Columbian days—a touch of which still lingers in the charming costumes of the Indian women of Yucatan. Perhaps it was the costume, white above the hips and black below, which made Bernal Diaz report many pretty women in Tepoztlan.

[163]

HEALTH

The contribution of Spain to the health of Tepoztlan was smallpox, whooping cough, diphtheria, syphilis, and fear of the Evil Eye. These maladies were unknown to the Aztecs. Yet against their inroads the only therapy continues to be the Indian one. Spain dumped the liabilities with no offsetting assets. There is neither doctor nor nurse in town. There are, however, thirteen *curanderos* or herb doctors, two magicians, one priest and ten midwives, dealing in the 110 remedial plants and herbs which are collected in the surrounding hills, together with a reasonably rich output of therapeutic hocus-pocus.

If one falls ill of *el espanto,* "the terror," one trembles and grows weak and does not wish to eat. Anything frightening may cause it, as waking up suddenly in the night and seeing a ghost. The patient must be bathed with laurel that the priest has blessed, and with orange and shaddock peels which have been placed on the altars during Holy Week." Or again, for *la mohina,* a kind of extended peevishness. "Children do not get this disease. The remedies are various quieting drinks. Spiced drinks are common, a tea made of lemon leaves, and especially an infusion of turnip peels."

The commonest explanation of sickness in Tepoztlan is that one has been attacked by *los aires* (the airs, the winds). They are the evil spirits of the air, and are found at water tanks, in ravines, at public washing places, in the rain. They are thought of as very little people. This concatenation of little people and water is most unfortunate. It makes washing extra hazardous. Remedies are various, including anointing with certain herbs and internal doses—such as a tea made from powdered woodpecker's head. Amulets compounded of *mucuna* seeds are also worn. The anointing with herbs should be done at the intersection of two streets. When completed, the bundle of leaves is flung away and the patient must rush into his house without looking back. "Sometimes los aires demand a chicken. Then you take a live chicken and tie it by the water tank or wherever the sickness came, and leave it there until it dies. If you ate it yourself you would die." Symbolic sacrifice, of course.

For a short time in 1925, a Bulgarian doctor moved into the town and attempted to establish a practice. He was well liked but people continued to patronize the curanderos; and he had to move on to Yautepec. There is a hospital at Cuernavaca, and doubtless by this time health posters in the Tepoztlan school. The central health authorities in Mexico City have an excellent habit of calling out the army, encircling a given village, and vaccinating every man, woman and child. Knowledge of modern medicine is making headway.

As it grows, it causes a certain amount of confusion. Here is J. S., perhaps the best educated man in Tepoztlan. His baby falls sick of an intestinal disorder on Monday. On Tuesday he goes to the shoemaker for medicine. The savant prescribes opium and mercury pills, and rubbing the baby's stomach with cold water. Fortunately the baby still breathes, but faintly. The father then (1) sends to Yautepec for a regular doctor, and (2) rides up into the mountain to find a special kind of rose, which, steeped, is held to be good for intestinal trouble. The rose tea is administered. The doctor's medicine is administered. The child is no better. More herbs are given at the advice of a neighbour, and its stomach rubbed with suet. The child is worse. Nothing is done about its diet. The next day the doctor rides up from Yautepec, barricades the herbalists, and cures the baby.

The interweaving of medicine and magic could hardly be better shown. The distracted father rushes from one to the other. There is reason to believe that the pre-conquest peoples, besides having fewer fell diseases to combat, came nearer to a genuine therapy. Their priests were very intelligent men, and had an extraordinary knowledge of herbs—certain of them, such as quinine, perfectly sound for specific disorders. Herb doctors to-day are less intelligent, the body of knowledge has de-generated, while the Spanish contribution of the Evil Eye has run riot in Mexico, complicating the situation. The miraculous Spanish virgins and santos offset the Evil Eye, and at the same time double the complications. When thousands kiss the same polished stone, contagions are uncontrollable.

Child mortality under ten years as calculated by Pani averages about forty per one hundred for all Mexico, rising to fifty in the capital. This compares most un-favourably with ten in Norway, fourteen in France, twenty-seven in Russia. The death-rate from the Spanish legacy of syphilis is more than seven times as great in Mexico City as in the United States. Gruening, himself a medical man, gives us a very gloomy report of the national health.

Village Mexicans, with rare exceptions, look healthy. They have to be, to survive the infections that come their way from faulty diet, spoiled meat, impure drinking water, concourses of invalids at miraculous shrines, pulque first sucked from the plant by peons and then fer-mented in pigskins. "It is not surprising," observes Flandrau, "that a population perpetually in the throes of intestinal disorder should be somewhat lacking in energy." Nevertheless those who escape the village graveyard, what with sun and air and exercise, *look* sturdy. Elementary hygiene would make them really so.

In an experimental school centre near Pachuca, which has trained physicians to serve the surrounding villages, as well as training classes for pharmacists and midwives, great emphasis is laid on proper diagnosis. The lessons are beginning to penetrate. An Indian boy with a stomach-ache refused the gory chicken his mother wanted to tie upon the afflicted part, walked several miles to the school where he again refused a hasty diagnosis, and insisted with dignity on having an examination to give "*los datos exactos.*" Which shows what Indian boys are capable of. The most striking piece of modern architecture in Mexico is the new *Salubridad,* home of the Department of Health. The building is there; its influence on the national death rate has yet to be established.

One morning the little plaza of the suburb of San Angel near the capital was audible five miles away. Coming to the centre of the pandemonium, I found every dog in town foregathered in leash and yelping his heart out. There must have been 500 of them, and they put Mr. Ringling's big tent completely at naught. Every last one of them had been, or was to be, vaccinated against rabies. Please, Mr. Presidente, remember the babies as well as the dogs.

Tepoztlan is indeed self-sufficient in respect to its medicine, but in this prime essential, contact with the outside world would be not a mixed blessing but a consummation devoutly to be wished. The door needs to be flung wide open for the sanitation and hygiene of the machine age. . . . With perhaps a shade of hesitation as to the descent upon the village, in full regalia, of a brigade of tonsil-snatchers.

CHAPTER IX

MACHINELESS MEN—THEIR WORK

THE first of the year finds the men of Tepoztlan engaged in late harvesting, coffee-picking and the drying of coffee berries, for which the only engine employed is the sun. In February some go off for a few weeks to work on the sugar haciendas. The state of Morelos used to be called "the sugar-bowl of the world." Fields of yellow-green cane and the tall chimneys of refineries dominated the landscape. Fortunes were made by hacendados, but peons led a miserable life. When Zapata came riding on a white horse, shouting "Land and freedom," they joined him almost to a man. Now the green fields are diminished and iguanas rattle over ruined hacienda walls. Nowhere in Mexico was there such ruthless destruction.

One has only to motor along the new road from Cuernavaca to Taxco to realize the vast underground pressures which Diaz had engendered. Like a new volcano, they burst the plains of Morelos, destroying not only the feudal system but its physical plant as well. It would have been wiser to oust the hacendados and spare their mills and buildings. But revolutions, like lava flows, do not intellectualize their courses. Some sugar-growing continues—indeed the industry is slowly reviving under different leadership—and there a group of Tepoztecans find a little work to help balance their annual budgets.

In a sense, it is so much velvet. Twice a week they return to the village for a load of food. Their women grind and grind.

In March and April comes the nadir of the agricultural cycle. There has been hardly a drop of rain for six months. At Santa Catarina, one of the encircling hamlets, the wells are empty, and a burro, a barrel and an Indian must go a mile for water. The fields are yellow and dry as tinder. Up the shoulders of Popo dust storms swirl, dense as thunder clouds. The air is acrid with smoke from the milpas, fired in anticipation of the next sowing. When all our northern world is blossoming into spring, Mexico grows drier, dustier, more barren. Except for the firing and a little brush clearing, field work is at a standstill. This is the time for putting new tiles on the roof; repairing the compound fence; choring about the house. It is the time for community work— repairing roads, walls, fountains, water tanks; for cleaning chapels, inserting new stones in the town laundry. Mexican town laundries consist of running water and massive washing stones in rows. They are never, at any season or any hour, deserted. Women washing beside a river are almost as much a symbol of Mexico as the sombrero. Community work is called *cuatequitl*. A group of men go from one house to the next announcing in Aztec: "Tomorrow it falls to you to do cuatequitl." The irrelevancy of the formal municipal government is sealed in these words.

Then the face of the world changes. In May the rains begin; the desert turns garden; the barrancas begin to roar; billions of tons of water fertilize the parched earth and slide to the sea. Corn planting starts at the hamlet of San Juan, the grains inserted with the same pointed stick the Aztecs used. In the main village, old ploughs are being repaired, and timber hewn into new wooden ploughs.

In June plough and oxen furrow the fields. The whole town is hard at work. By the fifteenth, the last kernel is in. Cultivation is done with the *coa,* a flat hoe, not quite Aztec, not quite Spanish, and so pure Mexican. Through the summer, the daily downpours and the cultivation continue. In the mornings the sun shines on a world washed and green. The flowers are incredible.

In October the showers slacken; by December they have altogether ceased. The corn stands high and green in the milpas; harvest has come. It is the season of the town's maximum activity. All other work is dropped; men, women and children are in the fields. The corn factors prepare to dispose of the surplus. The ears are pulled by hand, and the husks slit with a broad needle of wood or iron hung on the wrist. The cobs are piled into sacks for transport by back or burro to the circular storehouse in the family compound; the husks bound into bundles for tamales; the stalks cut down with machete for fodder, or in some cases left standing as poles for beans. In Michoacan I saw a great cornfield resembling a camped army, with rows of big stacks like tents, and smaller stacks like soldiers on parade—all in precise geometrical pattern.

It is impossible for Mexicans to produce the humblest thing without form and design. A donkey wears a load of palm leaves arranged on either flank in great green sunbursts. Merchants hang candles by their wicks to make patterns in both line and colour. Market cocoanuts show white new moon strips above the dark, fibrous mass. Sarapes are thrown with just the right line over the shoulders of ragged peons, muffling them to the eyes. Merchants in the market will compose their tomatoes, oranges, red seeds and even peanuts into little geometric piles. Bundles of husks will be tied in a manner suitable for suspension in an artist's studio. To the traveller from the north, used to the treatment of cold, dead produce as cold, dead produce, this is a matter of perpetual wonder and delight.

Work in the milpas goes on from dawn to dusk. While each family harvests its own field, community spirit is strong—as in old New England barn raisings. For machineless men generally, it is both necessity and pleasure to assist, and be assisted by, one's neighbour. The owner whose field is ripe announces cuatequitl. A group of men whose fields are not yet ripe, or already harvested, foregather to assist him. He has helped or will help them in due course. A minor fiesta is declared. The owner secretes "the little mule," a bottle of brandy, under the pile of corn; the housewife prepares a special dinner, assisted by the wives of the other men in the group, and the meal is carried with ceremony to the field.

The last loads taken to the village are the little round green squashes which grow between the furrows. The cattle are turned out to forage; harvest is over. In the yard of one of the houses near the plaza, a score of boys are sitting on the ground learning to sing the songs of Los Pastores, the shepherds, taught by the *maestro* who is the repository of this local tradition. The mayordomos begin to decorate the barrio chapels with flowers, boughs of cedar, and coloured tissue paper. To celebrate the harvest, the long fiesta of Christmas and the New Year is approaching.

So runs the work cycle of Tepoztlan. It is also the cycle of education. There are two small schools in the town but their influence is only beginning to dawn. About 100 children out of a possible 1,200 attend these schools for a few months in the year. Real education begins at about ten years of age. Boys are instructed—through the medium of helping their elders—in house building, construction and repair of furnishings, textile working, milpa-tending, community labour, fiesta work, all the home crafts. Girls learn to prepare food, grind and bake tortillas, sew, use the washing stones, and select food supplies at the market. Their sales resistance is very high. All children learn two languages. In actual preparation for life, Tepoztlan's educational methods are superior to Middletown's.

Agriculture, maintenance of household equipment, community repair—such are the chief tasks of the men of Tepoztlan, and of most Mexican villages. In addition we find some of them giving a varying share of their available hours to certain specialties. In earlier chapters we have specified some eighteen occupations concerned with food, shelter, clothing and health—bakers, butchers, storekeepers, masons, shoemakers, midwives and the like. To complete the list for Tepoztlan we must add:

One judge.
One priest.
Two school teachers.
Two "word-knowers," a curious profession. "These are men who know the traditional Aztec words used in summoning people to pay their contribution for the santos, and those used in thanking them when the contribution is paid." Mexicans are the politest people in the world.
Assorted musicians, particularly the village band and the players of the Aztec pipe, both constantly in demand during fiestas.
Fiesta specialists—dancers, mask-makers, decorators (spinning lovely ribbons of woven evergreen), candlemakers, manufacturers of fireworks.
Arrieros or transport men. With their loaded burros, they maintain Tepoztlan's material contact with the outside world.

On every trail in Mexico one finds the arriero and his patient beast, plodding along in the dust, teetering on the brink of precipices, hopelessly entangling motor traffic. The arriero is very important in a mountain country. He takes the place of freight car and truck; without him most mining operations would come to a standstill; yet before Cortez he was totally unknown. Aztecs used tump line, gourd, and crate of sticks on their own backs—methods still employed. The Spaniards revolutionized transportation by introducing the burro, mule, horse and ox. The equipment of these animals—saddles, bridles, lassos, yokes—is still substantially of sixteenth century Spanish design. "God," say the villagers, "made the mule to give the Indian a rest."

This gives us seven more occupations, and brings the total to twenty-five. And that is all. These are the only specialists this handicraft community of 4,000 people requires. Tepoztlan, furthermore, might be even better off if a few were stricken from the list—say the herb doctors and the magicians. We must remember too that most are part-time workers only, and that certain talented individuals appear in two or more categories. Here for instance is E. V. He is mason, woodcarver, gilder, mask-maker, and has a post in the city government as well. Here is L. V., cobbler, mason and musician. Both, of course, are farmers.

Middletown, with 40,000 people, has more than 400 distinct occupations. In an American town of 4,000 there are undoubtedly half that number, 200 against Tepoztlan's twenty-five. The machine age requires far more skills than the era it replaced, despite the lamentations of William Morris. Tepoztlan demands more in the way of all-round skill, but its craft specialties are few. Where would a journalist, electrician, garage man, clerk, stenographer, telephone operator, chauffeur, laundryman, movie actor, radio broadcaster, elevator boy, janitor, chef, pressman, street car conductor, advertising man, broker, realtor, engineer, professor or flagpole sitter get a job? A photographer might do a little business; a hot-dog vendor would certainly be sampled. Mexicans will eat anything. But most of the occupations north of the Rio Grande have no point or purpose in Tepoztlan.

Similarly with our staggering inventories of material equipment. In Sears Roebuck's catalogue are 30,000 articles, a good fraction of which will be found in every American town as large as Tepoztlan—I should guess at least 10,000 different sorts of tools and devices in a great variety of shapes and sizes. In Tepoztlan I doubt if there are 500 different sorts of things, and the size varieties are meagre. There are, perhaps, fifty items in the average family compound; sundry contraptions for harnessing animals, a few fixed styles of clothing, an assortment of very simple agricultural tools, and minimum equipment for preparing and serving food. There are a few devices—water pipes, hinges, bronze bells, office materials—in the public buildings. Food, shelter, clothing, education, recreation, are all provided for after their fashion. Certainly nobody starves spiritually or physically. Yet these groaning shelves, these heaving freight cars, these mountains of fabricated tonnage, simply do not exist. Nor is there the slightest demand that they should. What in heaven's name would Tepoztecans do with the stuff? There are no wages to produce purchasing power, to produce sales, to produce profits, to produce capital, to produce purchasing power, to . . . recurring decimal. So the village population get on with enough to get on with. They could stand a little more, as we shall see. Which does not mean that Middletown could not stand less.

To devote a chapter to work in Mexico will seem to

Diego Rivera 1931

BOSTON PUBLIC LIBRARY

many Americans a task of supererogation. It is a dreary business, but I suppose the time-honoured saw must be answered. Are Mexicans lazy?

Mexicans are never in a hurry; they like plenty of sleep, and are much given to fiestas. Unfortunately they have to eat. Eating involves, among other things, cultivating cornfields on top of *picos,* three or four thousand feet above one's village; it involves carrying one hundred pounds thirty miles in a day over a mountain trail. (When wheelbarrows were first introduced on railway construction work, Indians removed the wheels and carried the barrows on their backs.) It involves grinding corn with a heavy stone pestle for six hours on end; it involves arising normally at dawn. On occasion, Mexicans are the world's champion workers, though, being wise, they never labour any harder than necessity demands— a formula which, through the meshes of a New England upbringing, I am striving to make my own.

Americans receive their impression of the peon's laziness chiefly from plantation and mine owners. Indians, as we have seen, have been forced, often by the most brutal methods, to give up the free village, which they love, and go to work for a boss, which they hate. Is it to be wondered at that the bosses report a certain apathy? They tell us that even higher wages will not make Indians work harder, but the contrary. According to them, a man who does not want money and the things money can buy must be lazy and probably immoral.

THE POPULAR ARTS

Time was when Tepoztlan produced copper tools and fine paper; when it had, in common with most pre-conquest towns, a real handicraft specialty to exchange with other districts. During the colonial period it wove sarapes of tree cotton, and fabricated most of its own clothing. Today it possesses no outstanding specialty, and is the poorer for it. We shall have to turn elsewhere to follow that bright pattern known as the popular arts of Mexico. Twenty miles across the pedregal to Cuernavaca brings us headlong into them. Here we find Indians making hats, chairs, shoes of coloured leather strips—to which even young women on Fifth Avenue are beginning to take a fancy.

Tannenbaum gives us an excellent idea of regional specialization in eleven villages comprising one district in the state of Hidalgo:

Number one, like Tepoztlan, lives primarily by agriculture.
Number two lives by agriculture and wage labour on neighbouring haciendas.
Number three, agriculture and sarape weaving.
Number four, agriculture, pulque making, fibre weaving.
Number five, the same.
Number six is primarily a village of arrieros, engaged in transporting earthenware (which must be made nearby; he does not mention where.)
Number seven ditto. As a secondary line, its members have gained some fame as highwaymen.
Number eight, agriculture, pulque making, and transportation. The manufacture of bassoons, violins, and curious miniatures.
Number nine, hacienda work, pulque making.
Number ten, fishing and river crafts.
Number eleven, fireworks making, with a good fiesta trade. Land about this village is very poor.

We might divide Mexican handicrafts into three main classes:

First, articles made by the householder for his own use. These include all manner of devices and contraptions —furniture, saddles, bowls, gourds, cradles, basket work, metal work, tile, crude pottery. Most of it will be quaint and comely, but there will be little to excite the collector. Tepoztlan possesses handicrafts of this order.

Second, articles made for the tourist trade, and for urban demand. Some of these are exquisite and some are inexcusable. The tendency to date has been to debase the local crafts. Fortunately there are new forces working in the opposite direction, as we shall see.

Third, articles made by the Indians for exchange in their own village markets. Here lie the popular arts in their purest form. They fulfil both a utilitarian and an esthetic function. They are normally made by a village which specializes in one particular line, and which expects, in exchange, wares and even food from other villages. The items of this output constitute an important factor in regional economy. They are bought as household necessities, or because they are bright and pretty—the latter applying particularly to children's toys and inexpensive jewellery. Some of them show a high order of workmanship and design.

Let us take a turn around the Oaxaca market on fiesta day and note the things which are for sale. This market is reasonably "pure." We are the only tourists in town; indeed the harrowing twelve hours by narrow-gauge railroad from Puebla keeps tourist traffic at a minimum. These things are certainly not made to catch our eye. Again, Oaxaca is a small city of 40,000 people. There is little proletariat to cater to. The goods in these booths are largely made by village Indians for village Indians. Over a radius of a hundred miles and more they have brought them in. When the fiesta closes, the goods will go out over that same radius, though on different brown backs.

For each item on the following list, there will generally

[179]

be one or more booths. Each booth is presided over by two or more persons. One person fulfils every economic need, but two or three can gossip, comment on passers-by, and have a better time. This is a fiesta, not a bourse. Mexicans have an incurable habit of performing by groups rather than individually. Taxi drivers take a boy friend along and often two—one on the front seat and one supine on the mudguard. Kitchens drip with humanity; railroad trains sometimes have more crew than passengers. One can live in a ten-room hotel for a week and still be unable to compute the staff which drifts in and out of the lobby.

THE OAXACA MARKET, 1930

Handicrafts

Pottery. Green, smoky black, and the usual Oaxaca rainbow, all shapes and sizes. Chamber pots in olive green. Four-foot tan water jars. Plates, bowls, cups and saucers that one longs to buy by the dozen.

Hemp. Rope plain and coloured. Great waterfalls of unwoven coloured hemp. Bridles, lariats and cinches in white, black and rose. Bags in rainbow colours, from huge packs to little round purses for carrying pesos like a stack of poker chips. Hammocks, plain and varicoloured.

Leather. Thonged sandals with open toes. Saddles, bridles, belts, pouches, holsters, scabbards—plain and with embossed designs.

Sarapes. No booths. Sold by Indians wandering about the market and plaza with piles upon their shoulders. Rectangular shape, all sizes, in designs of white, black, grey and rose— some in red and black, some in royal blue. Eagle and tiger patterns are common. With difficulty one refrains from purchasing a dozen.

Embroidery. Some of it beautiful hand work. Cotton napkins and table covers from a local workshop, in bright, intricate plaids.

Baskets. All shapes and sizes, from six feet in diameter down. Mostly plain lemon straw, beautifully woven and very sturdy. Woven straw animals and toys.

[180]

Petates (mats). All sizes, many with coloured zigzag patterns.

Sombreros. Straw, with coloured designs. Some gorgeous charro sombreros in golden brown felt, three feet wide, embroidered with gold flowers. The latter may cost as much as a hundred pesos.

Lacquer. On gourds and on wood. Smashing colours outside and in. The display is small and probably comes from the north or from the state of Chiapas. Lacquer is not made locally.

Toys. Pigs, burros, devils, cows, dogs of clay or *papier maché.* Painted clay whistles in the shape of animals. Painted canes and whips. Sticks with animal heads.

Masks. Skulls, devils, monkeys, funny faces in *papier maché.*

Candles. White, brown and honey coloured; wax images of santos to burn with them.

Silver work. Milagros, crucifixes, ornaments.

Tin ware. Lanterns, cups, vessels, kerosene flares.

Wooden ware. Chocolate beaters, intricately tooled. Noble stirring spoons. Bird-cages—a green parrakeet in one.

Iron work. Machetes and knives. Beautiful tempered steel swords, daggers, hunting knives, stilettos etched with designs and bloodthirsty mottoes. This is one of Oaxaca's specialties. The iron comes from Monterrey but is tempered here. I was shown a sword that I could bend around my waist like a belt. The work has been compared to that of old Toledo.

Musical instruments. Hand-made guitars, violins, mandolins. Embossed bronze church bells in a smithy beside the market.

Stone work. Corn grinders, three-legged stools.

Glassware. Lovely blue and green goblets sown with air bubbles.

Fireworks. Rockets, roman candles, bombs. Master craftsmen in this art work to special order. They fabricate the costumes for the churchyard gladiators described earlier. They make huge set pieces, with the general appearance of the skeleton of a whale. In this fiesta one was touched off at midnight, a good forty feet high.

So much for the handicrafts. To complete the market picture we should note:

Local produce

Mountains of foodstuffs both raw and manufactured. Lovely booths of vegetables, fruits and nuts. Hideous booths of hacked meats and dried fish. Booths serving a hearty native meal—soups, frijoles, tamales, tortillas, enchiladas, for a few centavos. Breads and sweetmeats. Ice cream—made not by cranking, but by twisting the canister in the ice pack with the hand.

Flowers, mosses and boughs.

Herbs and charms. Humming bird bodies for safe journeys. Cures for snake bite, charms for pregnancy and anti-pregnancy. Shells and incense.

Junk shops. Reclaimed nails, spread on the counter in fan design. Bolts, locks, candlesticks, screws, lamps, bottles—grouped by sizes and colours. A stone idol or two; strings of old jadeite beads. Braziers made of half a square oil can.

Firewood and charcoal, weighed on scale in front of booth.

Soap. In bars of white or yellow, made locally.

Factory products. The volume is small. Lying amid the handi-crafts, they produce an effect like a cigarette advertisement in an art gallery. Some, we must admit, furnish necessities which are overcostly to make, or simply cannot be made, by local craftsmen.

Rebosos, mostly blue.

Bolts of linen and cotton in all colours.

Ready made shirts, blouses and skirts.

Factory shoes, a hideous display.

Handkerchiefs. Bright bandannas hanging in rows.

Musical instruments, for the village band.

Socks and stockings. Precisely why?

Second-hand books, nearly all in paper covers. One by H. G. Wells translated into Spanish.

Canned and bottled groceries, including beer.

Cheap jewellery and knickknacks, on the old five-and-ten level, reasonably ghastly.

Hardware and cutlery. Many useful gadgets here—steel ploughs, for example.

Postcards so luridly sentimental that one of our party bought a peso's worth to send her friends into hysterics.

I think it is fair to take the above as the standard pattern of the Mexican market. I saw much the same display at a big fiesta at Patzcuaro in Michoacan, at Tecal-

pulco in Guerrero, at the great festival of Guadalupe, on
the Alameda in Mexico City itself at Christmas time.
Many of these things can be found in the market of
Tepoztlan. In Michoacan the lacquer exhibits are finer
and the pottery less exciting than in Oaxaca. The accent
changes from region to region, colours and shapes
change, but the main classes tend to be constant. Con-
noisseurs come to know the exact village where a given
sarape or clay vessel is made. The ordinary traveller
picks up a working acquaintance with the crafts at about
the same rate as he picks up Spanish. It takes years to
master either. As good an introduction as any to the
popular arts is Susan Smith's *Made in Mexico*. But to
see them at their most typical, you should have some
article made to order. Everything depends on whether
your design catches the artist's fancy. If it does, he will
add a few embellishments which undeniably improve it,
and perhaps keep it half a day after it is ready (that is,
from a week to a month beyond the date originally agreed
on) to trace the pattern for his own future reference.
Nothing ever comes out exactly as ordered.

Let us recapitulate the outstanding handicrafts together with the most famous points of origin:

Pottery (glazed) ....from Oaxaca and Puebla
Water jars and unglazed ware.from Guerrero and Jalisco
Tiles ....from Puebla and Guadalajara
Lacquered gourds and wooden
    trays ....from Michoacan
Lacquered boxes ....from Guerrero
Glass ....from Mexico City and Puebla
Glass toys ....from Jalisco
Wood carving ....from Michoacan
Chairs ....from Morelos, Guerrero, Jalisco
Iron work ....from Oaxaca
Silver work ....from Puebla

Gold work ....from Guerrero and Oaxaca
Sarapes ....from Oaxaca and Tlaxcala
Embroideries ....from the Isthmus and from To-
                                  luca in the state of Mexico
Hammocks ....from Yucatan
Baskets ....from Guanajuato
Straw animals ....from Guerrero
Paper masks ....from Guanajuato
Woven leather shoes.........from Morelos
Filigree jewellery ....from Oaxaca

If you look at a map of Mexico you will see all these
names well south of the border states. The handicrafts
persist where the Aztec, Maya, or Tarascan influence
was strongest. The nearer one approaches the Rio
Grande, the weaker grows the craft influence. Indians in
these northern regions were more nomadic and less civilized to begin with, and latterly have been influenced by
cultural penetration from the United States. One does
not really get into Mexico until he strikes Guanajuato,
some 400 miles south of the border.

The old civilizations produced marvellous craftsmen.
Their pottery, though unglazed, was distinguished; their
feather robes, turquoise masks, silver and gold work,
carving of bone and obsidian, textiles, embroidery, wood
carving, frescoes, and sculptured stone were of the highest order. To this tradition the Spaniards added excellent
arts of their own, notably iron work, glazed pottery,
leather working, glass making. In addition, certain crafts
purely Mexican, such as sombrero and sarape weaving,
have been evolved since Cortez landed. But I am afraid
that, as in the case of basic civilization, Mexican handicrafts have been slowly declining since the conquest.
Working in bone and obsidian is almost gone; there are
only three feather robes left in the world—those robes
which Bernal Diaz used to count by the score of man-

loads; both feather-painting and certain lacquer work
have decayed to the point of copying the more florid
variety of picture postcard.

Despite these breaches in the wall, our stroll around
the Oaxaca market makes it clear that the handicrafts
are still amazing enough. Their freshness and vitality
cause the traveller on his return to wonder why American shop windows look so lifeless. The glare of neon
lights only makes the contrast gloomier. Mexico has
made Fifth Avenue a duller street for me, and I am not
sure that I am grateful.

Perhaps we can understand why this is so by looking
in at a shop where three men and two boys are making
glass. Two brothers are in charge whose family has produced glass for generations. The only machine in the
place is a blower, operated by a small motor, for the furnace. The raw materials are shovelled in by hand, the
clay bowlfuls of dye are mixed by hand; the blowing and
fashioning are done with long, hollow rods and curiously
shaped pincers. Had we looked in two hundred years ago,
the scene would have been identical—round, brick furnace with square apertures filled with blinding light; high,
smoke-filled room retreating into velvet shadows, the
stooping backs of men and boys bearing long staffs with
glowing ends, like huge fireflies. . . . The master craftsman welcomes the friend who has brought us. His face
lights up. "Presently I shall make something for you,"
he says, "something very beautiful. I have a new idea.
Wait and see."

We waited, and it was beautiful—a big-bellied pitcher
in pale green glass with broad flat handle, scalloped rim,
and spiral grooves from neck to base. With the help of
one of the boys he fashioned it, from molten mass to
oven, in fifteen minutes. "Nobody has ever made a

pitcher like that before. Tomorrow it will be cool and you will come and get it. It is for you." To have offered him money would have been to strike him in the face. That is why glassware coming out of a factory on an endless belt misses something that only a craftsman, in a hopelessly antiquated shop, with a beautiful new idea, can give. Incidentally this same maestro came to New York a few years ago. No interior decorator discovered him, and all he could find to do was run an elevator up and down, down and up, in a tall hotel. He did not stay long.

We are speaking of glass, and pottery, and sarapes. No craftsman, though bursting with lovely new ideas, could make an electric light bulb, or an automobile engine, or a bathtub faucet, a fraction as justly and well as machine and factory can.

All over Mexico today men and women, mostly Indians, are making the homely things which they need and their neighbours need, with something of this glass blower's spirit. I do not doubt that that spirit is repeatedly crucified with dull ritual, with monotony, but enough of it breaks through to make an Oaxaca market, or such a repository as that of Mr. Frederick Davis in Mexico City, as exciting to me as any art museum. This is the kind of work which millions of these machineless men engage in, sometimes in lieu of, but far more frequently in conjunction with, their agricultural labour. In front of looms as hoary as the glass blower's shop, at cottage benches, in the frowzy, colourful courtyards of town dwellings, in the market's dust, I have seen their dexterous fingers, their timeless patience, their concentrated interest as they weave and cut and hammer something a little different than anyone else has made. They punch no time clocks, prepare no job tickets, visit no employment office, receive no welfare work, say yessir to no boss. They work when they feel like it, stop when they feel like it, sleep when they feel like it. According to the doctrines of the Manchester School, under whose dispensation we of the north live, they are Ishmaelites, utterly beyond the pale. Yet all the masters, and all the men, and all the factories, and all the steam in Manchester, working day and night for one hundred and fifty years, have never produced a tithe of the excellence in human goods to be found in one holiday market in one small city in the south of Mexico.

We have touched on the debasement of certain crafts. Is the process to be indefinitely extended? Are the handicrafts ultimately doomed? I know of one positive counter-irritant, and at the same time I feel a vague foreboding. Rene d'Harnoncourt has to my certain knowledge revived the art of feather-painting and the lacquer work of Olinala. By showing the Indians the old designs, by finding a readier market for the revived as against the debased, he has started an eddy in the other direction. D'Harnoncourt did not teach, he only showed examples —and suddenly, mysteriously, something long dead came back to life. Perhaps other true friends of Mexico will follow his example.

My foreboding is concerned with the American tourist. In a few months (this is June, 1931) he will be able to drive his Buick clear through to Mexico City. Clouds of Buicks, swarms of Dodges, shoals of Chevrolets—mark my words, they will come. They will demand souvenirs to take back, and the souvenirs to which these cars are accustomed are found in shiny log cabins beside the hot-dog stand in the Profile Notch, New Hampshire, or at Niagara Falls, New York, or in Glacier National Park, Montana. Travelling up from Vera Cruz I asked a fellow national if he cared for Mexican popular art. Yes, he said, he was greatly taken with Mexican art. He had indeed bought two fleas, one dressed like a bride and the other like a groom; he had bought a walnut with a glass top and a whole landscape, mountains and everything, painted inside. Clever people, the Mexicans.

They will have to be clever to preserve their craft integrity against that southward-moving cloud of dust. . . . Perhaps the Buicks may fall off the unguarded hairpin turns which distinguish Mexican mountain roads. Even better, perhaps these cars will learn, following the chastening years of business depression, to discriminate between sound workmanship and junk.

CHAPTER X

MACHINELESS MEN—THEIR PLAY

THE fiesta is the outstanding exhibit of Mexican recreation. There is nothing like it in the States, unless it be Mardi Gras in New Orleans. The nearest thing to it in my experience was the old-fashioned Fourth of July, which meant much to me as a boy in New England. Perhaps the smell of gunpowder brought it back. The church bells at midnight, the salvos of rockets and bombs in the early morning hours, firecrackers at dawn, the parade of the Antiques and Horribles in masks, the overworked town band perspiring on the common, strawberries and ice cream for dinner, the blistering heat, uniforms and flags, fireworks and the set piece of Niagara Falls— which miraculously ceased flowing when it was supposed to cascade its hardest—there was something of the real fiesta spirit in all this. But the old-fashioned Fourth of July was chiefly for small boys. Little girls in those dark, pre-feminist days were equipped with nothing more deadly than paper torpedoes, while the grown-ups of my acquaintance regarded the day as the most nerve-wracking, forbidding and dangerous in the year. (They were certainly confirmed as the tetanus figures began to come in.)

In Mexico it is the other way around. The fiesta is primarily for grown-ups. Children down to week-old babies are all present, and those old enough to walk enjoy themselves hugely. But it is their fathers and mothers, their gaffers and grandams, who dominate the spectacle. Not boys, but adult men are shooting off the rockets, and dancing in plumed headdress and masks. Mexican children are without any exception the quietest and best behaved in the world. They never dominate anything. A ginger-whiskered Freudian might stalk among them scenting repressions, but I doubt if youngsters so exuberantly loved by their elders can suffer from this malady, while to the wayfarer their dignity and decorum is a source of never-failing delight. Charles Flandrau goes so far as to declare that if he were managing the world he would arrange for all children to be born Mexican and remain so till they were fifteen. I think he means Indian, not white Mexican children. The latter share with their Nordic cousins the usual percentage of the spoiled, peevish and intolerable.

Suppose we follow through the principal activities of a typical fiesta—say that of Oaxaca in the middle of December. In it we shall find, as we found in the market, the basic pattern for all. It begins before the announced date with a slow, often unnoticed, but very extensive human migration. Into every centre like the city of Oaxaca lead, say, one railroad, two motor roads—we will call them motor roads—and scores of valley and presently mountain trails.

The one train a day will suddenly fill to the bursting point, until Indians, surrounded by every sort of lumpy bag and parcel, begin to pop like so many chestnuts on to the roofs of the cars. The interior looks like nothing so much as a six o'clock express in Times Square—except that there are no straps, and everybody is good-natured. The railroad never dreams of adding more cars or an extra train. Mexican coaches in these parts run in two classes—the first class maintaining the approximate equipment of an Erie Railroad smoker in the seventies. Theoretically it is reserved for holders of first class tickets. But at fiesta time we are given a very pretty example of why Europe has never subdued Mexico. When the second class coaches, the freight cars, the tender and the roofs are all full, and only then, the Indians, like a dark brown river, come flowing relentlessly into the first class carriages. The train crew make no attempt to stop them, knowing its futility. The spare seats go, the spaces around the lavatories fill solid, the floor disappears under layer after layer of wicker lunch baskets, pottery, and knickknacks. Suddenly one finds oneself lifting a baby through the open window and delivering it to a waiting—and very polite—barefooted mother in the aisle. Miraculously a seat on which two of us were sitting holds four, and there is a little boy in white pyjamas leaning against one's leg. We are thoroughly uncomfortable but the philosophical implications of this invasion help our patience. And the smiling brown baby beside one's ear is certainly worth watching. We resign ourselves to the convocation of what Terry terms the entomological congress. Indeed there is nothing else to do; only a steam shovel could extricate us.

Meanwhile a few crazy Fords converted into busses are bumping over the so-called motor roads equally burdened. If the driver has room to manipulate his gears among the bundles he is lucky. But the real exhibit, the exhibit which accounts for nine persons out of ten, is the pedestrians and animals on the converging trails. If we should ride a horse in a circle at a radius of ten miles from Oaxaca, bisecting all the trails, we should gather something of the full impact of this extraordinary migration. It comes by families, at least one baby in each. A few travellers are on horseback, a few are mounted on the extreme rear end of a patient mouse-coloured donkey. More often the burro is loaded with produce or handicrafts, and the whole family, save the baby, walks. In Oaxaca, papa is not above carrying the infant. In other areas this does not do at all. Some of these people have come from inaccessible mountain notches a hundred and more miles away; places to make Tepoztlan look like Broadway. They have been travelling for a solid week; building a little fire beside the trail at nightfall, roasting their tortillas, and anon sleeping, wrapped in their sarapes, to take the trail again before dawn.

Perhaps the jolliest prelude to a fiesta I ever saw was on Lake Patzcuaro in Michoacan. I went down to the lakeside in the early morning of the opening day. It is a sheet of water, 6,700 feet above the sea, broken with islands and long bays, and rimmed with lofty mountains. On the foothills the milpas grow like checkerboards. There are a dozen towns and villages of Tarascan Indians about the lake, living from fishing and hunting as well as corn. When pursuing duck, they use the old Mexican *atlatl* or throwing spear. Now they are coming across the rose-coloured water in literally hundreds of dugout canoes, propelled by curious little paddles shaped like lollypops. Bark and paddle have not changed their shape in a thousand years. Some of the canoes are forty feet long, with all the family paddling. Some are full of women, a frieze of parallel rebosos above parallel oars. Heaped on the bows are flowers, vegetables, little white transparent fish strung on green rushes; mosses, boughs, pottery, nets; food for the days to be spent at the fiesta, and produce for exchange at the market.

Oaxaca has no lake, but from trail, road and rail, it

will add 40,000 people to its population, doubling it in a day or two. The fiesta proper begins at midnight, but a few anticipatory rockets will explode earlier in the evening. Hundreds of little booths have sprung up around the Church of the Soledad, and men are struggling with the erection of a merry-go-round and a diminutive ferris wheel at the foot of the church steps. Townfolk are running paper streamers across the streets. The migration is steadily seeping into town, populating the booths, crowding the churchyard, brimming the main plazas. Where are all these thousands to sleep? A tour of inspection answers the question. They are going to sleep where they finally come to a halt; in back of their booths, in the churchyard, in the market, around the plaza. On the bare ground—it is cold in the evenings at 5,000 feet in December—they are going to curl up like so many caterpillars. Elementary sanitation has been provided for. All the town fountains are flowing. Food they have in their bags, or can purchase for a few centavos at the booths.

At midnight, every church bell in town breaks into a raving delirium. Small boys, who ought to be in bed, have climbed the towers of a score of churches and chapels to set them somersaulting. A devastating explosion, on the general order of the Paris gun, takes place in the direction of the Soledad. Then another and another. The fiesta has officially begun. Through the remainder of the night, bells ring and bombs detonate, with another frantic zero hour at dawn.

This particular fiesta is in honour of the Virgin of the Soledad, and centres around her great church, which I described earlier when swinging architecture around the compass. Soledad means solitude, but the lady is nothing if not gregarious. She welcomes thousands to her festival, and in addition has to be locked up at night, for as patron saint of sailors she has a generous but indelicate habit of leaving her niche and spending the hours between sunset and sunrise in heaven knows what ocean-going company. Certainly she has been caught in the morning with salt water on her dress of black velvet. Or so we were solemnly informed. But the Indians like her all the better for this small dereliction; the old gods were not without their human foibles. She is a very great santa, and her miracles are known far and wide. She looks a little like a gypsy dancer with her slim figure and her enormous hooped, pearl-embroidered skirt. She is a waxen image, about life size, high up in the centre of the grand altar, which has been decorated for the occasion with silver ribbons and six-foot candles. Throughout the fiesta a moving multitude passes in and out of the church; some to pray devoutly, some to beseech material benefits, some to watch the show. Mothers and babies spend the whole day sitting on the floor. From time to time choir boys sing, and the organ booms. Sometimes there will be a thousand lighted candles in a thousand outstretched hands, smoke and incense curling up to the murky, vaulted ceiling.

At noon, the Apaches take their place in the courtyard. They will dance for five hours. There are twelve of them in headdresses of real aigrets dyed in bright colours. Violin, piccolo and guitars call the tune. They advance and retreat, turn deftly, break into fours, reverse, take their places—something remotely like the figures in New England country dances. Their rhythm is sharper, their masks prevent any change of expression; they hold themselves a little stiffly, but they are well drilled and tireless. A crowd gathers, and the circle, through outside pressure, narrows until it cramps the

Diego Rivera. 1931.

BOSTON PUBLIC LIBRARY

dancers' movements. The music stops, while the spectators are pressed outward.

Meanwhile the merry-go-round and the ferris wheel are doing a thriving business, mainly with adults. A variety of centrifugal swinging seat, attached by a chain to a central pole, is, however, just dizzy enough to attract small boys. The military band begins to thunder on the plaza, its first number a movement from a Beethoven symphony, extraordinarily well played. The Oaxaca band is known all over Mexico. There are about fifty pieces. If they loaned some of their brass to the Mexico City symphony orchestra, one might be more enthusiastic about the latter.

The gambling games are in full swing under their canvas sunshades, particularly *loteria,* played with a peculiar deck of cards with pictures of animals upon them, and with kernels of corn as counters. One may sit in for five centavos. Mexicans of all shades adore to gamble, but they do it stolidly. Shooting galleries and ring toss are taking in the coppers. Everybody seems to be chewing sugar-cane. Here a packed ring in the street encircles two corrido singers; a fat man with an immense sombrero and guitar, and a youth with sweet, high tenor, singing a third above the fat man, and now wearing a little thin. Since early morning they have been delivering the interminable ballads which the Indians love, their only payment the sale of the words on brightly-coloured tissue paper.

Presently more dances start. "The Moors and the Christians" enact their ancient battle. After sundown comes the solemn procession into the church of the vestments of the Virgin and the great iron lanterns, followed by the fireworks dancers in the courtyard. Then bombs, pinwheels, rockets, and finally the detonation of the huge set piece, forty feet high. This is the climax of the day, and indeed of the fiesta. There will be plenty of activity tomorrow but at a slower tempo. In another day or two the migration will reverse itself.

The inroads of the machine to date are not great, even in a city fiesta like this. The chief contribution is the substitution of electric lights for flares and torches, making the night less picturesque but far more visible. The ferris wheel and some of the merry-go-rounds are run by motor. Others are propelled, as heretofore, by small boys pushing them around from the inside. There is usually a photographer's booth. Many, of course, will attend the town movie, where Hollywood dumps its more dismal failures, titled in both Spanish and English. This is about all. Coney Island would utterly collapse without its huge allotment of horsepower, but a Mexican fiesta functions today much as it did a century ago.

The two focal points are the church with its dances, processions and fireworks, and the market with its wares. It is impossible to tell which is the more important, but I suspect the latter. In Oaxaca, the market is half a mile from the Church of the Soledad; crowds surge back and forth from one to the other. Food booths are thick in the street below the church, candle and milagro sellers thick in the churchyard itself—I have even seen them inside churches during mass. But most of the handicrafts, the precious purchases which are to go back over the trails, are to be found at the market. Its wares we have already described; its spirit remains beyond description. People come to buy, yes, and to sell; they come to gossip, and to tell the news of the villages, there will be no such news again for many a long day; they come to look at the crowds and the colours and the goods; they come to herd together, to feel the hot breath of impacted humanity, to press upon the flesh of their own kind. This means more to lonely mountain folk than you and I, living in Megalopolis, can sense. Through hungry pores they drink in the market; they drink in the whole fiesta. It becomes as integral a part of their lives as harvesting corn or making love.

I cannot conceive Mexico without the fiesta and the spirit it engenders. Once I was caught in a gold mine by a sudden flood of water, long pent up. There was no danger, but before we reached the mouth of the tunnel we were wading to our knees. Our host, the mine owner, was divided between commiseration for his guests' discomfort and relief that the water had been released. Presently the Indian miners came wading through the zinc-white flood, wringing wet and smiling from ear to ear. "See, we have made the water come! *Bueno, muy bueno!*" They trooped down to their little village. To change their clothes? No indeed. To start a miniature mountain fiesta. In five minutes rockets were hissing; bombs cracked; a large pinwheel began to turn. It was still broad daylight but that was a detail. After many weeks of hard and dangerous work the water had been tapped and led harmlessly away. The victory demanded immediate celebration. Could you duplicate the scene—and the spirit—in West Virginia or Cornwall?

In Tepoztlan, Mr. Redfield has probably given us the most careful schedule of the fiesta cycle ever prepared. We find nearly thirty of them in the year, accounting for more than a hundred holidays. On roughly one day in three, the year around, Tepoztecans are celebrating a major or minor festival. This reminds us of the machineless men of the Middle Ages in Europe, when a hundred saints' days and holidays a year were common. The Aztecs had market and compulsory holiday every five days, together with a certain number of general celebrations— of which the thirteen-day period at the close of the fifty-two-year calendar cycle was probably the most elaborate. There are four types of fiesta in Tepoztlan:

General or national	13
Barrio	9
Village	5
Regional	1
Total	28

The first type is celebrated all over Mexico, including Tepoztlan. The second is the special fiesta at the chapel of one of the barrios of the town. Sometimes it interests only the residents of that barrio, but usually all the village attends, and not infrequently Indians come from outlying villages. Through some obscure process, developed over centuries of time, a given fiesta in a small barrio or a tiny village becomes "important," attracting an extensive migration from the surrounding region. Thus I saw a fiesta at Tecalpulco in Guerrero, a poor village of not more than a hundred houses, visited by 15,000 people from all over the state. The santo in the local church had taken on especially miraculous powers.

The third type concerns not the barrio but the whole town, and centres around the plaza cathedral. The last is not in the village at all, but twenty miles away at Yautepec. This is the nearest trading centre—you can actually drive from Mexico City to Yautepec by motor. It is a very important fiesta, and everybody who can walk tends to migrate thither. It corresponds to the call of the big festival at Oaxaca to its hinterland. In addition, many Tepoztecans make the rounds of other regional fiestas, either with goods to sell or just to enjoy them, and some make annual pilgrimages to such distant shrines as Guadalupe or Chalma when the great fiestas occur there. Here in abbreviated form is Mr. Redfield's schedule:

January 1. Fiesta of *Santa Maria de Tepoztlan*. Three days. Not very important.

January 6. Fiesta of the barrio of *Los Reyes*. Four days. Includes a bull fight and rodeo. Fairly important.

January 12. Fiesta of the barrio of *Santo Domingo*. One day. Not important.

January 16. Fiesta of the hamlet of *Santa Catarina*. Three days. Very important. Apaches from Jalatlaco come to dance. Huge fireworks castillo.

January 20. Fiesta of the barrio of *San Sebastian*. Eight days. Very important. Apaches of San Juan. Toros (bull-figures of fireworks) and Chinelos—leapers.

February 2. La Candelaria (Candlemas). One day. The doll Christs which were put to bed on Christmas eve are taken up and dressed. Parties. Rockets. Strong drink.

February 5. Signing of the National Constitution. One day. Not important in Tepoztlan. School children parade. Speeches. Music.

February 28. Carnival. Six days. Most important secular fiesta of the year. Masked dancers. Ice cream from Cuernavaca. Huge market.

March 14. Fiesta at *Yautepec*. Many go from Tepoztlan. This inaugurates a round of fairs at five different towns. Many Tepoztecans make the rounds.

Palm Sunday. Palm, laurel and cedar to be blessed at church.

Holy Tuesday. Last Supper allegory.

Good Friday through Easter. Ceremonies, processions, feasting.

April 29. Fiesta of the barrio of *San Pedro*. Three days. Important. Little boys dance.

May 3. Fiesta of the barrio of *Santa Cruz*. One day. Not important.

May 7. Fiesta of the barrio of *San Miguel*. One day. Not important.

May 8. Fiesta of hamlet of *Ixcatepec*. Eight days. Very important. One hundred Indians come from the village of Milpa Alta

in the State of Mexico carrying their santo, who is the same as
that of Ixcatepec. Apaches. Cock fights. Horse races. Toros.

June 12. Fiesta of the barrio of *La Santisima.* One day. Not
important.

June 16. Fiesta of *Corpus Christi.* One day. Not important.

July 22. Fiesta of hamlet of *Amatlan.* Three days. Fairly important. Apaches.

July 25. Fiesta of hamlet of *Santiago.* Three days.

August 4. Fiesta of hamlet of *Santo Domingo.* Three days.
Dance of the Moors and Christians.

August 16. Fiesta of the barrio of *Santa Cruz.* Two days.

September 8. Fiesta of the pueblo of *Tepoztlan.* One day. Com-
memoration of Tepoztecatl, the god of the pyramid above the
town. Aztec *teocalli* (pyramid-temple) is built. Drums. Pageant.
Attack in pantomime.

September 29. Fiesta of the barrio of *San Miguel.* One day.
Unimportant.

October 31. The *Festival of the Dead.* Three days. Very important. Peculiar ceremonies straight from the Aztecs.

November 7. Octava los chiquitos y los grandes. Two days.
Death ceremonies completed.

December 8. Fiesta of *La Virgen Purisima.* One day. Not
important.

December 12. Fiesta of *Our Lady of Guadalupe.* One day. Not
important in Tepoztlan, but at the church of the virgin, near
Mexico City, the biggest fiesta in the country. A hundred thousand people. Some Tepoztecans always attend.

December 16. Christmas fiesta. Nine days. Posadas. Processions,
rodeos, singing.

December 24. Noche Buena. Christ doll put to bed. (On Christmas Day itself nothing happens. The spirit has been exhausted.)

This is, we must admit, a schedule to appal even
George F. Babbitt. What professional joiner could hope
to keep up with it? Special foods, special dishes—the
women grind and grind—special costumes, special drinks,
special behaviour, for each occasion. The ritual is slowly
disintegrating, according to Redfield, but the markets
and the general spirit of relaxation are unimpaired. A

[202]

hundred days of playtime, more or less. Sunday is also a day of markets and relaxation, which gives us fifty more —with some overlapping, of course. A Puritan Sunday is unheard of in Mexico. Everything is wide open. You can even work all day if you choose.

It may seem strange to conjoin death and play in the Festival of the Dead. Yet this is one of the great fiestas, observed throughout the nation. On the evening of October 31 at eight o'clock in each home in Tepoztlan a candle, decorated with flowers and ribbons, will be lighted for every dead child there remembered. In front of the candle food is set—bread, chocolate, chicken. Every utensil used must be new. Copal incense is set burning. Each *muertito*—"little dead one"—is called by name and the food is offered him. Plates and wooden spoons are laid out. The family keeps vigil all night long. At six the next morning, people come to the plaza church and ask the priest to bless the remembered children. Then all return to their homes and eat the food laid out the night before. In the evening the same ceremony is enacted for the adult *muertos*. The candles are larger, are hung with black ribbons and decorated with flowers of black wax. A large incense-burner is lighted. Food is laid out for the dead—tamales, rice, mamones, oranges, lemons, bananas, melons, *mole verde*—a hot spiced meat dish. As it is offered, one says "Now comes the Day of the Dead. I will await my departed." The city is again awake all night. Torches are alight on the streets. The church bells strike the hours with double strokes. At four o'clock a group of men from each barrio goes about asking tamales for the bell ringers. At six, the blessing is given, and the food offering in front of the candles is eaten.

The dead come back to feast with the living. There is no wailing and lamentation, but flowers, candles, bells and festival in an orchestral minor. Those who have seen these ceremonies, particularly in the more remote villages, report them as indescribably impressive.

To the outsider, the organization of the fiesta is a mystery. There are no masters of ceremonies, no committeemen with badges, no bureau of information, no policemen discernible. The thing seems to run itself. When are the Moors and the Christians to dance? Nobody knows, or else everyone asked has a different theory. Where are they to dance? Nobody knows. All that one can do is to keep watchfully circulating, an exhausting matter. A day at a Mexican fiesta is more debilitating than ten sets of tennis; it is indeed the most tiring experience I know.

Somewhere, deeply hidden, worn smooth by the tradition of centuries, there is organization. Most of it lies in the unconscious behaviour of the participating crowds; they feel when this should be done, and that. They drift "right now at three or five o'clock" to the proper ceremony at the proper place. Part of it lies in deliberate planning by the group most concerned with the particular celebration. Barrio fiestas are the responsibility of their inhabitants. Men of the barrio must decorate the chapel, prepare the fireworks; women must grind mountains of corn, cook the special dishes; boys must ring the bells. Arrangements must be made for the extension of market space, for toilet facilities, for the clearing of refuse, for stringing flags and threading streamers of pine and cedar. Without any frantic chief of staff, surrounded by telephones, messengers, secretaries and typewritten orders, it all gets done. It may be at three, it may be at five, it may be at midnight—but it occurs. The responsible group, whether barrio, church or municipality, sets the stage, each member, through long experience, doing his alloted share. The visiting Indians, through long experience, do the rest. Lines never form on the right; church aisles become all but choked; crowds congest to the bone-breaking point—but suddenly the pressure gives, nothing serious seems to happen; no fists are shaken, no irate voices raised, no lost children wail. The only arrests are the steering of an occasional gentleman, overfull of pulque, to the side lines.

To the northerner, used to rules, regulations, uniformed direction, orderly queues and one committeeman to every two spectators, the whole phenomenon is astounding. Something is going to break loose; something terrible will surely happen. It never does. Ultimately one comes to trust this strange unplacarded, automatic type of organization, and to realize that despite the baffling want of information, it has a broader base, handles crowds more safely than our own Coney Islands, football games and Fifth Avenue parades.

In my time I have criticized play in the machine age with some severity. I have said that it was over-commercialized, mechanized, standardized; that it tended to compound the strains and stresses set up by monotonous factory work; that there was too much sitting, watching, listening, rather than first-hand participation. I have cited the movies, the radio, the stadium complex, the funny papers, the motor car. How does this major form of recreation among machineless men differ in spirit; is it, when all is said and done, any more rewarding? Do Oaxaca and Tepoztlan really have more fun than Middletown?

I think they do. They take their fun as they take their food, part and parcel of their organic life. They are not driven to play by boredom; they are not organized into recreation by strenuous young men and women with badges on their arms and community chests behind them; they are not lectured on the virtues of work and the proper allocation of leisure hours. In short there is no "problem." In the second place, while the dancers and active performers in a given fiesta are comparatively few, the crowd is not standing still waiting to be fed recreation with a spoon at so much a gulp. No. The crowd is moving, exchanging news, absorbing new impressions, bargaining in the market, participating, in a very fundamental sense. You can have a football game without a crowd, you can have a talkie, or a radio program. But a fiesta without a crowd would be unthinkable. The dancers, bands, rockets, ferris wheels, booths, are only the higher tongues of flame in a furnace.

The fiesta is the spirit of play released on a vast and authentic scale. The body receives very little exercise in the form of sport. Perhaps it should receive more. Perhaps these holidays could be improved by mass dancing, opportunities for games, races and competitions in muscular skill. Certainly I should not object to the experiment. But we must remember that Indians are almost never fat. As the full significance of this observation dawns, we realize that we are dealing with a population that never has time to sit down long enough to take on weight. It is exercising from cradle to grave. One glance at perpendicular mountain cornfields is enough to establish this point. It is reasonable to suppose accordingly that their recreation does not demand muscular exercise in the form of sport, and that the fiesta produces less active but to them even more rewarding forms of play.

In the case of children this conclusion is less tenable. The fiesta, as we have observed, is primarily for adults. Mexican children ought to have more sports and games.

Fortunately the Revolution has engendered a strong movement in that direction. In front of every new village schoolhouse stands a basketball court. It was strange to see little Indian boys playing basketball in the sleepy plaza of Tsintsuntsan amid the mouldering churches and the ancient graves—a town a million miles from nowhere, once the capital of the Tarascan race. In Yucatan they are taking avidly to baseball. Mountain-climbing clubs have been organized. I spent the hot hours of two days in a Oaxaca swimming pool, and wished I could stay a fortnight. The boys were so pathetically eager to learn the crawl stroke, and proper form in diving. They were fearless in the water, but nobody had ever taught them the techniques which would add vastly to their enjoyment. Although the famous Latin game of Fronton—a kind of glorified handball in which the players wallop the ball with an enormous claw strapped to the wrist—is played publicly by Spanish professionals, many Mexican amateurs have their own courts. Newspapers carry articles promoting athletics. "Every child," says one, "will become a propagandist for sport . . . and interest, inevitable as gangrene, will infect the grown-ups."

I see room for a great development of this sort of thing. But I see no field at all for bridge tournaments, Marathon dancers, tree roosters, or publicity gained by pushing a peanut up a mountain with the aid of one's nose.

CHAPTER XI

MACHINELESS MEN—THE BASIC PATTERN

WE have perhaps gone far enough to glimpse the basic pattern of the machineless men of Mexico and to see that it is possible to lead a normal, reasonably creative, and rewarding life without thirty slaves of energy at one's elbow. It is true that there is no progress. It is also true that there is no visible material decay. Such an equilibrium causes a Nordic philosopher acute katzenjammer, but that only proves him an indifferent philosopher. Progress has never been adequately defined, while decay is all too plain. Look at Rome; look at the Mayas; look at Spain herself. We Westerners may even now be on the brink of a gorgeous toboggan slide. A people like the village Mexicans—done with "civilization" for four hundred years, sturdy enough to keep going without economic lifts and nose dives; with sense enough to make beautiful things with their hands, to see a fair world about them, to produce the best behaved children on earth—may leave something to be desired, but only an ignoramus may sneer at them. These people possess several qualities the average American would give his eye-teeth to get; and they possess other things completely beyond his purview—human values he has not even glimpsed, so relentlessly has his age blinded and limited him. All of which does not prevent it from being true that machineless men, in their turn, must sacrifice cerain positive goods if they are to maintain their way of life. I could not—you could not—live among them indefinitely and be happy, conditioned as we are. Individually we might, like Mr. William Spratling, buy a house in Taxco, compromise between standards of living, and be happy for a number of years. But if a dictator had the power to convert Tepoztlan into Middletown, he would belong in the lowest and hottest corner of hell if ever he gave the word.

Let us briefly summarize the findings of fact set forth in the last four chapters, and attempt to get into focus the basic pattern of this handicraft culture.

Most Mexicans are Indians and they live in villages. The urban population does not exceed five per cent of all. Around the villages are milpas, and the culture is solidly based now, as of old, on maize. These villages, according to Dr. Eyler Simpson, may be roughly divided into two economic groups. A minority will be almost entirely self-supporting, growing and fabricating nearly everything they need. These tend to be the more remote and the more primitive. Far commoner is the village which forms part of a self-supporting region. Such a one raises the bulk of its food, but many of its necessities come from other villages in the region, exchange takes place in the markets and during the cycle of the fiestas. The exchange medium is both barter and silver pesos, but as a buyer is often also a seller, a large volume of exchange can be executed with a small volume of silver. The motive of the market as a whole is not a pecuniary one. People do not go to make a profit; they go to deliver what they have made, get what they need, and pass the time of day. The Aztec marriage of market day and holiday has never been dissolved.

Such money as they have, and it is very little, comes

primarily from two sources: sale of their surplus products, both crops and handicrafts, outside the region; sale of their surplus labour to mine or hacienda. We have seen how for a few weeks in the winter the men of Tepoztlan go off to the haciendas for money wages. We have also noted how at harvest time they sell their surplus maize to the two corn factors of the town, who in turn market it in Mexico City. There are no figures, but I should guess that, except the money which takes the place of barter in regional exchange, not ten per cent of the household budget is bought with cash. Money could be absolutely eliminated, and the region still carry on.

Within a given region we are likely to find both handicraft centres and unspecialized villages like Tepoztlan. The former will give more time to their special art—lacquer, pottery, toys, fireworks, musical instruments, or whatever it may be—and less to their crops and other necessities. They must accordingly lean more heavily on regional exchange.

The unconquered tribal village is self-supporting, and profoundly communistic in its economic habits. "We have," to quote one of them, "1,300 hectares of second-class non-irrigated lands, and 600 hectares of mountain land to which there are 585 properties with rights to the land among men, women, widows and orphans, all in equal parts in proportion to the possibilities of each." The free village, so-called, is more accessible, more civilized and more directly descended from the Aztec and Maya cultures, rather than from outside tribes. It also is strongly communistic in its land habits. When Diaz forced it to assume individual land titles, citizens deposited their deeds with the cacique, and continued to accept his allotments as theretofore. The most recent estimates show free villages and tribal villages account-

ing for more than sixty per cent of the population of
Mexico. Hacienda villages account for some twenty-five
per cent of the population, and vary from self-sufficiency
to complete dependence on money wages, according to
the hacienda policy. Here the old traditions and communal habits have been greatly modified. On some of the
big plantations, the Indians have degenerated to a rural
proletariat. The Revolution of 1910 favoured the free
village and weakened the hacienda system.

Mexican agriculture is predominantly that of the hand
and the hoe. The hoe, pick, iron bar, pointed stick,
machete and axe are the common tools. When a plough is
used it is generally of wood, rarely rimmed with iron.
There is a widespread belief that iron ploughs hurt the
land, offend the maize god. A recent survey shows, per
hundred villagers:

    66.3 chickens
    30.1 goats
    14.6 hogs
    10.5 oxen
     8.3 cows
     7.8 horses
     6.9 asses
     6.9 calves
     1.8 mules

and

     1.8 carts
      .9 cultivators
      .3 sowing machines

We have spoken of Mexico as a country set on edge,
with the resulting difficulties in transportation. Here are
the figures for free villages, sampled over ten states:

Sixty-four per cent can be reached by burro trail only
Twenty-seven per cent by horse and cart
Five per cent by railroad
Two per cent by motor car
One per cent by water

Beyond the economic pattern, yet linked closely to it
through the market, is the fiesta with its attendant religious ceremonies. About one day in three, the year
around, is devoted to play or worship—the latter very
tolerantly defined. The normal locus of the fiesta is the
courtyard of the church, with the market immediately
adjoining if not in the yard itself. A fiesta is a mosaic of
pilgrim shrine, regional exchange of goods and news,
pagan dance, Coney Island, gambling joint, sidewalk
café, camp ground, rodeo, subway jam and Fourth of
July.

Scientific medical care is non-existent in the pattern,
the health of the community being taken in charge by
the time-honoured law of the survival of the fittest, and
by herb women, far less clever than their Aztec and
Maya progenitors. Education is a feeble but growing
spark, in respect to formal schools. Probably two thirds
of the population over ten can neither read nor write.
But great numbers speak two languages—their Indian
dialect and Spanish; while education in the sense of preparation for life is compulsory for every village boy and
girl. By the time they are fifteen they have mastered the
arts of house building, cookery, agricultural work, and
may have mastered a genuine handicraft such as pottery
making or sarape weaving.

By way of illustrating the self-supporting village not
dependent on a region, come with me on horseback up a
trail so steep that we must dismount and walk from time

to time. Up a roaring river we go, and into deep pine woods. At 9,000 feet we come out upon cleared cornfields at frightful angles, and the little town of San Pablo Cuatro Venados in the State of Oaxaca. There are a fine old church, a school, a rickety town hall, a little plaza, and 850 people according to the 1930 census. It has gained just 200 inhabitants since 1910. A priest makes the rounds twice a year, and a government teacher somewhat oftener. Three per cent of the couples living together are officially married. Two herb women care for the town's health. There are about ten fiestas a year, and the Day of the Dead is observed with much ceremony. The old cacique system of local government is in effect, and the ancient communal land system. Villagers hold their lands only so long as they cultivate them. When crops cease, the fields go back to the community for redistribution. Corn is the main food, supplemented with peaches, apples, honey and beans. Timber is exchanged for a certain amount of strong drink. Fuel is plentiful; charcoal is burned. Beautiful hand-woven sarapes are made on local looms. A little cotton cloth is toted up the dizzy trail. This, with the brandy, is about all the outside world provides. There is an old Zapotec idol not far from the town, and from time to time one may find fresh turkey blood in front of it. By and large the village is sufficient unto itself. It will of course send its delegation to the great fiestas in the city of Oaxaca. Its own fiestas are not visited by people of other villages. It is perched, flanked with pine, on one of the most commanding sites in the world—a site chosen hundreds of years ago as a watch-tower for the Zapotec army.

Tepoztlan is lower, larger, less backward, and 500 miles to the north. It is part of an economic region which comprehends a good fraction of the state of Morelos—

[213]

say an area half as big as Connecticut. It has seven encircling hamlets locked in its immediate economic orbit. The great bulk of its food is home grown, and nearly all the rest obtained in regional exchange. Practically all its shelter is home manufactured. Not much of its clothing originates at home but most of it is cut and sewed there. Of other things, the home area provides the bulk—pack animals, wooden saddles, drums, fireworks, rope, candles, coffins, ploughs, hoes. From regional exchange come tobacco and gunpowder.

The above accounts form perhaps ninety-five per cent (this is my own estimate) of the economic budget of Tepoztlan. This is the tonnage provided by the region *from its own soil*. The other five per cent comes from the outside world.

The inroads of the machine into Tepoztlan may be simply told. As everywhere the phenomenon advances in two divisions, material and spiritual: the iron horse and his products, and the behaviour patterns he engenders. Of the former we find:

Specific machines	*Factory and refinery products*
Sewing-machines	Cotton cloth
A small flour mill	Store clothes
One or two phonographs	Steel tools and implements
Probably a radio	Printed matter and paper
A typewriter in the church	Kerosene
Firearms	Alcohol tins
Clocks and watches	Furnishings for the houses of los correctos
	Rebosos and coloured handkerchiefs
	Cheap jewellery
	Canned goods
	Bottled goods
	Matches
	Musical instruments

[214]

These things make life in Tepoztlan a little easier, but the interpenetration is so light that, with the exception of cotton cloth, all could be given up without disrupting the economic structure. The town would slide back to say the time of Maximilian, with no serious dislocations.

In respect to behaviour, the impact of the machine age is even more nebulous. Failing that great modifier of habits, the automobile, it consists of a growing stock of new ideas rather than of specific acts. A few Tepoztecans have been to Mexico City, ridden in motor cars, read the newspapers, seen the movies at Cuernavaca. Some have learned not to feel too uncomfortable in the hideous clothes affected by western civilization. Some doubtless look forward to the day when Fords will come chugging for the first time in history upon the cobbled streets of the town. One might conclude that the machine age has affected local behaviour hardly at all, but does affect the behaviour of Tepoztecans when they are, for example, in Mexico City. A slight mental shift has taken place, but it finds expression only in foreign parts.

In Middletown, for all its location in the western cornbelt rather than the urbanized east, both machines and behaviour flowing therefrom are transcendent. There is one motor car to every five people, a radio in every other house, a wholesale retreat from the kitchen to the delicatessen store, an enormous subdivision of labour to the practical extinction of the jack-of-all-trades, a growing emphasis on money as the measure of all things, a growing uneasiness as to one's economic security, chronic unemployment, declining illiteracy in letters and mounting illiteracy in the knowledge of the worth of the goods one buys, a sharp increase in longevity, a growth in clubs and organizations at about the same dizzy rate which marks the decline in church activity, while "most people over thirty get their recreation sitting down."

A hundred years ago, Middletown, as a frontier community, would have possessed many of the behaviour patterns and something of the philosophy of Tepoztlan. Today the whole pattern has been uprooted and flung aside. There is no trace of local or regional economic self-sufficiency; the community is locked beyond recall into the highly delicate and interdependent economy of two hemispheres. If rubber from islands in the Indian Ocean should fail, the life of Middletown would go to pieces. Without tires for its cars it would be a child lost in the wilderness. Ninety-nine per cent of the products its own people make are shipped to the four quarters of the globe. Only one per cent is locally consumed. If these far markets fail—as they do today—repercussion is quick and deadly. The men of Middletown are on the streets. Cash they must have or starve. As wages and cash decline, purchasing power sinks with them, local merchants cease to make their usual attenuated margins, "for rent" signs appear on Main Street, a bank gurgles and expires, carrying the savings of a thousand households.

Middletown in the upswing of the business cycle is a gaudy and in some respects an exciting spectacle. But when the spiral starts downward it is one of the saddest spots on earth.

As new forms of life emerge, new parasites appear for their bedevilment. The business cycle is the microbe especially created to plague, if not ultimately to kill, the vast, sprawling body of mechanical civilization. In this body, Middletown is but a single cell, while Tepoztlan is aloof and unincorporated, an organic, breathing entity.

The questions before us are two: Should Tepoztlan be incorporated? Will it be incorporated?

Diego Rivera. 1931

BOSTON PUBLIC LIBRARY

To the first we can answer an unhesitating no. In the spring of 1929, two years ago, when Middletonians were watching their stocks, retained on margin, advance ten points a day; when factory furnaces were roaring—we might have had a shade of hesitation. No judgment was quite sane as the fifth great period of American prosperity drew to its dramatic close. Today it is only too evident that Tepoztlan had better remain aloof until a serum has been developed for the parasites of overproduction and unemployment.

The question as to whether Tepoztlan will be thrust into the system, willy-nilly, is at once more complicated and more to the point. Mexico City has been all but pushed in; even little Merida in Yucatan is suffering from the depression today—though far less poignantly than Middletown. Mexicali in Lower California reports, in the spring of 1931, food riots with soldiers guarding grocery stores. Here Indians have lost self-sufficiency and become dependent on wages. Mexico as a whole is not a completely self-sustaining area, but with flattened curve, goes up and down in the business cycle. I do not clearly see the handwriting on the wall which commits Tepoztlan to western civilization. I realize that many thoughtful observers do see it. My reasons I shall reserve for a later chapter, where the attempted answer to this basic question more properly belongs.

We have tried to sketch the economic pattern of the Mexican village. From its regional independence flow certain material values, particularly noticeable at this time of world-wide depression. In addition there are psychological values permanently operating; values which always belong to a stable handicraft culture.

Money as a force in itself is not important in Tepoztlan; it is not important in most of Mexico. Some years ago an agricultural concession was granted to a friend of mine, who was also a friend of labour. He found that the going rate of wages in this particular area for hacienda work was twenty-five centavos a day. He examined his estimated cost sheets and concluded that he could afford to double the prevailing rate. Fifty centavos seemed little enough. The peons were duly hired and work begun. At the end of the first week the men were paid at the advanced figure. Everybody seemed pleased. Monday morning when the gates were thrown open not a soul appeared; operations came to a standstill. A few interviews shortly established the reason. The peons could make ends meet on twenty-five centavos a day; they had earned in a week enough for two weeks, so why should they work any more? Why indeed? Utterly devoid of pecuniary behaviour, their logic was unassailable. The only way my friend could secure a steady labour supply was to swallow his principles and reduce wages to twenty-five centavos.

Another authenticated case is less amusing. Some years ago a sugar plantation was organized in Tehuantepec. Labour was hard to get. The neighbouring Zapotec Indians were not interested. The company bribed a *jefe politico* (local political boss) to arrest the Indians on a trumped-up charge—alleged drunkenness is usual in such cases—and deliver them at so much a head to the hacienda. The victims made a few polite motions of an agricultural nature and presently escaped to their village. Here were fine mango trees, manna coming down from heaven. Why work for aliens in the hot fields? In desperation, the company finally sent its own men in the night and *cut down the mango trees,* starving the village into serfdom.

An Indian carpenter did some cabinet work for a woman I know in Mexico City. After he had left she discovered another piece of work for him to do. For three weeks my friend tried to locate the man, with increasing impatience. Finally she found him.

"Why haven't you come before?"

"Señorita!"

"I owed you five pesos for the other work, and you did not come."

"Ah, that was the reason. If I had come, you would have thought it was to get the money."

Not cash but goods, indeed frequently not goods but happiness and peace of mind, is the prevailing Mexican desire. This centres values in innately valuable things, rather than in the artificial, unreal things—rows of figures, ink marks on ledgers, pieces of engraved paper—which govern us in the north. We have first to grope our way through this heavy litter of symbols to find life itself—and increasingly we never find it. To the village Mexican, life lies clear and sharp beneath his eyes, its values uncoated with cash considerations. Yet American business men and bankers go to Mexico to return puzzled if not infuriated. These people, they say, are lazy, shiftless, improvident. They must be taught to save, they must be taught to want more things, they must be taught the value of money. This is all very well from the point of view of bankers who want interest, and business men who want installment contracts. But it is exceedingly ill from the point of view of Mexicans. Why should they be made money-conscious to their everlasting torture?

Another psychological asset is the sense of economic security. Many students believe that the greatest single liability of American life is the lack of this sense. Following, like the docile folk we are, the advice of our advertisers and our captains of industry, we buy and buy, we spend and spend, ignoring the still small voice of sales resistance. The wheels of industry must be kept turning, even if the installment payments do come round like a wheel of fire. We keep right up to the margin; and many of us, attending to that newest school which proclaims that the successful man is one who is not afraid to bond himself, go valiantly over it. But the uneasy thought of where we are finally coming out will not down. What is going to happen to us in our declining years, aye when middle age arrives—with industry refusing to hire men over forty? What is going to happen to us in a business slump, if we cannot go a month on our cash reserves? What is going to happen when the boss installs the new machine he is talking about, or when the time-study men come into the shop, or when the next merger fastens upon our particular line, and begins to prune its over-head costs? What is the use of sending Jim through college when there is a plague of college men in business, and Helen to the School of Journalism when there are twice as many students as actual reporters? The house and the car, the overstuffed davenport and the new refrigerator are all very nice, but they are not paid for yet, and how long are they going to last? . . . This editorial says we ought to spend more. Is our duty never to end?

The future hangs like a great black raven over Middletown. In Tepoztlan the sky is clear. The corncrib takes the place of mortgage and installment contract. There is no car, no electric refrigerator, but there is economic security.

Finally we have to note an acute difference between the two cultures which revolves around the word *function*. Handicraft peoples produce only for a specific need; all their output is essentially custom made. They fabricate

the articles which enable them to cope with their environment, and little more. Their houses, clothing, utensils
are adapted to maximum economy, with no more motions
than are absolutely necessary (except when housewives
grind corn). On top of prime essentials they demand the
ageless human overlay of non-material goods—light,
colour, dances, music, festival, worship—again with
maximum economy.

With us, on the other hand, there is no clean-lined
functional pattern. With our billion horsepower we can
defy our environment, and do. We can even defy our
human nature, and do—as when we keep young people
from marrying until an average age of twenty-eight. We
have a wide margin for experimentation, in the process
of which we tend to forget function altogether. Necessities for us are a blurred mass of both the functional and
non-functional; we have lost all idea of where one leaves
off and the other begins; we have no conception of what
our basic biological and psychological needs are. As a
result a vast tonnage of our production serves no need
save emulation, keeping up with the Joneses and con-
spicuous consumption. Our clothes make us abnormally
uncomfortable; our food abnormally constipated; our
apartments and our cities abnormally compressed and
deafened; our recreations abnormally weary. We are
surfeited with an undigested mass of functionless material, fabricated by the mile in mass-production units,
sold to us by appealing to our baser appetites. We are
cluttered up with things essentially meaningless, and, being human, we flounder, puzzled and perplexed, trying to
find the values which will give meaning back to life.

Tepoztlan has never lost these values. It works, plays,
worships, attires itself, composes its dwellings in the
normal rhythm of *homo sapiens* upon this planet, without

[223]

abnormal effort, without waste. It knows what life is for because every move it makes contributes to a legitimate function of living. Or better, it never bothers its head about the meaning of life. It lives.

But with all these assets of the spirit Tepoztlan is no rustic Utopia. Certain attributes of western culture could not fail to improve and enrich the processes of living. Properly controlled, only the gloomiest of backward-gazing philosophers would paste a sign "no trespassing" across its gates.

Indeed there is little question even of proper control involved in applying modern hygiene and sanitation. I should not hesitate to lift this department out of Middletown, and transpose it *in toto*. This does not cover of course the patent medicine shelves of Middletown's glittering drug stores, or the educational brochures released therewith. But I would take the doctors—split fees and all—the nurses, the clinics, the hospitals, the city health department, the sewers, the water supply, the dentists (who would not have much to do), an osteopath or two—the whole kit and kaboodle of them, and dump them down without a tremor. The herb doctors may not be so dangerous as their cousins, the patent-medicine men, but they have served their time.

Again, every Mexican village without exception could stand a reasonably stiff injection of scientific agriculture. Control would need to be exercised here to guard against overproduction and overspecialization. An immense amount of dreary work could be avoided by a better knowledge of crops, seeds, fertilizers, irrigation, stock-raising, and a larger cash crop grown for ready absorption in Mexican cities—which are now buying corn from Africa, eggs and butter from Texas, vegetables and fruits from California. Mexico could readily be fed entirely from her own soil, but it will need modern science, better tools, steel ploughs, and a few brigades of tractors to bring about this common-sense result. In the five months I zigzagged through the hinterland, I noted precisely two tractors.

Thirdly, I see no ominous concomitants in a wide extension of electric power, *properly controlled*. The Electric Bond and Share Company is busy in Mexico, and, judging by its activities in the north, control vesting exclusively in this single-minded organization might leave something to be desired. There is 6,000,000 horsepower to be derived from water falling down Mexico's mountains, and if a sizable fraction of this were linked to long-distance transmission lines and deployed into the larger villages, we can readily see some excellent uses to which it might be put, including:

Lighting.

Milling of corn to save housewives interminable grinding.

Refrigeration, thus stimulating the milk supply, now abnormally low. To say nothing of the unsavoury condition of the present meat supply.

To operate cottage industries through the use of small motors—sewing, pottery, looms, metal work, wood turning.

To operate cement and mortar mixers. Mexico, a country of stone, uses huge amounts of these materials.

To operate pumps for good drinking water and for irrigation. Both are sadly lacking at the present time. Some villages, indeed, like the hamlet of Santa Catarina near Tepoztlan, go completely dry for several months a year, suffering a grave deficiency of water both internally and externally. Irrigation is desperately needed in many areas. Electric power would help provide it. Cornfields at sixty degree angles on 10,000-foot mountains would be less mandatory. Forests could come back where they belong.

A telegraph line and one long-distance telephone could hardly do a village any harm. In emergency they might do it a large amount of good. They would serve, furthermore, to unify the country, give it more of a common purpose than it now possesses. There is such a thing as being too independent.

At mention of a motor road my eyes drift to the ceiling. It would be both a blessing and a curse. Trucks would save an unconscionable amount of slogging over mountain trails with a hundred pounds on one's back, or steering a plodding burro thereover. Supplies, newspapers, the world outside, could come flooding in. But in that flood, alas, might come car ownership, snobbery, motor accidents—Mexicans are even worse drivers than we—high-powered salesmen, the annual model racket, cheap factory goods, and cheap urban ideas. I am not so sure about the motor road unless it were most carefully and specifically controlled.

Movies, talkies, radios are in the same general category. Sensibly used, as they are in Russia, they could be made instruments of unparalleled educational and social value; the more so as most Mexican villagers cannot read. Used on the Hollywood, sponsored-broadcasting formula they would be a useless, if not vicious, expense. Hygiene, sanitation, improved agricultural and handicraft methods, dietetics, could all be enormously stimulated by movies and radio, intelligently directed. News of the world could be communicated, the vast cultural inheritance of Mexico could be graphically shown, the unification of the nation actively promoted.

Dreams only. But enough to make it evident that we are not quarrelling with the machine as such, nor are sentimentally satisfied with machineless men. Between, however, cleaving to what they have with its manifest shortcomings, and bolting industrialism raw as Middletown has bolted it, they had best hold hard to their basic pattern.

CHAPTER XII

CORNUCOPIA

WE shall leave the cobbled streets of Tepoztlan, and, boarding if you like one of the sturdy tri-motored planes of the Pan-American line, take a bird's-eye view of the whole nation. To fly from Mexico City to Brownsville, Texas—plateau, mountain ridge at 14,000 feet, the long glissade to the Gulf—is one of the most glorious experiences any human bird can have. In six hours' time, all three empires of the republic pass in review: temperate lands, cold lands, hot lands. We can see cities, unvisited villages, tilled fields, mines, a few factories.

How far is Mexico urbanized; how far industrialized; what is the composition of the population? Mexico has been called by no less an authority than Cecil Rhodes the treasure house of the world; others have likened it to a horn of plenty; how true are these glittering observations?

POPULATION

In 1790, the year in which the United States Census Bureau first opened its doors, the population of the young republic and that of Mexico were approximately equal. Each had something less than 5,000,000 souls. By 1840, the United States had grown to twice the size of Mexico. Today she is almost eight times as large, 123,000,000 against 16,000,000. Tannenbaum gives us five sound reasons for Mexico's slower growth:

Restriction of immigration
Feudalism and serfdom
Continuous revolutions
A large proportion of barren soil, partly due to lack of irrigation
A high death-rate

America welcomed the whole world to Ellis Island, confined feudalism to the South, had only one serious revolution—in 1861—possessed almost unlimited areas of flat rich soil, and turned science loose on the problem of public health. While its hundred and sixty-acre homesteads and sprawling cities rolled westward, Mexico stood pat on her haciendas. The clustered huts remained isolated and scattered in gulleys and on mountain sides, the only line of communication a burro path impassable in the rains. The covered wagon and the iron horse creaked and snorted to the north. "The Mexican rural community remained almost completely indifferent to changes in other parts of the world." The basic pattern held.

By 1900, population had crept up to 13,600,000; adding another million and a half by 1910. (No Mexican census of course can be better than a rough approximation. How would a census enumerator (a) ever get to hundreds of remote villages, and (b) escape if he got there?) During the first decade of the revolution, to 1920, population shrank a million persons, to 14,300,000 —due, however, more to Spanish influenza in 1918 than to war and famine. Now, in 1930, it is at the highest point ever recorded, 16,400,000. Applying Tannenbaum's ratios to this total:

	Per cent	Persons
Free villages (and tribal villages)	60	9,900,000
Hacienda villages	25	4,000,000
Mining villages	2	300,000
Urban and industrial...........	13	2,200,000
Total.....................	100	16,400,000

Thus eighty-seven per cent of Mexicans live in the country, as contrasted with forty-four per cent of Americans. To state it in another way:

Living in places of	Per cent	Persons
Less than 100 population........	12	2,000,000
100 to 1,000 population.........	57	9,300,000
Over 1,000 population..........	31	5,100,000
Total.....................	100	16,400,000

Tepoztlan belongs in the last, and is hence less typical than the middle group, which averages about 300 persons per village. Free villages meanwhile are typically larger than hacienda villages.

Not more than 300,000 Spaniards, according to Paul S. Taylor, ever settled in Mexico, and they were mostly men. History records 15,000 Chinese and 6,000 Negroes —both races being now excluded. This is literally all the immigration Mexico ever had—save for the shifting foreign residents and colonists. There were 1,000,000 "whites" in the census of 1790, but the figure refuses to make sense. If only 300,000 whites came in, the bulk of the group must have had Indian blood. The census of 1921 exhibits 1,405,000 "whites," again a ridiculous statement. Few Spaniards have colonized in the last century, with the inevitable genetic result that *Indianization is steadily increasing*. There must be far less white blood today, both relatively and absolutely, than in 1790. Gruening doubts if there are now as many as 500,000 Mexicans who can properly be called white, say one person out of thirty. The observer travelling about Mexico would agree that this is an outside figure. Ladies, particularly maiden ladies, wreck the purity of American census figures, by reporting their ages at the nearest round number below their actual age. A forty-two will put herself down at forty. Similarly, "white" being the hall-mark of the ruling class, Mexicans are prone to claim that colour, though it flows in halves or quarters or even eighths. And the census man is a tolerant fellow.

Following Gruening and Taylor, I estimate that the present population looks something like this:

	Per cent	Persons
Indian and mestizo.............	96	15,700,000
White, not more than	3	500,000
Foreign, not more than	1	200,000
Total....................	100	16,400,000

To calculate the number of pure Indians in the first group would land a statistician in a hospital for the incurably insane. My guess—a reasonably wild one—would be at least half the total, or something under 8,000,000. Millions with dashes of white blood live and behave like pure Indians, leaving the distinction primarily an academic one. (Biologically Indianization, we must remember, is increasing.) Far more relevant would be an enumeration of those who eat wheat bread against those who eat maize tortillas. This is the real cleavage between the Indian and the white Mexican way of life. The count has never been made, but I should estimate it at one to ten. In the recent cabinet of General Calles, there were eight whites, three mestizos, and one pure Indian.

Two million Indians speak no Spanish, another 2,000,-000 speak their own dialect by preference. This gives us some 12,000,000 persons, or seventy-five per cent of all, normally using the official language of the country. At the time of the conquest, 150 dialects were identified in Mexico. Fifty-two are still spoken; fifteen in the state of Oaxaca alone. It is estimated that ninety per cent of the population of Oaxaca is pure Indian. In central and southern Mexico, Indian blood and the Indian languages survive most sturdily. The northern and border states run to mestizo stock. A decade ago, sixty-five per cent of all Mexicans over ten years of age could neither read nor write. This figure will be less today as the little white schoolhouse advances.

NATURAL RESOURCES

If population classifications are dubious, the count of natural resources is even more so. Mexican antipathy for statistics is profound. We do not know how rich the country is, for its assets have never been tabulated properly—or even explored. We do know that these assets are extraordinarily varied, comprising probably a longer list of items than in any equal territory in the world, and we know that some of them have yielded great fortunes in the past. But whatever the final balance sheet, nature has provided two major handicaps to exploitation—jagged mountains and steamy jungles. The former present terrific and often insuperable problems of transportation, the latter a nice problem in keeping alive.

Suppose we select at random two of the thirty-one states for specific examination. Here is Chiapas in the

VIVA MEXICO

Diego Rivera. 31

BOSTON
PUBLIC
LIBRARY

south, and Durango in the north. Chiapas comprises
71,000 square kilometers, bigger than Belgium plus Holland. It is compounded of heaving mountains and fertile
valleys in the tierra caliente. Its resources have been little
explored. The population is 521,000, nearly all Indian,
speaking fourteen languages. Travellers even report that
peculiar telepathy, or long-distance language, common
among African tribes. The capital is three days on horseback from the nearest railroad. The flora and fauna are
innumerable. The economic output includes orchids, in-
digo, lumber and cabinet woods, copal, fruits, quinine,
coffee, sugar, cacao, rice, vanilla, henequen, rubber, cattle,
and alligator skins. Craftsmen produce lacquered gourds,
and the *marimba,* an enormous xylophone, requiring
sometimes four operators, which is used throughout
Mexico. The ruins of Palenque, perhaps the most impressive of all the Maya cities, are within the state's
borders, while learned scientists have debated whether
Chiapas, rather than the Caucasus, was not the real
cradle of the human race. Much of the pre-conquest
population committed suicide in preference to being captured by the Spaniards. Once for a time the state abandoned Mexico altogether and combined its government
with that of Guatemala.

Durango is in the tier next below the northern border
states. Its area is 100,000 square kilometers, more than
Portugal's, and its population is 395,000, with a large
infiltration of mestizo. The savage tribe which occupied
the region at the conquest was driven out in 1554. The
country is very mountainous and abounds in game, from
grizzly bears down. It grows some cotton and supports
a few cotton mills. There are one hundred and twenty
mines in the state, producing iron, sulphur, rubies, gold
and silver. In a certain district is a mountain, seven hun-

dred feet above the plain, of almost solid iron—six hundred million tons of it.

So, if space allowed, we might go from state to state, finding drama, history and nuggets of fabulous wealth. But nuggets do not necessarily make an entire nation rich. Of more importance is the matter of plain dirt. The soil of Mexico leaves much to be desired, as the following figures show:

	Millions of acres
Land actually cultivated................	30
Pasture land	120
Timber land	44
Desert, waste and unutilized..............	296
Total area of Mexico.................	490

Thus only about six per cent of the soil of Mexico is under actual cultivation. How much could be brought under? Dr. Eyler Simpson estimates that ten per cent is possible without irrigation, and another twenty per cent if huge outlays were made for impounding waters. The outside theoretical limit is thus 150,000,000 acres, with perhaps 60,000,000, twice the present area, as the practical limit of cultivation. Mexico can just about feed herself, at the present time. (She is now importing corn from Africa, but this is probably due to abnormal conditions following the Revolution.) By improving her technical methods she could more than feed herself, especially if she also improved her diet, substituting more milk and eggs for the present excessive bulk of cornmeal. If she cultivated every foot of ground that would raise a crop, including a considerable outlay for new irrigation works, she might conceivably support twice the present population, say 32,000,000 people. This is about the limit unless, like England, she turned industrial and traded her manufactured goods for corn and wheat, a most unlikely programme.

There is no great potential wealth in Mexico's soil, save perhaps for a plantation owner here and there. There is still wealth in her forests, but a constructive policy would demand more woods rather than less. The Spaniards denuded the country to make it look like the barren hills of Spain, and brought down the blight of drought. For both soil preservation and moisture, more forests are badly needed. Happily the government is encouraging them. Grazing land is—well, grazing land. Ask your banker about fortunes to be made from that. Deserts are emphatically deserts.

At sundry points under the soil lie pools of petroleum, a black, viscous and disagreeable fluid which causes prospectors to unlimber their Winchesters and bankers to leap from their armchairs. Here lay wealth for Mexico—or at least for somebody—beyond the dreams of avarice. And so, for one dizzy decade, it proved. Then salt water came meandering into the viscous pools, and government restrictions into the financial structure. From a peak of 193,000,000 barrels in 1921, oil production has fallen steadily to 45,000,000 barrels in 1929. Tampico is a city of ghosts. Certainly for the moment this asset moves into the portfolio marked "frozen."

This brings us down—or up—to mountain rocks, and, whimsically enough, more cheerful matters. The mines of Mexico constitute an indubitable asset to any nation; an asset proved, furthermore, by four hundred years of activity. If the hacienda did more than any other institution to modify Indian civilization, the high drama of the colonial epoch was furnished by the hewers of mountain rocks. The Aztecs were competent tunnellers and miners, but the matter never greatly excited their interest. Their attitude towards rare metals was normal rather than pathological. When the use of iron became known to the natives of Central America, "they valued that metal above anything," says Bancroft, "and considered it an excellent bargain when they could obtain a hatchet or a knife for an equal weight of gold." As indeed it was.

Not so the Spaniards. "I came to get gold" was the formula of Cortez. Alas, there was not much gold to get. After the current supply had been lost or stolen or shipped to Spain, it was found that the output obtainable from the known mines was meagre. In some cases the Indians abandoned their workings and out of hostility concealed the location. (I visited an old gold mine in Oaxaca surreptitiously worked by the Zapotecs for two hundred years after the conquest.) Gold is widely distributed in Mexico but infrequently in bonanza quantities.

So the Spaniards turned their attention to silver, ultimately with phenomenal success. Veins of altogether fantastic dimensions were discovered, and, despite the crude technology of the time, yielded their owners incredible riches. The Conde de Regla made a net of 5,000,000 pesos in a short period from his mines at Pachuca. He presented Carlos III with two warships, one carrying 112 guns, and loaned him 1,000,000 pesos (never repaid) besides. A mining grandee in Zacatecas had the street between his house and the church—the chroniclers neglect to state the distance—surfaced with silver bars for the wedding of his daughter. Regla, not to be outdone, repeated the performance for his son's christening, and invited the king of Spain to visit Mexico City, promising to pave the road from Vera Cruz to the capital with bullion for the royal coach. We know how far that is— some two hundred and fifty miles! Jose de la Borda left two outstanding landmarks for the modern tourist. From the proceeds of his silver mines in Taxco, he built a great rose-brown cathedral, one of the loveliest in Mexico. When he had lost that fortune and made another, he constructed the famous Borda Gardens in Cuernavaca, at an outlay of 1,000,000 pesos. The curious traveller may still wander about the walls and pools and from their luxuriant disorder reconstruct the grandeur of two hundred years ago. Altogether Borda took nearly 40,-000,000 pesos out of the mountains of Mexico.

From 1537 to 1914, the nation dumped 90,000 tons of pure silver, to a value of more than $5,000,000,000, upon the markets of the world. In the first hundred and fifty years of that period, she doubled the world supply. A single nugget weighing 2,750 pounds is said to have been found in Sonora. Mexico's oil declines, but not her silver. The Purisima vein, probably the richest single deposit ever mined anywhere, was discovered as late as 1910. Up in the mountains the wayfarer can hardly remain a day before somebody is showing him ore samples of a new silver strike. Today in China, the going currency is still "a dollar Mex." Indeed the chief difficulty at present is not exhausted mines but too many mines. Silver is falling headlong in world markets, taking Mexico's chief industry down with it. Thus even her most promising asset is today a little tarnished.

There remain iron, copper, lead, antimony, graphite, mercury, zinc, precious stones and the pearl fisheries of Lower California. Some of these workings are very prosperous; some of them will undoubtedly prove bonanzas in years to come. But I heard nothing which tempted me to pawn my personal property and invest.

Of available water power Mexico is said to possess 6,000,000 horsepower. In comparison with the 35,000,-000 of the United States this is not a startling exhibit.

[239]

Water runs in Mexico perhaps faster than anywhere else on earth, but it confines its galloping to the wet season in the summer months. To make power available the year around, huge and very costly storage reservoirs must be constructed. There is utility and some wealth to be gained from the present resource without storage projects, but the margin is hardly one to excite Mr. Samuel Insull.

The inventory is indicated if not complete. Mexico is not a poor country in natural resources like Italy or Norway, but the tale of her riches has been somewhat overtold. To my mind her greatest wealth lies in her scenery, her sunshine, her architecture, and her brown people—not as lure for tourist dollars, but for her own life and enjoyment.

MARCH OF THE MACHINES

Mexico introduced the machine into North America early and briskly with the falconets of Cortez. She followed by printing the first book on the continent in 1536, and the first newspaper in 1693. Then she rested on her laurels, and has been resting ever since.

The industrial revolution proper entered the country in 1850 when thirteen kilometers of railway track were laid on the line from Vera Cruz to Mexico City. By 1876, when Diaz came into office, there were 691 kilometers of track; in 1910, when he fled to Europe, 24,717. In the latter year 33,000 textile operatives were working in 135 factories, and the mines, hand operated for 400 years, were putting in motors, automatic pumps and mechanical conveyors. In the Diaz generation thousands upon thousands of horsepower came marching into Mexico, and if the same rate had been maintained for the last two decades, we might have seen a pretty little industrial exhibit in the nation today. It was not maintained. Industrialization has moved but slowly since Diaz. Electric power and automotive engines show sharp advances; railway mileage, trolley lines, factories, have hardly more than held their own.

In 1926 there were 2,877 manufacturing establishments in the country, employing 95,775 workers, with a total investment of $1,700,000,000. The state of Texas in 1925 had 3,606 factories employing 106,792 workers, not including light and power plants. (Included in Mexican figures.) Mexico with richer resources, three times the area, and three times the population of Texas, *is the less industrialized of the two*—not relatively but absolutely. Texas is but one state in the union, and with the highest respect, to regard it as an industrialized area is a quaint conceit. Little Rhode Island has more machinery to show. In the United States, one person in fifteen is working in a factory; in Mexico one person in one hundred and sixty.

Let us enumerate all workers conceivably industrial:

Factory workers	96,000
Miners	70,000
Railroad employees	40,000
Oil workers	8,000
Total........................	214,000

If we added chauffeurs, typists, aviators, motor cops, even machine gunners, everybody who has anything directly to do with machines, we could hardly swell the total to 250,000, or one person in sixty-four. A similar computation for the United States would run something in the order of one person in ten. If the comparison is permissible, one might say that America is more than six

times as industrialized, relatively, as Mexico. Out of
every hundred men, women and children, one and one-
half are in Mexican industry; ten in American industry.
In the light of these figures the title "machineless men"
is not quite so apt for the whole country as it is for
Tepoztlan, but it is apt enough.

The principal factory industries and the number of
their workers may be shown as follows—the figures are
for 1929:

Textiles	49,600	Paper	2,300
Boots and shoes	10,500	Flour milling	2,200
Tobacco	5,500	Soap	1,900
Breweries	3,000		
Distilleries	2,900		80,600
Tanneries	2,700	Miscellaneous	15,400
		Total	96,000

Of factory-made articles, Mexico supplies her own re-
quirements of beer, gasoline and twine—a curious cocktail. All else must be imported in whole or in part. She
is far short of cotton cloth, the item so important in the
village market. Her only large steel plant, in Monterrey,
turns out 100,000 tons a year, where the United States
turns out 60,000,000 tons. Monterrey, however, is en-
larging its capacity in the teeth of the current depression.
The production of electricity has reached 500,000 horsepower, about two thirds of it from falling water. We
produce 42,000,000 horsepower, from coal and falling
water. There are 60,000 telephones against our 19,000,-
000; 75,000 motor vehicles against our 30,000,000; 400
miles of stone-surfaced highway against our 625,000
miles. Mexican manufactured goods, like Russian, tend
to be notoriously poor in quality. To the beer, however,
I can give more than a passing grade.

MARCH OF THE TRADE UNIONS

With an industrial population of only 250,000, labour problems in Mexico sink into relative insignificance, compared with agricultural problems. The rise of the labour movement since 1910, however, has been dramatic, and in a political sense, important; it deserves a word. The first modern labour union was organized by the railroad workers in 1887, but not until 1904 did it attain stability. From the turn of the century, the ideas of Bakunin, Henry George, and French socialism began to filter in. The cotton mill workers tried to organize in 1906, to be promptly shot down by Diaz. Copper mine employees shared the same fate in the same year—curiously the one that followed the great abortive Russian revolution of 1905. A railroad strike in 1908 was squelched with the threat of gunpowder. By this time there were some 16,000 unionists in the country, a negligible number.

Organized labour first became a power after the split between Villa and Carranza in 1915. "Red battalions" of workers saved Carranza's tottering standard. Article 123 of the Constitution of 1917 was their reward—a document to which we shall presently return. At the time it was the most progressive labour code ever drafted by any nation. In addition, Carranza turned over to the unions the management of the telephone and telegraph lines. In 1918, the C. R. O. M. was founded, a sort of Mexican A. F. of L., headed by a cabinet officer, Luis N. Morones. Its membership, including agricultural workers, has run as high as 2,000,000. In 1927, it claimed one minister, eleven of the fifty-eight senators, forty of the 272 deputies in the national chamber, two of the twenty-nine state governors. From time to time it has controlled the municipal government of Mexico City.

Today the C. R. O. M. is in eclipse, for a number of reasons. The peons have transferred their support—such as it is—to the Agrarian Party. The Labourites made many enemies by attempting to destroy independent unions, such as the railroad workers. They created great bitterness among employers by pressing them over-hard under the new labour code. More flexibility would have saved both employers' balance sheets and workers' jobs. Finally, and most disastrously, the organization has been run by a small inside group, some of whose members were exceedingly corrupt. The gun-toting politician has wrecked the labour movement as he has done his best to wreck everything else in Mexico. "Today," says Dr. Simpson, "Mexico is without an effective labour organization."

Wages have been rising steadily since 1910, but the cost of living has been rising even faster. Real wages show no appreciable advance and thus run contrary to the curve of real wages in the United States. A study made in the Federal District in 1928 set a necessary minimum wage for a labourer's family of five at 3.36 pesos per day. Actual wages averaged about 1.50 pesos—less than half the required minimum. Undernourishment, on a calory basis, is all too common among industrial and urban workers. In short, labour in Mexico is less important than in the United States; it has, on the whole, a more dignified standing and, until recently, far more political power, but its standard of living is distinctly lower. The movement has won revolutionary status but not much in the way of bread.

On October 1, 1930, in the very trough of the world-wide business depression, the Mexican government reported 87,000 unemployed the country over. This is just a little more than one half of one per cent of the population. On the same day in the United States there were at least 6,000,000 unemployed, or five per cent of the population. These figures measure to a nicety the difference between a handicraft and a mechanized system. Man for man we suffer just ten times as badly from unemployment as does Mexico. We gain when the business curve is up, perhaps; certainly she gains when the curve cascades. A representative of one of the great American mining companies in Mexico told me of discharging 3,000 men from a silver district. The company was worried. Would they have to be fed? Was rioting imminent? The fears were groundless; the next day the 3,000 had disappeared. Investigation showed that they had gone back to the corncribs of their villages.

MARCH OF THE DOLLARS, FRANCS AND POUNDS

Finally let us examine the investments of foreign capital in Mexico, and the gross movement of foreign trade as indices of industrialization. Between 1886 and 1910, Diaz persuaded almost 3,000,000,000 pesos of foreign investment into the country. The bulk of it went into mines and plantations, but a substantial amount was devoted to factories, railroads, light and power companies. In 1912 a rough estimate shows:

American capital	$1,058,000,000
British capital	320,000,000
French capital	143,000,000
Other foreign capital...........	118,000,000
Total.......................	$1,639,000,000

Today, after two decades of revolution, the figure has shrunk.

When one enters a hardware store it is highly probable that it is owned by a German; a grocery store by a Spaniard. The overwhelming bulk of the output of the mines, the oil wells, the factories, the power companies, is controlled by foreign capital. Railroads are heavily mortgaged to American and English bondholders. The plain conclusion is that industrialization in Mexico—such as it is—has been taken over by aliens, and is not an affair of native Mexicans. Since the Revolution, however, these alien hands have not had matters altogether their own way; their sometime carefree methods of exploitation have been seriously hindered by new property conceptions, by labour codes, agrarian laws.

In 1873, Mexico was so emphatically an independent economic area that its total foreign trade reached the ridiculous figure of only $25,000,000. Diaz attempted to clamp the nation into the world economic system by raising the total to $250,000,000 in 1910. Today it has advanced further, to $487,000,000 in 1929—$192,000,-000 of imports, $295,000,000 of exports. Some fifty-one per cent of the total is with the United States. Imports run heavily to manufactured goods—machines, automobiles, iron and steel, cotton cloth, chemicals; exports run heavily to raw products—silver, lead, zinc, petroleum, coffee, raw cotton, henequen. Only a tiny fraction of goods manufactured in Mexico finds an export market, mostly with other Latin American countries.

We must indeed modify the conception of Mexico as a horn of plenty, brimming with material wealth. As far as evidence is available, it is a country relatively poor in soil; inadequately irrigated; declining in oil production; rich in minerals—for the moment the least profitable variety of minerals; with but the merest beginnings of the paraphernalia of industrialism—an equipment if you please inferior to that of the state of Texas. That there is room for expansion in the latter item goes without saying, but it will have to progress in the face of bitter transportation difficulties, a lethal climate in certain areas, a government policy which has executed a right about face from the come-hither attitude of Porfirio Diaz. Personally I am enchanted with the prospect. It is obvious that the rhythm of Tepoztlan is in no immediate danger, and that the basic pattern may be modified only slowly if at all. The enforced delay, furthermore, should give Mexicans opportunity to contemplate the cavortings of the machine in the nations of the West— particularly during periods of business depression—and should steel them to admit it only on compulsion of more civilized behaviour.

Meanwhile handicraft economics supplies virtually all fundamental needs of the population, as we have seen in detail. Mass production obviously cannot compete in charm, and probably not in quality, with most Mexican handicrafts. I am convinced, in the teeth of all the doctors of economics, *that it cannot always compete in price*. Here is a village potter, making let us say five hundred articles a year. What are his costs? Try and find them. His clay and colours came out of the nearby soil, his wheel is beyond the laws of depreciation. He has no interest or insurance, and normally no taxes. He cultivates a milpa for his living, and makes pots for fun in his spare time, thus dispensing with the charge for direct labour. To make matters worse, his expenses of distribution are so involved with the spirit of the fiesta—he goes to market for the amusement he finds there—that they collapse to a practical zero. In short, the fellow has no costs at all; the cash he receives for his pots is so much velvet. (In regional exchange we should in justice allow a small expense account.) He sells a fine bowl for two cents, a great five-foot jar for a dollar, a lovely yellow water bottle for thirty cents. Try to beat that, Mr. Ford! He has no rent, no bookkeeping, no advertising, no spirited salesmanship. The only cost is his own time, and that he gives willingly, often lovingly. Much the same holds true for basketry, sarapes, woodworking, simple ironwork, leather-working, toys, sandals, sombreros, simple furniture, varying with the price of the raw material. The Indian system, for many products, in respect to both quality *and cost,* has mass production completely whipped.

Mrs. Ralph Borsodi, at Suffern, New York, produces floor wax in her own kitchen, made to Bureau of Standards formula, for $1.50 a gallon. An inferior product, purchased at the store, made with all the alleged economies of quantity production, costs her at least $3.50. She can show you jellies, preserves, canned goods, home produced at a fraction of the going market price, and far superior in quality. Her cost-accounting system, furthermore, would be approved by any certified public accountant who knew his business. Some day the practical men of the machine age will have to face the implications of Mrs. Borsodi's kitchen, and the potteries and looms of Mexico. Mass production has its place, but not necessarily sprawled over the whole bed.

ASSORTED STATISTICS

in round numbers

Year

1930	Total population	16,404,000
1930	Population of Mexico City (Federal District)	1,218,000
1930	Area of Mexico—acres................	490,000,000
	square miles	767,000
1929	Total exports	$296,000,000
1929	Exports to United States	$118,000,000
1929	Total imports	$192,000,000
1929	Imports from United States.............	$134,000,000
1929	Government receipts including	$161,000,000
1929	import duties	$ 42,000,000
1929	public services	$ 30,000,000
1929	tax on industry	$ 23,000,000
1929	Government disbursements including.....	$138,000,000
1929	war	$ 45,000,000
1929	public works	$ 17,000,000
1929	education	$ 14,000,000
1927	Railroad mileage	14,000
1929	Tons of freight carried................	10,000,000
1929	Passengers carried	16,000,000
1930	Federal surfaced highways—miles........	850
1930	Budget for federal highways............	$ 7,000,000
1930	Motor vehicles in Mexico..............	75,000
1929	Gasoline consumption, gallons...........	68,000,000
1926	Telegraph lines, miles.................	84,000
1928	Paid telegrams sent...................	3,700,000
1928	Free telegrams sent (official, etc.)........	1,300,000
1930	Number of telephones	60,000
1929	Post office pieces handled, domestic.......	130,000,000
1929	" " " " foreign	62,000,000
1929	Insurance in force (mostly fire).........	$684,000,000
1928	Corn production, metric tons............	2,079,000
1928	Wheat " " "	324,000

[249]

Year

1928	Bean production, metric tons	195,000
1930	Sugar " " "	198,000
1928	Henequen " " "	133,000
1926	Number of cattle	5,600,000
1929	Silver production, kilograms.............	3,381,000
1929	Gold " "	19,000
1929	Lead " "	248,700,000
1'929	Copper " "	86,500,000
1929	Zinc " "	174,050,000
1929	Mercury " "	82,000
1929	Oil " barrels..............	45,000,000
1926	Electric horsepower capacity............	464,000
1930	Estimated foreign capital...............$1,500,000,000	
1930	" U. S. capital including bonds...$1,000,000,000	
1928	Number of schools....................	17,923

CHAPTER XIII

THE YANKEE INVASION

THE village Indian has resisted the twentieth century as he resisted the Spaniards, the Church, the industrialism of Diaz. He has taken only such aspects of the machine as do no violence to his basic pattern. The same cannot be said for urban areas. Cities are made of softer stuff. Both the physical structure of Mexican cities and the people who live therein have been profoundly influenced, first by Spain, then by France, now by the United States. In such a town as Oaxaca or sleepy little Acapulco on the Pacific, the influence is at a minimum, in Mexico City it attains its maximum.

It was in the capital that Aztec civilization received its most deadly stab; the Indian pattern being all but erased. Its inhabitants were butchered, its leaders hunted down and tortured, its gods obliterated, its temples and public buildings razed. As a result it became a Spanish town, with colonial architecture throughout. The same red lava brick was used, many a new foundation was compounded of carved stone idols, but the whole aspect, physical and spiritual, of the city changed. Here the viceroys and the archbishops took up their headquarters, here the hacendados and the silver-mine grandees built their noble palaces. Here the treasure trains—long files of loaded mules guarded by soldiers—came swinging in from the mines, and from the distant Philippines— via galleon to Acapulco. Here as late as the 1840's

Madame Calderon found a gay creole society, the ladies covered with diamonds, and, like so many Amy Lowells, smoking long, black cigars. And here the little boys of the Military School, some of them not fifteen, died defending the castle of Chapultepec against the invasion of General Scott.

Another invading army from the United States was in Mexico during my last visit. It came on horseback but carried polo sticks in place of sabres. It was sternly repulsed by the Mexican army team in three straight games. When the engagement was over, the defeated American officers made a gracious gesture. They hung a wreath of flowers on the monument where the little cadets lie buried:

As late as 1880 we find the United States minister to Mexico letting the cat out of the bag with these words. "Certain gentlemen interested in the administration of President Hayes have conceived the idea that in view of the disturbances in the southern states, it would divert attention from pending issues and greatly consolidate the new administration if a war could be brought on with Mexico and another slice of territory added to the union." First and last we have collected fabulous slices of territory hitherto Mexican. We took Texas by force of arms in 1847. California and New Mexico we bought —more or less at the point of the gun—for $15,000,000 in 1848. This sum today would not buy one minor movie company in one suburb of one California city. In the Gadsden purchase in 1853, we lifted another 30,000 square miles of border territory, while the vast northern area west of the Mississippi fell to us via international transfer involving France and England.

Mexico City has seen revolution, earthquake, bombardment, resplendent viceroy, emperor, dictator, president, and a deal of history in four hundred years. But the real spirit of Mexico it has seldom seen. It is a hybrid, as shifting as the soft lake bed upon which it stands. It has denied its own inheritance and held out its arms to Madrid, to Paris, to London, and now, as one Mexican critic remarks, to Hollywood. Its architecture reflects all these moods, and its literate citizens, vibrating from east to west, from south to north, suffer from acute inferiority complexes.

I feel perpetually ill at ease in the capital, and spend most of my time mapping out the next trip into the provinces. Yet indubitably it is one of the great cosmopolitan cities of the world, with only New York, Chicago, Philadelphia and Detroit outranking it on the continent. Its site is magnificent, its climate superb for those who like unlimited sunshine at 7,500 feet above the sea. It rests in a great valley rimmed with mountains. To the east Popocatepetl and the White Woman lift their everlasting snow fields; from street, plaza, balcony, their glittering masses can be seen. The old cathedrals and colonial palaces—such as the Viscainas—are lovely; many of the avenues are regal; Chapultepec, where the cadets were slain and Maximilian ruled for a few short years, is one of the most beautiful parks on earth, with its ahuehuete trees six feet through and a hundred feet high. The city has a variety of admirable features, and deserves unlimited pages, richly illustrated, in any guide book. But I am not a guide book, and I do not like it very well. I do not like its architectural jumble; its altitude gives me a dull ache abaft the right ear; above all I do not like the Yankee invasion, painfully reminiscent of Zenith and Middletown.

As one approaches it, sign boards begin to roar familiar soaps, motor cars and drugs. The same ruddy, vacant faces are upon them, but the words have changed to Spanish, and the emotional appeal is stepped up: "Do not let other tooth pastes scratch his tender teeth." Filling stations sprout to right and left—but happily no hot-dog stands. A gas tank looms. Upon a far volcano a tobacco product screams in letters of white cement, fifty feet high and ten feet thick. And here, if you please, is a subdivision, with realtor's office, dreamy title, half completed villas, and nuzzling steam shovel, all complete, labelled "El Hollywood de Mexico." Presently we come to the "High Life" building, in good plain English, but pronounced to rhyme with fig leaf. It indicates the first flutterings of the skyscraper. But between the boggy soil and the constant threat of earthquakes, flutterings mark the limit of the technique to date. Which is just as well in view of a traffic jam that, at certain hours of the day, would bring a blush to Herald Square.

We station ourselves, notebook in hand, at a street corner in the heart of the city, and proceed to analyze the extent of the invasion—interpreting it broadly to mean modern industrial civilization. We shall collect as well patterns of old Mexico, and what for want of a better term we might call the Victorian infiltration. We shall sit on the broad stone rim of a fountain, allowing a crippled mestizo boy to shine our shoes interminably, and try to mark off the old, the intermediate and the new, in everything we see around us.

OLD MEXICO

A beautiful colonial pink church on the opposite corner; carved stone doorway, fine grilled ironwork, leaning gargoyles, grass growing on the roof. An Indian beggar in dirty white pyjamas squats in the shadow of the arch, a ragged sombrero held out for centavos. (We are back in a pecuniary economy.)

In front of us a tiled kiosk with clock and bells surmounted by a metal star and crescent, inscribed "Turkish Colony."

A pink and white three-story colonial building; a virgin in carved stone in a corner niche. Wrought iron balconies.

The little plaza in which we sit, with fountain, benches and fine shade trees, manifestly of the old regime.

Sidewalk vendors—Indian and mestizo—squatting at the plaza's edge precisely as they squat in the market of Tepoztlan. Most of the wares are identical—tortillas cooked on charcoal brazier and smelling divine; sweet bread, beads, embroidery, hand-woven baskets, nuts, carved wood, medicinal roots. The chestnut woman has a baby in her reboso; so has the woman selling red seeds.

One person out of three who comes within our line of vision is dressed in Indian clothes—pyjamas and sombrero, or full skirt and reboso. This, remember, is the centre of the shopping district. Out on the city's periphery the proportion of native costumes will run far higher. A very common type for city worker is an adaptation of the pyjama made of blue overall cloth. On our corner we see many barefoot Indians wrapped in colourful sarapes. Two of them are even now standing enchanted before the last word in nickel-plated, copper-returning weighing machine.

In the distance, the arcade of an old colonial building devoted to little shops. Madame Calderon may have bought French laces and Spanish shawls there in the 'forties.

Plenty of specimens of the Mexican dog, an ageless, bedraggled, gaunt and cowardly beast.

An Indian with twelve living turkeys in a wicker basket on top of his head. Another with a huge trunk on his back, supported by a tump line around the forehead, his sombrero still miraculously in place.

"VICTORIAN" MEXICO

The neo-classic building of the Hipotecario Bank—a ghastly piece of architecture, doubtless cemented home in the days of Diaz.

El Gallo de Oro (golden cock) *cantina*. Abbreviated swinging doors, brass rail, white-coated bartenders, great mahogany bar.

Two money-exchange booths, beplastered in front with lottery tickets. As we sit on our fountain, no fewer than twenty persons, of both sexes and all ages, try to inveigle us, with long coloured streams of coupons, into the great Christmas state lottery—600,000 pesos to the winner. As he will be paid in silver pesos, he had best call for his prize in a truck.

A very fancy confectioner's shop, its windows loaded with exotic and somewhat dubious piles of sweets. It is equipped with corrugated iron shutters which roll down to the ground at night and at the noon siesta period, completely barricading it. Shops such as this roll down at one o'clock, and roll up at three, or later. Then they may stay open until seven.

A newsstand with bright coloured magazines in Spanish, and plenty of shrilling newsboys.

The office of the London, Liverpool and Globe Insurance Company, and above it, "Dr. Ezguerro, Dentista."

Policemen, heavily armed, in the gaudiest of uniforms, with Sam Browne belts.

Patriarchal gentlemen with flowing beards, silver-mounted canes and long frock coats. Mammas in black bombazine leading little boys in long-trouser suits and round sailor hats.

THE YANKEE INVASION (SYMBOLICALLY SPEAKING)

Trolley cars, thumping tremendous bells.

Shoals of taxis. They are mostly model A Fords, without meters or the heraldic accoutrements of their northern cousins. They are called *"Libres,"* meaning free, because of the cardboard sign displayed on the windshield when a fare is wanted. When the fare is captured, the sign usually stays in place. One can go almost anywhere in the city for twenty-five cents. The overproduction is stupendous; the driving superbly reckless.

Fleets of trucks and motor busses. Chauffeurs of the latter consider the day ruined when they have not capsized, or at least stripped the mudguards from, a brother bus. They do not, however, have the range they should in a flat region like Mexico City. To see them at their best, one must ride behind them to Acapulco—double reverse curves on a fourteen-foot road, with a good thousand-foot drop into a gurgling river over the unrailed road edge. This is where their talents have real scope, and where passengers crawl out with hair gone grey.

Floods of private cars. If you see an Auburn, a Cord or a Rolls Royce without license plates, you will find the traffic officer—with a silly little whistle on a silly wooden stand—saluting rather than arresting. Mexican generals, you learn in due course, do not bother their pretty heads with license plates.

Steel post boxes; neon advertising signs over shop windows; bicycles—a lot of them; street arc lights; radio antennae; telephone cables on poles (they have not yet gone underground); a steel rubbish can; "no parking" signs; a weighing machine; an ice-cream vendor; a *cine* with huge poster heralding Bebe Daniels in *Dixiana;* another advertising *Radio Pictures* in English; another, Paul Whiteman's band.

A sports shop with window full of tennis rackets, golf sticks, basketballs, fielders' gloves, backgammon sets and weight-lifting machines. An electric appliance shop with heaters, toasters, griddles, ice boxes, flash-lights, and all the standard gadgets. The day being cold for Mexico—say 60°—one heater is going full blast on the sidewalk, wafting a hot breath on every passer-by. This strikes us as sound advertising. A gas stove and heater store. A Johns Manville window display. A plumbing store with the basic instruments in pink, purple and baby blue. We stare through the window enchanted at a lavender toilet seat with cover of mother-of-pearl. These Yankee plumbing salesmen know their customers.

The two persons out of three not in native costume regale us with Arrow collars, the cheaper grades of Messrs. Hart Schaffner and Marx, sleazy rayon frocks all but sweeping the ground, near silk stockings, close-fitting felt hats, extra high heels and legs whose curves are subtly wrong. Every man wears a felt hat out of deference to the winter season. The sun has no such deference; on some of these December days it is strong enough literally to strike one down.

This, then, is a street corner in our city. It serves, I think, to give the pattern of the whole; a confusing cocktail of machines, Maximilian, colonial façade and Tepoztlan. The Indian still provides colour and vitality, but he shrinks before forces which descend upon him primarily from the north.

[258]

BOSTON
PUBLIC
LIBRARY

Diego Rivera. 31

Side by side on the same continent, the area known as Mexico and the area known as the United States (here we are always referred to as the "United States of North America" to distinguish us from the United States of Mexico) have commingled and interpenetrated one another for uncounted thousands of years. The Rio Grande is less formidable than its name, particularly in the dry season. According to the theory of Paul Radin, the mound builders of the Mississippi Valley came up from Mexico. Certainly migrating Indians came down from the great plains upon the Mexican plateau. We find the maize culture spread generally over North America. Once, as we have seen, Mexico held title to Texas and most of the far west. Our cowboy fiction, our cowboys' very habits, would be something far less picturesque, without the Mexican range culture which lies back of both. It gleams in such words as vamoose, hombre, corral, mesa, sombrero, mesquite, rodeo, remuda, reata, bronco, nevada, poncho, no sabe, canyon. Nor should we forget that Mexico and Spain fought the English in Ohio and Florida, and so helped us win the Revolution of 1776. Millions of Mexicans have crossed the Rio Grande to work for a time in mine or field or on the range. Some have drifted to the cities. Scores of thousands have gone back to their milpas, particularly since the market crash of 1929. On June 30, 1928, there were 883,000 Mexicans in the United States. They constitute a migratory population of great importance to the American food supply. They move, according to Paul S. Taylor, in great seasonal cycles, following the crops; thinning sugar beets in May, chopping and picking cotton in June, "following the fruit" in the summer, harvesting grapes in the early fall, and later walnuts and lettuce in the Imperial Valley. Winter finds them, the whole family of course, camping beside their ramshackle Fords, in southern California. Their cycle ebbs and flows from Pennsylvania, to Michigan, to the Coast.

I was constantly meeting, in the most outlandish places, young men who had been in Chicago, Los Angeles, New York. They recognized me instantly as an American (which the Indians, I am glad to say, often did not) and approached with a warming assortment of my native slang. I found one youth who had driven a truck all the way from Seattle to Oaxaca, a route theoretically impossible for even a Ford. Yes, they like the States. No, they do not want to stay there indefinitely.

The migration of Americans into Mexico is on a much more restricted scale, compounded of business men, concessionaires, adventurers, oil men, miners, prospectors, and a sprinkling of ranchers in the border states. It is estimated that about 30,000 American citizens now live in Mexico, half of them in the capital. Few become Mexican citizens except for strictly business reasons, although they may live out their lives in the southern republic. We shall return to them presently; they constitute a strange phenomenon.

Today we are exporting words, habits, technical methods, and our peculiar type of modern goods to the urban areas of Mexico. Among the words we note:

Sandweeches
Girl—flapper
Mitin—meeting
Lider—leader. There is no Spanish word for civil leader; only
    for political and military
Spot—spot cash, in market reports
El dumping
El boicot
Futbal
El goal

Basebal
El umpire, el pitcher, el bat, el bateador
El box—a boxing match. Plural, los matches
El tren—train
Como el Pulman—very, very plush
Los sleepings—Pullman berth
Los smokings—dinner coat
Foxtrotear—a new verb, to dance
Socket, sweetch, and electrical terms generally

Dr. Eyler Simpson estimates that 50 per cent of all technical terms are in English.

In the States we acquire merit by giving our cigarettes British names—Pall Mall, Herbert Tareyton, English Ovals, Three Kings, Philip Morris. In Mexico distinction is achieved by facing north; we note the "Country Club" packet, and "Jazz." Out of 4,196 inches of display advertising in the two leading daily papers of Mexico City for a Sunday in December, 1930, 2,509 inches dealt with American products, 1,056 inches with Mexican products, 631 inches with European—or unidentified—products. America outranked Mexico two and a half to one, and Europe at least five to one. The American things advertised were, in order: Equipment for the household, primarily radios and electric devices; other machinery, primarily automobiles, cameras, typewriters, firearms; Hollywood movies and talkies; cosmetics and soaps; drugs and patent medicines; clothing and textiles —silk stockings, shirts and collars, Stetson hats; travel by air, rail, and water; watches and jewellery; schools and instruction; hotel equipment, chiefly plumbing.

Does it not all make one feel at home?

Head-line in Mexico City paper in January, 1931:

"Nueve Chicos, Emulos del Famoso Capone de Chicago"—Nine Kiddies Go Capone. (Head-line writers, you will note, have still something to learn from America. Spanish is, however, a devilish language to compress.) Nine boys, according to the story, averaging eleven years of age, formed themselves into an armed gang. They began by forcing their way into houses, under pretext of reclaiming a baseball from the patio, and stealing what they could. They advanced to cutting squares of glass out of shop windows and lifting soap and trinkets. They planned to steal a car as soon as the leader learned to drive. All came from well-to-do families, and all were devoted movie fans.

Mexico, the originator of the three-hours-for-lunch club, is headed for gastric ruin by quick lunch counters which are beginning to appear all over the capital. Pigglywiggly stores have their noses under the tent. There are four Tom Thumb golf courses on the San Angel road alone. Indian vendors with their heaping baskets of native flowers are disappearing before florists' shops, tin foil and fancy boxes. For all I know Mothers' Day has been introduced. Bathtubs and showers are making phenomenal progress. A Little Theatre movement is under way. *Nuestra Ciudad* is obviously patterned after *Vanity Fair*, while newsboys chant in singsong *"Graf-i-co, Graf-i-co,"* the capital's new picture weekly. O'Sullivan's heels are to be found on native shoes of woven leather strips; Indian artists skilled in silver filigree jewellery are making earrings fashioned like automobile wheels with tires, spokes, and hubcaps. The talkies are all over town; the flappers have their fine black eyes unswervingly on Fifth Avenue. Mexican butter-and-egg men are building homes in the new subdivisions copied from the Los Angeles copy of the Spanish villa— a case of cultural diffusion to excite the anthropologist, and a boomerang in all senses of the word. . . . Instalment selling has long applied to sewing-machines, even in the villages, and now moves on to brass beds, chromos, phonographs and radios. The traffic, however, is not entirely one way. Mexico makes possible perhaps the vilest of all our nationally advertised habits. She ships annually some four thousand tons of chicle into North American jaws, hacked from jungle trees in Yucatan.

We note the Ritz, the Regis, and the Geneve, all in the throes of endeavouring to superimpose Statler standards upon the slippery foundations of normal Mexican inn-keeping. The two systems have nothing in common save boarding and bedding. When the stream of Buicks arrives over the new Laredo road, I prophesy piteous outcries from Americanos deprived of their usual quota of steam heat, hot water and snappy service.

If I may be permitted to digress for a moment, I should like to lay a small garland upon the hostelry of the old regime. It takes time to become used to it, but once acclimatized, one cannot deny the charm. In Mexico City I lodged at one of the antiques, in preference to one suffering from the Statler infiltration.

It is only in the provinces that one finds the Mexican hotel in its purest form. The keynote is a sublime casual-ness. It is normally a huge stone building of two stories, built around a patio. Here one eats, frequently among flowers, banana trees, parakeets in wooden cages, and wandering flamingoes, turkeys, hens, dogs and cats. The huge bedrooms surround the patio on both floors, some of them with no ventilation save the corridor door. One can usually take one's choice of two double beds and assorted cots in the same room. The lobby is normally a dingy little hall with a register chalked on a blackboard, an electric bell signal case in deplorable repair, and nobody about when the traveller meets his crises. Indeed there may be nobody about when he arrives. At other hours everybody, including most of the town, will be in attendance.

We are breakfasting, let us say, at 9 A.M. in Puebla's leading hostelry. It has a giant tiled patio with three tiers of bedrooms and a glass roof. The linen is clean, the waiter is attentive, the food is good. Directly in the centre of the rear patio wall is a large sign: "W. C. Caballeros." A gentleman at the next table has beaten up three eggs in a huge glass beaker, the waiter has poured in about a quart each of hot coffee and hot milk, and the gentleman is now dipping his roll into the foaming mixture and sucking it into his mouth with enthusiasm. A boy, with a wicker crate of beautifully arranged onions, cabbages, beets and other vegetables upon his head, makes his way straight across the middle of the dining room from front door to kitchen. He is followed by another boy with a great basket of flowers, also on his head; an Indian woman with a tremendous bundle of dirty sheets; a man with raw meat in a tray; a woman with a skinned pig held tenderly in her arms; a ragged old gentleman in pyjamas with two live white hens—the price of which is a matter of lengthy bargaining between himself and the proprietor; assorted citizens in sombreros and rebosos—obviously the staff reporting for duty; a boy with a hatful of eggs; a mestizo woman with a load of beautiful inlaid boxes which she carries from table to table.

Down each side of the patio a sweeping brigade is hard at work, dust flying in clouds. Four cats are jumping upon chairs and occasionally upon a table top. They are reproved tenderly by a porter—whose life work seems to be just this—and as tenderly borne away in the direc-

tion of the kitchen, immediately to reappear. We ask—
it is always an adventure—for butter. The waiter beams.
He brings a large platter of delightful yellow morning
glories, but before it reaches the table we are aware that
the adventure has not been successful.

To secure a hot bath in a country hotel is a major
operation, shaking the whole establishment to its foundations. Porters, firemen, chambermaids, waiters, all join
in the process, converting it into a small fiesta. It is akin
to getting up steam on an ocean liner. It takes time, it
takes approximately half a day, but ah, what triumph
when the tap is finally turned and water, choked with
steam, rushes out. Everybody must see the triumph; indeed it is only with the greatest difficulty that the bath-
room is cleared. One gets into the tub, one bathes
luxuriously enough, one pulls the stopper, hears an alarm-
ing sound, and springs for the door. The bathtub is
draining directly on the floor, a wild freshet headed for
one's shoes. Just as one is about to recall the staff re-
gardless, the freshet dodges the shoes and drops down
a drain in the far end of the room.

Sheets are clean, towels are supposed to last a week,
there are never enough blankets on cold nights, and no
bell is ever answered—provided it is technically capable
of ringing—after 10 P.M. Nor is water or light to be
had. Nights are for sleeping, not for gallivanting around.
In each room there will be a wardrobe about twenty feet
high with no coat hangers. There is never a wastebasket
nor an ash tray; to attempt to read in bed by the single
dim bulb somewhere up aloft would send one to the
oculist. There may be a toilet, washstand and cold
shower partitioned off the corner of the room—and there
may not. If there is, part of the impedimenta will be
chronically out of order. There will certainly be a

motherly Indian chambermaid calling the lady of the party *"niña"* (child), and smiling so beautifully that it becomes impossible to reprimand her for neglecting more material attentions. She will take one's laundry and return most of it, in twenty-four hours, admirably done. The missing articles invariably reappear sooner or later; nobody ever steals in a country hotel.

The uncounted staff is willing, helpful, graciously polite and marvellously inefficient. The food is good and served in enormous quantities. The prices are ridiculous, two to three dollars a day, including more than one can possibly eat. Tips are often not expected, and if they are, amount to nothing. One is as likely to be undercharged as overcharged on the final bill. This is not a pecuniary civilization. Repeatedly I have called the proprietor's attention to telegrams, laundry, baths which he had overlooked—in itself a strange phenomenon, quite contrary to my behaviour north of the Rio Grande. One takes no pride in "getting away with something" in a land where money is not God.

You are let alone, you are fed well, you are charged little, you are bathed in friendliness if not hot water. After all, what more does one want? But the Buicks will never tolerate it. . . . Even now the authorities are planning modern hotels along the new roads, and admitting plumbing fixtures free of duty.

Which brings us back to the Yankee invasion. Of all the $200,000,000 worth of goods imported into Mexico each year, the United States supplies two thirds or more. By far the largest item on the import list is "machines and accessories." This does not include automobiles, which rank second. More than ninety-nine per cent of Mexico's 75,000 motor vehicles were manufactured in the United States; they are now being shipped in at the rate of about 16,000 a year. Seventy-five thousand cars for 16,000,000 people is not many. There are more than 16,000,000 people in the States of New York and Massachusetts, and 3,700,000 motor cars. I should estimate, however, that more than half of all Mexico's cars and trucks are located in the capital. Forty thousand cars for a million people is an advance, but Detroit with a somewhat greater population has six times as many. There is one car for every four persons in the United States, and one for every two hundred in Mexico.

The invasion of American capital stands at something under a billion dollars, a total less than it used to be. More than $200,000,000 has been squeezed out of the oil investment alone in the last ten years. Mining and smelting now come first with $230,000,000, controlling eighty per cent of Mexico's gold and silver. Oil is second, with $200,000,000, half of what it was in the peak of 1922. The investment in public utilities amounts to $90,000,000, with many companies recently taken over from British capitalists. It includes light and power, telephone and telegraph, street railways, water works. The hacienda investment reaches $64,000,000, sugar plantations first, followed by livestock, fruit and rubber. From here we drop a long distance to the investment in manufacturing and selling establishments.

Americans own some eight per cent of the land of Mexico, a little more than half of all foreign holdings, according to Tannenbaum. Next come the Spaniards, and then the English. In certain districts, the word "Spaniard" is identical with the word for "thief." Spaniards own a fertile belt in the central states. American holdings run to range lands in the north, and are less valuable per acre.

In the light of these figures, I found it difficult to

become overheated as to American imperialism—old style—in Mexico. A billion dollars is dangerous anywhere, but it is not so threatening as once it was. A greater danger to my mind lies in the invasion of gadgets, ideas and habit patterns.

There are four kinds of Americans in Mexico.

Tourists. Like tourists anywhere, except possibly a little hardier. They do not like Mexican hotels, and their conversation turns mainly on indignities suffered therein; that and their customs' grievances.

Students. We might term them the popular arts boys (and girls). They are tough, intelligent, enormously enthusiastic, a little mystical, and in various stages of going native. Mexico has got them and it is doubtful if they can ever break loose. On their right flank march the more stolid battalions of archeologists, investigating scientists, and even a lonely economist or two, like myself. They seldom have a settled place of residence.

Residents. A very small and select group which loves the country, likes the Indians and associates freely with government officials and other white Mexicans. It may be identified readily by the excellent display of native handicrafts in its houses.

The American colony. A larger group, representing primarily commercial interests, and oriented about the Country Club. Vestiges of it will be found in all the larger cities, but the prime exhibit is the capital. It has little or no handicraft work in its houses; all members sigh for the good old days; all have the Diaz reflex, dependable as the knee jerk; all dislike Mexicans in any form, and are interested in Indians only in conjunction with the servant problem. This they discuss interminably. They were, as a class, bitterly disappointed in Mr. Morrow because he gave more consideration to the viewpoint

[270]

of Mexico than to their own particular grievances—their mines, haciendas, franchises and oil wells. They hold that an American woman who associates with Mexicans is no better than she should be. They conceive it sometimes inevitable, but no part of their duty, to learn Spanish. They try to keep their children spotless from local contamination. They move in a close, unventilated circle of club, dinner, bridge, golf and Sanborn's tea and gift shop. They are not averse to alcohol in all forms and unlimited quantities.

I am not proud of what I have seen, or the reports I have had, of the American colony in Mexico. I am afraid, as an item in the Yankee invasion, it will have to be classified on a level with signboards and patent medicines—probably below the lavender plumbing. My criticism may be made somewhat plainer if we swing the picture around. Suppose there were a group of Mexicans resident on Park Avenue, New York, with powerful financial holdings in many of our leading corporations. They keep strictly to themselves; despising and looking down upon the United States, criticizing its customs, sneering at its government, refusing to learn English, sending their children to school in Mexico, looking upon any woman of their group who might associate with Americans as a moral liability. They publicly deplore the American Revolution, and sigh for the good days of King George. They appeal to their government in Mexico for armed intervention to protect them against a probable attack of bandits from Chicago. Their protests against all forms of local, state and national taxation are vociferous and unceasing. . . . One hesitates to state in plain words the fate of such a group; enough that the end would be comprehensive and sudden. The inborn courtesy of the Mexican is proved by the fact that a similar fate does not overwhelm the American colony. . . . That, and one hundred and twenty millions against sixteen.

Though the manners of the American colony leave much to be desired, its business methods have been slowly changing in recent years, on the whole for the better. American business, Diaz model, came to Mexico to make a maximum of profit in a minimum of time, by any available method, and retire with the loot. The stench, aye, and the blood left upon the trail could be disregarded, for one did not plan to pass that way again. American business, 1931 model, is tending to pass and repass the same trail; to trade, to operate public utilities, to *stay* in Mexico. For obvious reasons, stenches must be kept at a minimum. If the Electric Bond and Share Company proposes to put millions into electric light plants and operate them, it will have to get along with its customers. If Mr. Ford desires to keep saturating the available highways with model A's, he and his agents must be polite to prospective buyers, and keep them pleased after they have bought. Oil, the great mother of the exploitation regime, is passing out of the economic scene as salt water comes into the Tampico wells. In brief, the accent is more on long-time trade and services, and less on short-time exploitation. With this gradual change of front, is it too much to believe that the American colony will, in a generation or two—the Diaz reflex dies hard—civilize itself from within?

I cannot leave these business relations without a story. A mine superintendent, and thus allied to, if not a member of the American colony, is speaking: "I was inspecting an elevator shaft in the mine when something went wrong and I started to fall to certain death. My helper, a Mexican boy, watching above, had seen the break.

Instantly he threw himself on the loose end of the counter to balance my weight, and was hoisted up into the pulley. He had risked losing a hand and perhaps his life, but he had saved mine. . . . He was no model of virtue; just an average Mexican."

American penetration is confined primarily to the cities, especially Mexico City. Along the border it seeps into the towns and rural districts. In these states it is not unusual for Mexican farmers, like Texas farmers, to come down to the station in Fords. But in comparison with Canada, the penetration of Mexico by the machine has been slow indeed. The chief difference, culturally speaking, between Canada and the United States is prohibition (waiving an area in Quebec). But one has only to cross the river from Brownsville to Matamoros to enter a different world, and the farther south one goes, the more different it becomes, until Mexico City provides a partial hiatus. They call us in Mexico "Blond Beast" and "Colossus of the North," as well as *gringo*. Colossus we are. We have done our best to roll Canada flat, and it is inevitable that we should try to roll south as well. The wonder is that we have not rolled faster and more heavily.

Rural Mexico, below the border states, is almost completely unconquered. Cities smaller than the capital have taken to automobiles, electric power, Hollywood and jazz in varying degrees. Mexico City has gobbled a sample of practically everything except skyscrapers and subways. But as our street-corner survey shows, she is still far from a typical American city; great blocks of colonial, European, and Indian still survive. The invasion is not to be measured so much in capital investment as in American words, American attitudes, American sports, American goods.

Nor is this invasion wholly to be deplored. It has some excellent features. Even in rural areas, as we noted in the last chapter, certain technical importations would be very welcome. The health work of the Rockefeller Foundation, the archeological work of the Carnegie Foundation are splendid importations. Dr. Hugh Darby of the United States Department of Agriculture, stationed in Mexico City, represents a scientific liaison of incalculable future benefit. The popular arts students are forcing Mexico to realize the wealth of her Indian tradition. American sports for Mexican youngsters will do them a world of good. There is nothing the matter with electric lights, or, if you please, with automobiles in moderation—provided Mexicans could divest themselves of the conviction that they are a nation of Barney Oldfields. Even imperialism, turning to the long-time view, is a less sinister menace than it used to be.

The sad aspects of the invasion are to be found primarily in diluting and debasing a colourful and vigorous culture quite capable of standing on its own feet; quite capable, indeed, of exporting a philosophy of life which industrial civilization needs even more than Mexico needs gadgets. One is loath to see pecuniary values displacing human values, economic insecurity growing for the urban dweller as Mexico is tied into the world's industrial system. I have no enthusiasm at all for the inroads of high-pressure salesmanship, quick lunches, Arrow collars, screaming radios, squawking motion pictures, jazz, plus-fours, tabloids, subdivisions and copies of California copies of Spanish villas. Mexico could throw all this stuff into her deep barrancas with advantage to her appearance and to her soul.

CHAPTER XIV

PISTOLS AND POLITICS

I MET a man in the south of Mexico who was in charge of excavating one of the most exciting ruins in the republic; a modest, competent little man with more than a dash of Indian in him. He was gentle, kind, and seemed the perfect example of quiet government servant. In due course I learned that this man had been a highly placed officer during the Carranza administration. As the president neared the end of his regime, he sought to stave off liquidation by executing his enemies right and left. For some mysterious reason the executions in a certain district failed to eventuate per schedule, the marked men subsequently emerging in the best of health. The difficulty was finally traced to a night telephone operator, a very beautiful girl. She received the fatal orders and for reasons of her own withheld them. She was watched; her dereliction established; she was sentenced to be shot on a given morning—all without her knowledge. My archeologist was ordered from the capital to keep his eye on her through her last night on earth. Next morning neither guard nor prisoner was to be found. They had escaped together through the lines, out of the city, and up into the mountains. Not long after, Carranza fell. Our hero came out of hiding with his beautiful bride, and eventually secured a new government appointment in the department of archeology. Such stories abound in Mexico; the demurest people have the wildest backgrounds. For the last twenty years crisis after crisis has swept the country, and few there are who have not been seared by the flame of revolution.

We left Porfirio Diaz a few chapters back, breaking all speed records to Europe. As he fled, Mexico for the first time in four hundred years turned inward to her Indian tradition, and the only real revolution she had ever known was on. The muse of history has had to sit up nights to keep abreast of Mexico ever since. I shall have to leave the story to the muse; it is too involved to sketch more than a faint outline. I refer the reader to Gruening's definitive account of the major—and the bloodiest—period.

The Indians wanted land and the urban workers wanted relief from intolerable industrial conditions. Under the impulse of these two generative forces, the revolution waxed and waned. Leaders flared up and were shot; dictators arose and fell; factions formed, split and disappeared; laws were passed and forgotten; elections were announced and usually torpedoed; "plans" were formulated and disregarded; wise men limned a path and were pumped full of lead; Tepoztecans fled to the crags above their village; haciendas flamed; priests were thrown from their churches; towns were sacked; railroads dynamited; wild riders came storming over the mountains, Indians in ragged pyjamas at their heels; whole populations, their fields in ruins, turned to banditry as the only means of supporting life. (With fields cultivated again, banditry has lately suffered a grave decline.) Meanwhile the United States, with a billion dollars in jeopardy, stormed at the gates of Vera Cruz and sent General Pershing galloping over Sonora looking for a gentleman named Pancho Villa who could gallop even faster.

[276]

Out of this kaleidoscope came two men, two laws, and some of the noblest painting which the world has ever seen. One of the men is dead, and the laws are dying—or at least changing their form. Men are more important than laws in Mexico; generals have a following while principles are soon forgotten. It so happens, however, that these two laws fitted the grievances of the revolution, and had more body behind them than ever had happened before. The men were Alvaro Obregon and Plutarco Elias Calles, and the laws were articles 27 and 123 of the Constitution of 1917. The painting was done chiefly by Diego Rivera and Jose Clemente Orozco.

Diaz was ejected in 1910. It took seven years of terror to formulate the basic grievances and adopt drastic remedies—on paper. Carranza sponsored the Constitution of 1917, but it was forced down his throat. It was, and perhaps still is, one of the most enlightened constitutions ever adopted. It has nearly every principle, every political gadget, that a liberal could wish, and many that radicals cannot fail to admire.

This beautiful document remained on beautiful white paper for three more years while the dictators rose and fell and the kaleidoscope whirled ever faster. In 1920, Obregon, a small ranch owner from the north, risen to general in the army and with one arm shot away, assumed the presidency. Note the word assumed; few Mexican presidents have been genuinely elected. (The story runs of one Latin American gentleman, who, when notified that he was to run for president and would certainly be successful, chartered the fastest motor boat on the coast and fled to a British island.)

Obregon proceeded to put the two laws, and various other provisions of the Constitution of 1917, into tan-

gible effect. He had his failings, but he did honestly
attempt to give legal sanction to the villagers' cry for
land, and labour's cry for protection. It plunged him
into boiling water with hacendado, industrialist, Church
and foreign capitalist, but he persisted; the free villages
behind him, the "red battalions" of industrial workers
behind him. The laws began to bite; presently to cut deep
into outraged flanks. American oil men roared for armed
intervention, the Church groomed likely generals for another revolution; great landowners refused to cultivate.
Obregon kept on. In 1924 he was succeeded by General
Calles—an ex-school teacher whose power had been
growing steadily. Calles hewed to the line. More revolutions were launched and choked. Obregon came back
again, and was shot in a Mexico City restaurant. Soon
the corrido singers in village markets were strumming
a plaintive ballad with unending verses and the refrain:

> Obregon fue presidente,
>   General y buen ranchero
> Y dondequiera la gente
>   Llora con dolor sincero.

Presently Mr. Dwight Morrow arrived and to the vast
surprise of everybody, except possibly himself, captured
the goodwill of the Mexican government and threw
strong support to a practical interpretation of the two
laws. He advised modification, but he did not question
the soundness of underlying principles. He insisted—in
the teeth of the American colony—that Mexico was for
Mexicans and not a happy hunting ground for Yankee
dollars, and he filled his house at Cuernavaca with native handicraft products. I was able to find hardly a
Mexican who distrusted him, or an American business

man who had a good word for him—thus establishing beyond cavil his point of view.

Calles has not returned to the presidency since 1928, but with the death of Obregon he became—and remains —the strong man of Mexico. At the thought of a bullet finding him, there is a universal and doleful shaking of heads. The bullet would have to turn several sharp corners, for seldom has a man been better guarded.

In 1917, Russia and Mexico were proposing, with roughly equal relative vociferation, a new heaven and a new earth. Mexico's constitution, moreover, was born nine months before Russia's. The peasant and the worker, the sickle and the hammer, were on the march. But Russia had the better organization, the better temperament for concentrated effort, the better background for leadership. Today her revolutionary engines are developing ever greater horsepower—while Mexico chokes her throttle. Communism is dead or in exile, and official socialism has paled to a faint pink. The revolution as a dramatic and dynamic force has passed to a slower tempo, but in passing it has deposited by-products of profound importance. Indians have land—14,000,000 acres of it —trade unionists have legal status and protection, the old hacienda system is hopelessly smashed, a vigorous rural education movement is in process, the Church has moved down from its pedestal, and an artistic renaissance born of the Indian revival has thrown up perhaps the world's two greatest living painters.

Here was Zapata, the most indomitable figure of the Revolution, who set our friends in Tepoztlan to climbing crags. A boy in a free village in Morelos, he was driven to desperation as the enclosure acts of Diaz crowded that village almost out of existence. In Mexico City as hostler boy, he tended horses housed in marble stables. He wanted the land and the dignity of his people restored, and in 1910 put himself at the head of a ragged army. He razed nearly every hacienda in Morelos, and once came marching into Mexico City, to its infinite terror. He never enriched himself, contrary to every precedent. He mistrusted and fought each shifting central government until he was killed in 1919. When Carranza was spending millions to destroy him, his soldiers, dressed as peons, would come into the capital, sell trinkets in the market, and depart with a load of cartridges. Their wives would make the federal soldiers drunk and steal their guns. Rivera has his portrait on a white horse among the glittering new frescoes at Cuernavaca—Cortez at one end, Zapata at the other, four hundred years of history between them. This village boy was no intellectual giant— he never learned to read until he became a general— but he embodied the fundamental spirit of the revolution. His single aim, to quote Tannenbaum, was "to redeem the forgotten mountain race, making it feel master of the land on which it treads, creating a nation of dignified human beings." His grave is now a sacred shrine among the Indians of all southern Mexico.

Here again was General Saturnino Cedillo, who kept the railroad between San Luis Potosi and Tampico blocked for six years, a terror to the region. Obregon sent a messenger to ask what, specifically, he wanted. "I want land. I want ammunition so that I can protect my land. I want ploughs and I want schools for my children, and I want teachers, and I want books and pencils and blackboards and roads. And I want moving pictures for my people too. And I don't want any church or any saloon. That's all." He got his land and his blackboards, and the railroad was open again. The line between a bandit and a forthright revolutionist is very fine.

THE LABOUR LAW

Of the two laws which sought to give expression to the revolution, one dealt with land, the other with labour, but as Mexico is an agricultural not an industrial nation, the former is by far the more important. At certain points, however, the two overlap. The "red battalions" of trade unionists demanded official recognition and they received it unreservedly in article 123. The law provided an eight-hour day, one day's rest in seven, rest periods for working mothers to nurse their babies, six hours a day for children under sixteen, no overtime for women and children. It directed employers to provide sanitary dwellings for their mine and plantation workers at a rental not to exceed one half of one per cent a month on the assessed value of the property; to provide schools, health stations, a market space (the Indian touch), and a playground; and *not* to provide saloons or gambling houses.

Minimum wage boards were to be established in local areas, not only to define wages but to go into the matter of profit sharing. There must be no sex discrimination in wage rates, no private labour exchanges, not more than one month's wages in any year withheld to liquidate a debt to an employer—a solar plexus blow at hacienda debt bondage—and double pay for overtime. All workers' debts to 1917 were summarily discharged; the slate wiped clean. Labour insurance was accepted in principle —old age, accident, compensation, unemployment. The right to organize unions was thrown wide open. Arbitration boards were set up for labour disputes. If an employer discharged a workman for joining a union or a legal strike (public utility workers were enjoined from striking without due notice to the arbitration board), he must either reinstate the worker at once or pay him three months' wages—at the option of the worker. Employers were liable for accidents and occupational diseases "arising from work." Provision was made against "inhuman work," wages paid in company script, obligatory purchasing at company stores. Finally, the document veered strongly in the direction of compulsory trade unionism.

Article 123 was, in brief, a bill of particulars to make rugged individualism foam at the mouth. The American colony did and does. A good fraction of the law's provisions remained strictly on paper, but Obregon and Calles put enough into effect to give Mexican labour an entirely new status. It is to the credit of the late Samuel Gompers that he threw all the influence he could bring to bear—the American Federation of Labor was a power then—to strengthen this new movement across the Rio Grande. At present the tendency is toward a less stringent interpretation, but the basic principles hold.

THE LAND LAW

If the villages were to have their ancestral lands, present owners must cede the area. This meant the partitioning of the haciendas, which meant a revision of the going concept of private property, which meant undermining the property claims of all foreign investors in Mexico. Here was a pretty kettle of fish. Obviously the Indians could not be satisfied without creating the bitterest dissatisfaction in the $1,500,000,000 or so of alien capital. The Indians, I believe, would never have advanced farther than the wind which went into their battle cries, if the outside world at the moment—1917— had not been too busy attempting harikari to give

Mexico any concentrated attention. There is this small credit item on the profit-and-loss account of the World War. It gave Mexico an unprecedented opportunity to clean house without the kind of aid and comfort normally vouchsafed her by outside parties.

Mexico put the land law on the statute books, though the protests and lamentations—particularly from American oil interests—were piteous to hear. Two interlocking problems faced her: the legal delimitation of property, the actual distribution of land. Article 27 begins boldly with the first. It lays down the principle that the physical territory of Mexico belongs at long last to the nation. Its subsoil and waters can never be alienated to private ownership, but only exploited by limited concession. The nation retains rights and powers over the surface of the land even when passed to private title, including specifically condemnation for public-utility purposes. The lands of the free villages are adjudged a public utility. What is or is not a public utility is a matter for government to determine, not subject to review by the courts. Ownership of lands, waters, and rights to concession shall be enjoyed by citizens of Mexico only. Foreigners may acquire such rights only on condition that they agree to act *as though they were citizens,* powerless to invoke the protection of their governments. Churches of whatever creed may not hold real property, the title shall vest in the nation which in turn may lease to the church organization. Stock companies may not hold agricultural property or administer the same—a thrust, and I think a fair one, at absentee, irresponsible ownership. Banks may not hold real property except their own premises and except temporarily in execution proceedings. Villages may hold land communally, but the law looks towards an ultimate division to the individual. In Tepoztlan, we remember,

[283]

land is held under individual title, but the administration of the milpas themselves is communal—a happy compromise.

The specific formula proposed by article 27 for the solution of the agrarian problem—for the prime grievance of the Revolution—is short and sweet. All alienation of village lands subsequent to June 25, 1856, is null and void. Villages which cannot establish title shall be given such lands and waters (irrigation waters primarily) as they need. The state governments shall administer the partitioning of the haciendas and the restoration of village lands. Hacienda owners—mark this provision— shall be compensated for their property so condemned, in the form of twenty year, five per cent government bonds. Land they must give up at a price beyond their control, but government bonds they shall receive. Mexican bonds to be sure are not instruments before which one has hitherto stood in awe. We must remember, however, that the haciendas secured their lands in the first place by calmly enclosing them, the only compensation in the premises being the enslavement of the villagers. In Aztec times to move a boundary post was a capital crime. The Spaniards turned it into a virtue, leaving the Indians no redress short of banditry. The present law, in comparison, is mild revenge and only partial reversion to the ancient tradition.

The formula for land distribution had to comprehend a wide front, reaching from a roving Indian tribe with no conception of legal ownership, to a modern high-speed corporation. Generally speaking, article 27 favoured the small owner against the large, the native against the foreigner, the individual against the corporation; but provided a place, however modest, for all. It certainly could not be classed as socialism or communism. We might term it an agrarian *status quo ante,* plus a move in the direction of rural individualism.

When Obregon proceeded to an actual enforcement of this piece of parchment, the local hacendados yelped, to be silenced by superior force, but foreign capital turned like a wolf at bay. It called on all its gods, all its sacred rights of property, all its navies and armies. The phrase most in evidence was "inalienable rights." But, as Gruening lucidly points out, property concepts of Nordic and Mexican are two different things. Inalienable rights never had standing in Mexico, revolution or no revolution. Mexico was not a Spanish colony but a patrimony of the kings of Castile and Aragon. Grants of property to vassals were in the nature of revocable concessions, and the great *encomiendas* (land allotments) were commonly given for "two lives" only. The enormous properties of the Jesuits had been blandly revoked in 1798; indeed revocations were reasonably common. After independence the same flexible conception dominated Mexican thought and practice—the state merely replaced the king. Diaz never hesitated to confiscate—from his own nationals.

Battle was joined. The United States, on behalf of its billion dollars, argued that Mexico could not expropriate the property of Americans, referring specifically to plantations, oil lands, mining lands and citing the sanctity of property in international law. Mexico argued that a nation always has a right to adjust its internal property, otherwise its sovereignty is a myth; if the United States pursued its own argument in internal affairs it would find itself a government without sovereignty, incapable of protecting anything. Whether Señor Obregon pointed to the Eighteenth Amendment, I do not know, but it would have been an apt citation.

[285]

Certain Americans sensed the inner drift of the Mexican argument. I append a quotation from Mr. Amos Pinchot:

It is perfectly all right for me to take my dollar to Mexico or any other place and get all I can out of it by every decent means. But for me—after subjecting my dollar to the larger and fully anticipated risk for the sake of the larger and fully anticipated return—to come running to the American tax payer the moment the risk materializes and the return does not, demanding that he, who has never invested a cent in Mexico, shall send his son and his money southward to get my hazarded dollar out of trouble, is obviously a performance which requires diplomatic description lest it be called by its correct and disagreeable name.

Mr. Morrow, given the task of adjusting the deadlock, saw the problem in its proper historical and national setting. He allowed, according to Tannenbaum, most of the Mexican case. "The only compromise of any significance on the Mexican side has been to convert a fee simple into a perpetual concession. In theory and in the long run, as matters now stand, rights in subsoil acquired before 1917 are retained by their present owners only by accepting their conversion into a concession." Fortunately Nature, as well as Mr. Morrow, contributed to the settlement. By sending salt water into the oil fields she greatly diminished the American investment and, with it, opportunity for international bitterness.

So much for concepts of property and armed intervention. The matter is for the moment adjusted, thanks to Nature and Mr. Morrow, nor have I heard any proposal, however delicate, to take our minds off our present economic difficulties by inaugurating a war with Mexico. A senator has indeed proposed to buy a pair of border states, only to be met by counter proposals from the Chamber of Deputies that Mexico buy back Texas and

California. Far more important at the present writing is the other aspect of article 27: How much land have the villages actually received, what use are they making of it, and have their revolutionary impulses at last been satisfied?

In 1910, when the Revolution broke, government lands had shrunk to twelve per cent of all land in the republic, so prodigal was Diaz of his property. By 1925 some 35,000,000 acres had been reclaimed, mainly under article 27, sending the government holdings to nineteen per cent of all. The condemned acreage, however, was to a large extent poor or desert land. By 1927, 2,246 villages had actually received their ejidos, or land distribution under the law. This is only seventeen per cent of the 13,388 villages which have an ascertained right to such distribution. Up to that year, five per cent of the total rural population had received some three per cent of the total land of the republic—not an impressive transfer. Conditions varied greatly in different regions. In Morelos, Zapata's stronghold, hacienda lands were cut squarely in half; the free villages now own (or better, have perpetual use of) seventy per cent of all land in the state, including communal mountain areas, and the haciendas only thirty per cent. In Colima, on the other hand, land concentration has actually *increased* since 1910. One hundred and fourteen persons still own a quarter of all the land of Mexico. In 1910, haciendas of more than 12,000 acres accounted for just half the land of the republic; by 1927 the proportion had shrunk to forty per cent. In Zacatecas, 160 persons in the 12,000-acre class own ninety-three per cent of all private rural land; in Coahuila, 282 persons own eighty-eight per cent. But in Puebla there are only twelve estates of more than 12,000 acres, accounting for about four per cent of the

[287]

state's territory. And so it goes. Excessive concentration has been dented but far from eliminated.

To 1931, the latest government figures show 14,000,-000 acres distributed in ejidos. The more piercing outcries are quieted, but it would be ridiculous to suppose that satisfaction has been achieved. In another direction, however, more progress can be recorded. There has been a heavy shift of population from hacienda to free village. Hacienda population declined from 5,500,000 in 1910 to 3,900,000 in 1927. Ten thousand hacienda villages have completely disappeared. The free village population has increased from fifty-one per cent of all Mexico to fifty-eight per cent. Agricultural labourers are declining, and independent farmers gaining. There are today some 400,000 heads of rural families entitled to free use of land, marking a very large gain over 1910.

Above all, 6,000,000 peons have been freed from serfdom. Dignity, if not unlimited land, has been won back. They come and go from the haciendas as free men, while wages have risen from twenty-five centavos a day to seventy-five centavos or more. Hours of rural labour have decreased to not more than ten a day, in many cases eight. Two millions have joined agricultural unions. The poor peon's mule, so often spared by revolutionary armies, can now be rented out to the hacendado—whose draft animals were killed or driven away.

Americans, up to January, 1931, had lost just 300,567 hectares—750,000 acres—by virtue of article 27. The largest single expropriation was in Chihuahua, totalling 50,000 acres. Altogether, 261 Americans were ordered to give up their fees simple, representing some six per cent of the 14,000,000 acres expropriated. The law provided, we remember, that owners who lost their lands were entitled to five per cent, twenty year bonds. The bond business has not been flourishing. Many owners, both foreign and native, refused to take bonds, holding that to do so validated their retirement. Of 50,000,000 pesos' worth of bonds actually authorized, only 8,000,-000 have been issued. Interest is being paid on the nail, but the instruments are in such poor esteem that they are quoted at fifteen per cent of par value. In property-loving America, however, brewers and distillers received no bonds at all.

Mr. Morrow did not like these bonds. He advocated setting aside a flat amount, say 6,000,000 pesos, out of each annual budget and paying cash for condemned land —a sounder fiscal procedure, *provided* 6,000,000 pesos could be squeezed out of a Mexican budget, always a dubious operation. For the moment the question is academic, for actual land distribution has now, May, 1931, come to a standstill. No more applications are being allowed. Certain grave difficulties have arisen which need more thought and probably a drastic amendment of the law. Where lands have gone to villages still close to the communal tradition, distribution has worked well enough, but where they have gone to villages corrupted by the haciendas over centuries, the distribution has worked badly. Proper use has not been made of them because communal habit patterns had broken down. Land these villages received, but no seeds, fertilizers, credit, above all, no *agricultural education* wherewith to cultivate effectively. As a result the acreage has been grown to corn where other crops were more advisable; irrigation has been badly managed; soils have been leeched, production per acre has drastically declined. Hacendados were models of inefficiency, but hacienda villagers on their own are frequently even worse.

Here, for instance, is a hacienda in the state of Mexico, four hours from the capital. It was valued at $500,000 before the revolution, raising wheat, cattle and sheep. Ejidos took the cream of the land, leaving the owner with a small strip of poor soil and no dependable water supply. Into the good soil, the Indians have run an excess of water from the irrigation dam, leeching it badly. No fertilizer is available to make good the potassium shortage which characterizes the soil. Corn has displaced wheat, and stalks which a few years ago were eight feet high have shrunk to four. The villagers have been actually forced to *import* corn. The land is ruined, the owner is ruined, a splendid irrigation system lies useless, the Indians are losing self-sufficiency. In this case everybody loses—nation, worker, hacendado. A friend of mine, an agricultural expert, would reclaim the land with alfalfa, and breed 25,000 cattle on it. He would preserve the Indians' freedom and dignity and rehouse them. The property is readily capable of being made the basis for a rich and flourishing community, without the feudalism of Diaz, and without the handicaps of ignorance. Along some such approach as this, the ejido system must be revised.

Theoretically it is sad that the Indians for the moment have ceased to receive land; practically it is not so mournful. This is the more true, alas, because of the very considerable acreage delivered not to Indians but to politicos, many of them sometime fiery revolutionists. It recalls strongly the outcome of the war for independence when revolutionary creoles stepped into the shoes and haciendas of retiring Spaniards. And this brings us face to face with the white, educated Mexican. We have discussed Mexican Indians hitherto, but the small class of preponderantly Spanish blood, which speaks officially for the nation, deserves a word. I wish it might be kinder than it is going to be.

BOURGEOIS MEXICO

White Mexicans tend to live in houses filled with plush, gilt, crayon portraits of ferocious gentlemen with mustachios, and a black plaster sambo holding out a card tray. Their taste in house decoration is indescribably bad, worse than old Timothy Forsyte's. Their taste in European clothing, which they generally affect, is dubious. In the open, to be sure, the gentlemen run to picturesque costumes, in which a cartridge belt and a huge pistol or two figure prominently. The story runs of two deputies lately embracing each other in an anteroom of the national chamber—the classic Mexican embrace where A puts his arms around B and slaps him affectionately down the rear, while B performs similarly. A slapped the trigger of B's sixshooter, discharging it harmlessly but noisily down the leg of his trousers. Instantly, according to my informant, the seated chamber to a man arose and drew a gun, ready for whatever might develop.

As a class, white Mexicans know very little about their own country, but cleave to the cities. They strain every resource to be educated abroad; they value only imported goods, buying nothing if they can help it of native manufacture. They have little use for Indians. They are lazy and self-indulgent above the average Nordic. They are unsure of themselves in the presence of westerners, whom they at once admire, emulate, and bitterly hate—sure index of an inferiority complex. At the same time courtesy and hospitality are cardinal elements of their natures. "My house is yours," they say,

and if you admire any personal possession, "It is yours."
This courtesy is part formula and part a very authentic
warmth of temperament. They give marvellous parties,
surrounding the guest in a glow of human kindliness as
well as alcohol and spiced sauce.

They are given to flights of rhetoric which would put
even a senator from Alabama in second place, while their
indifference to cold facts and figures is profound. They
are emotional, undisciplined, reasonably ignorant, and
often charming. I was invited to climb Popocatepetl by
a young art student. He spoke with sincere feeling. "We
will climb Popo together. Ah, it will be beautiful, the
white snow, the silver ice. It is the dream of my life. I
have never climbed a mountain. Perhaps I am not able
to climb. If not I come back to Mexico and shoot myself.
But it is the ambition of my life." We were to arrange
the details at a subsequent dinner, but he never appeared.

Nobody ever thinks of being less than half an hour late
to an appointment, and the traveller must learn to excuse
complete non-appearance. Mexicans, like Russians, have
no time-sense, but go on doing what they are doing so
long as it amuses them. While they lack acquaintance
with exact fact they have a fairly acute sense of reality.
They can undergo the most gruelling discomfort without
complaint, and have no difficulty in vacillating between
glittering opulence and the starkest and plainest of fare
and travel. (They travel, normally, with fourteen bundles per person including infants, most of the inanimate
parcels done up in baskets, mats, wrapping paper, or
coloured gauze.) They never, as it were, complain to
the management, but take life as it comes, and thus share
something of the Indian's philosophy. A hundred white
Mexicans—I refer to men—are more individual, unique,
and, on the whole, human, than a hundred members of

the Rotary Club of Zenith. But they are not so dependable. And they are capable, on occasion, of a cruelty which Zenith with its Red Cross and its community chest has long outgrown.

There is a group of Mexicans, normally with more white blood than Indian, known as *rancheros*. They are independent farmers and cattlemen, occupying the wide ground between hacendado and village Indian. They are to be seen in the smaller cities and towns, and many still affect the picturesque charro costume—wide felt sombrero, short embroidered jacket, skin-tight trousers with buttons like flute keys down the side. They do not suffer from feelings of inferiority at all, and are a joy to look at. They ride like centaurs, and adorn their sturdy little ponies with costumes as gay and lavish as their own. One feels, somehow, as if all white Mexicans ought to be like this—fearless, self-reliant, intelligent (within reason), and beautifully accoutred.

They are not. As a class I prefer the Indian. There are twenty Indians to every one of them; they float, a thin olive deposit, on an ocean of brown. If they should be obliterated overnight, Mexico would still function, and save for the cities, look about the same. For all I know it might develop leaders—statesmen, philosophers, artists, who would serve the nation better than it is now served. Juarez was an Indian, and so was Felipe Carrillo. Five hundred years ago, great statesmen, artists, philosophers and mathematicians were coming from this brown soil. If the Indians were obliterated, Mexico would cease to be. I should look for annexation within a year; Chambers of Commerce, skyscrapers, Antique Shoppes, unemployment queues, the year following.

We might divide white Mexicans into three classes: the normal bourgeois, the gun toter, the genuinely civilized. The former is the largest and the least interesting group. It is vulgar, kindly and dull, sharing with the American colony the Diaz reflex. It has been markedly impoverished by the Revolution but does not propose to do anything about it except continue the customary lamentations. I grew reasonably weary of those lamentations; weary of the pictures of viceroys, governors, archbishops, and ambassadors to France in the family album. These people hark back to their ancestors as persistently as a resident of Charleston.

The gun toter—specifically the militarist and swaggering politico—is the curse of Mexico. He runs to fancy uniforms, fancy women, Rolls Royces, unbridled arrogance, peculation to give a Tammany politician pause, and a complete and sublime indifference to the welfare of his country. He stems, I suspect, directly from Cortez. Wherever one goes in Mexico, one sees the black, ugly headed zopilote, half crow, half vulture, wheeling to drop on carrion. These birds always put me in mind of gun-toting politicos, soaring and plundering their own people and their own land. But the simile is not altogether apt: zopilotes have a scavenging function of some utility; militarists are pure parasite. Carleton Beals has given us the portrait of General Barragan, Carranza's chief of staff. He was under thirty, good looking, a dude, a braggart and a sadist. He affected a gold-headed English cane and foreign mistresses—note the imported goods. He had condemned and seized a string of mansions on the Avenida de la Reforma, the finest in the capital. He was superior to all traffic regulations and tore through the streets in a great yellow car, his feet on the windshield. . . . Such is the general style. The species may be observed in full flower at the Regis bar on any afternoon.

GRAN EXPOSICION
DEL
MENSAJE PRESIDENCIAL
OBJETIVO

Diego Rivera. 1931

There is normally one general to every 350 soldiers in the Mexican army. The fleet, three ancient gunboats, almost too decrepit to leave their anchorages, had at last accounts 603 men and 555 officers. At least four commodores were tried for treason last year, and acquitted. Mexico, of course, needs no army whatsoever. The only power she could pick a fight with is the United States; which is absurd. She could not reach Cuba or South America, and the Monroe doctrine prevents the Eastern Hemisphere from reaching her. If she were foolish enough to want to swallow a Central American "power," she might mobilize her traffic officers. She needs an internal police force and that is all. It may be objected that the army protects the nation against revolution. It does precisely the opposite. It incites revolution. Its minor generals are forever fomenting revolts that they may become major generals, and its rank and file is always ready to desert by divisions to the revolutionists; an accredited fact upon which every incipient revolution bases its whole strategy. Where else, pray, would it get its arms and munitions?

My private formula for keeping revolutions at a minimum is compounded of 10,000 national police, a picked, well paid and efficient force; and a fleet of one hundred airplanes, half of them bombers. Nothing discourages a bandido centre like a few well placed bombs. No mountain headquarters, however remote, is safe from airplanes. (On the whole I am glad my formula was not in effect in Zapata's time.) Fortunately for Mexico, the generals have not had things all their own way under Obregon and Calles. General Amaro, the present chief of staff, is actually reducing the army, and the huge outlays for military expenditure. He is said to be honest and efficient, and a harsh disciplinarian. He has, however, a grotesque and ghastly tradition to combat in his officers, and, for all I know, in his own soul.

Peculation reaches its finest flowering among military gentlemen and gun toters generally, but alas, it is not confined to them. It is manifest throughout all classes of white Mexicans. It is even more the normal course of business, if you can believe it, than in the municipal governments of Chicago or New York. With a few honourable exceptions, everybody who has opportunity grafts. It is part of the perquisites of public office. It goes back to colonial days when the only opening for an ambitious creole was to buy a sheriffship or judgeship, Spain having closed all other careers. Never a day went by in Mexico City that I did not hear from one to ten specific accounts of haciendas annexed, mines alienated, commissions received for awarding government contracts, town houses condemned, water rights purloined, new businesses blackjacked, even hotels pilfered from their builders. Discount these stories as you please, and I discounted them heavily, there is no escaping the plain fact that land laws, labour laws, the entire administration of national, state and local governments are honeycombed with peculation—most of it petty, some of it gigantic, all of it deplorable. I am convinced that the Revolution has made inroads in the custom, particularly in recent years, but only a romantic deaf-mute could believe that it had been stopped. Mexicans graft the way Americans drink, in easy and conscience-free disregard of the laws against both. We may amend our law and make ourselves honest men once more, but Mexico has no such easy exit. She must break the zopilote habit if she is ever again to become a great nation. Indians do not graft unless first corrupted by white Mexicans.

This is all reasonably discouraging. It would be perfectly possible of course to gather statistics of assorted peculations, say in New York City in the year 1930, which, ranged row on row, would put a Mexican general to shame, in gross receipts if not in daring. It would be possible to call the roll of Chicago racketeers to the same end. This, however, is but the vulgar argument of kettle against pot. In terms of relative wealth, the bill for graft in Mexico is certainly heavier than in the United States, but even if it were lighter, the situation is not one to be condoned by exclaiming "You're another."

Turning to the other side of the ledger, there is reason to believe that never before in her history have there been so many able, idealistic and genuinely patriotic white Mexicans. At intervals, during the revolutionary turmoil since 1910, they have actually controlled the ship of state. They dictated the Constitution of 1917, they have forced reform after reform, they crystallized the movement which led away from Europe and back to the Indian. They have fought—and died—for rural education, for public health, for the destruction of serfdom, for the economic independence of the village, for the restoration of dignity among their fellow citizens, for the cultural unity of Mexico. The group has been small, but it has been select. Its leadership and its tangible achievement have been far in advance of any kindred group in the world, barring Russia, during the past two decades. Mexico, in 1910 a feudal state, with a few Victorian trimmings, has blocked out, and partially achieved, programmes in labour legislation, education, land reform, stimulation of the arts, national economic planning, as progressive as they are daring.

I have said that the group has had to fight. Listen to one of its members:

I would have resigned from office a dozen times had it not been that one can feel the hope of the nation centred in our department. (That of Education.) We have had to fight for money; we have to criticize others for spending on things that are not educational; in some instances we have had to take the attitude of the "Anti-foreigners" because we opposed the spending of money in propaganda when we needed it so much for real work. . . . The millions spent in the celebration of the centennial broke up our budget and actually stopped some of our construction work on school buildings. Our worst enemy is politics. Another serious drawback is the army. While one hundred million pesos are spent in maintaining a military establishment that is useless for all purposes of progress, a really fundamental work cannot be undertaken in either public works or education. . . . More thought given to the future of the race and less to selfish present-day interests would go further than all the propaganda printed about our achievements. The work of education must be continued if Mexico is to come out of medievalism—not only that, but it must be increased at the expense of personal sacrifice.

The utopia of which these leaders caught a glimpse has not been achieved. Indeed they have been forced time and again to retreat from outposts already captured. Their ranks have been enfiladed by fire from militarist, politician, hacendado, cleric, foreign capitalist. What they hoped to do in 1920 is decimated in 1931. The curve of the revolution is slowing down, but even if it comes to a dead level it will remain far above the Diaz bench mark.

The government itself is compounded of black and white strands—the gun toter and the idealist. The latter is more articulate, speaking for Mexico on outstanding issues; the former is more active, lowering the whole character of the administration on a hundred fronts. Democracy, as we have hinted more than once, is an empty phrase. There are no well-organized blocs in Mexico— farmers, workers, "corn belt," even associations of busi-

ness men, to whom the politician is responsible. He goes
his own prima-donna way. The explanation of a political
manœuvre may be discovered only after long searching,
and it consists of answers to such questions as: Whose
nephew are you? Whom did his brother's niece marry?
Who is so-and-so's mistress?

Lord Bryce has given us four outstanding reasons why
democracy has failed in Latin American countries, to
which J. Russell Smith has added a fifth:

> The lack of racial unity
> The lack of a middle class of small property owners
> The lack of transportation and communication facil-
> ities by which ideas may be interchanged
> The lack of experience in self-government, such as
> the American colonies enjoyed before 1787
> The lack of popular education

Rural education is today the most hopeful feature in
the political and social scene. Here the idealists are con-
centrating their efforts, with encouraging results. Nothing, of course, is more fundamental. There are some
2,500 village schools in 703 circuits, supported by the
federal government. They are for adults as well as children, and the average attendance records show one
grown-up to every two youngsters. I visited a number of these federal schools and was excited by
them. They tend to grip the imagination of the whole
community.

One goes in a whitewashed doorway to hear little
Indian girls reading from a Spanish primer in soft voices;
one emerges presently to the strains of the village band.
It has appeared from nowhere to welcome the visitor
and show him how well it can play. Here comes the presi-

dente—in pyjamas and sandals like anybody else—to make a little speech about the village, its crops, water rights and problems. A boy is tugging us by the hand to see his blooded fowls in an immaculate runway in the school courtyard, and another, with enormous enthusiasm, begins to belabour a small hand pump that we may view the new shower-bath in action. The teacher proudly leads us through the new *casita campesina,* model country house, explaining the advantages of plumbing, real windows and three separate rooms. Two teams of mature youths are giving an exhibition basketball game. By this time the entire village has congregated in the plaza, and the high mountain air is stirring with enthusiasm, interest, pride in achievement. We gravely shake hands with every pupil in the school—thirty children or so—and most of the town besides, and depart, filled with an unreasoning affection for these people; convinced that there is no limit to their possibilities.

The Obregon-Calles regime, men who led the revolution, and who listened, if they did not belong, to the idealists, are still weaving in and out of office. No powerful reactionary group has seized the central power. Education is progressing with more vitality than ever before. Health work is moving slowly forward. The political power of the Church has been broken, perhaps for all time. Labour unions are losing ground, but the industrial worker is still protected by the most advanced labour code extant outside of Russia. Foreign capitalists are making no headway in reclaiming the happy hunting grounds provided by Diaz. Land distribution has come to a full stop, the accent on agrarian reform shifting to rural education. One is not sure that it should not stop, to catch its breath. The acid test will lie in the figures of land concentration. If concentration gains year after year, agrarianism is defeated. . . . And that means another revolution from the bottom, against which no army, no police, no airplanes will ultimately prevail.

CHAPTER XV

ADVICE FROM A PARVENU COUSIN

I LIKE Mexico. I like its colour, its violence, its raw tumbling mountains, green checkerboard valleys, dizzy trails, purple blue sky and stabbing sun. I like its crumbling monasteries and cathedrals with cactus growing from their roofs, and even more its ancient pyramids rising earth-covered and defiant from jungle plain and mountain top. I like the great Pacific rollers pounding on the beaches of Acapulco where the crags come down to the sea; the patio gardens, the little shaded plazas, so cool when all the world is hot. I like the quiet, grave-eyed children; the patient, stubborn asses; the compact villages each with its ruined church tower; its compounds set about with organ cactus, and corncribs like great stone vases. I like the noble frescoes of Rivera and the paintings of school children. I like the village markets, the lacquer, the pottery, the carved chocolate-beaters; and the tumbling bronze bells welcoming in the fiesta. I like the way Indians look, the way they walk, the polite "buenas tardes" they fling one on the trail; their dignity I like, their utter lack of pretence, their disregard of clocks, the tilt of their sombreros, and the fling of the sarape across the shoulder. Above all I like their magnificent inertia, against which neither Spain nor Europe nor western civilization has prevailed.

I do not like white Mexicans so well, nor the cities they live in, nor their taste in interior decoration. I do

[304]

not like politicos and gun toters—particularly generals —nor their mistresses, bars, or bullfights. Their personal manners, I am forced to admit, are often as impeccable as their social behaviour is atrocious. I do not like all Mexican odours, especially when cross-referenced to sanitation. I do not like travelling for more than two hours in so-called first class coaches on narrow-gauge railroads. I do not like the frequency with which entomological congresses are convened. I am convinced that all native chauffeurs, outside of Yucatan, are stark, staring mad; nor do I like driving a car myself up a thirty-four per cent grade on a slippery road eight feet wide with a 2,000-foot drop under my right wheel. I do not like Mexican dust storms, *moles,* newspapers, beggars, meat shops, money systems, thorns, matches, postcards, dogs, butter, hornets or coffee.

These are, however, the trivia of the unacclimatized wayfarer, fading before the grandeur and mystery of the total scene. It must be a great experience to be born in Mexico, and to have such a land to come back to and call home. Humboldt has characterized the country as "a beggar sitting on a bag of gold." He is wrong. Natural resources are not so lavish as they have been painted; human resources are far more splendid. A fairer metaphor would be "a brown philosopher astride a white volcano."

Mexico is our chief neighbour on the continent of North America, outranking Canada in population though not in area. In a vital sense she stands for all Latin America as well, and thus swells before our eyes to comprehend another great continent, unnumbered islands of the sea, and 80,000,000 people to add to her own 16,000,000. When we touch Canada we touch England. When we touch Mexico we touch not Spain,

[305]

but Latin America. With the exception of the belligerent ex-mayor of Chicago, we have outgrown our hatred of the mother country; Mexico has not outgrown her violent distaste for Spain. As a race, Mexicans are less Spanish than Americans are English; they comprise indeed the citadel of early American stock. America has been their continent for at least 20,000 years.

From the Rio Grande to Tierra del Fuego are 16,-000,000 white men and 80,000,000 Indians, the former European in their outlook, the latter indigenous American. Contemplating this racial cleavage, certain savants, such as Wallace Thompson, become panic-stricken and visualize a "brown peril" on all fours with the "yellow peril" of timid Californians. "That Indian culture . . . is perhaps the most sinister threat against the civilization of the white man which exists in the world today. Its strength is in its inertia; its threat is in the fact that it is the dominating factor in the political and social life of Mexico, the keystone nation of Latin America. . . . Behind the flimsy curtain of their Spanish language and religion . . . they leap in savage war dances and look forward to the day when Indian communism shall rule; when the white man with his mines and oil wells shall be forgotten."

Sound and fury signifying nothing. It would be a matter for universal congratulation if the white man with his mines and oil wells could be forgotten, allowing Mexico her own patrimony; the drift to date is in the opposite direction. The threat lies not from Indian to white but from white to Indian. Will the machine roll Latin America flat, trampling down the last vestige of the authentic American culture? Even if it does not, the notion of Tepoztlan arising in flaming zeal and marching on the White House is preposterous. There may be peril to white investments in Mexico, and elsewhere, and I sincerely hope there is. Foreign investments should be conducted at peril of good behaviour—a policy overlooked for four hundred years. But peril beyond the confines of ancestral milpas and communal mountain slopes is a vision of a disordered mind. What the Indian desires above all else on earth is to have his land and be let alone.

No. Dr. Gamio gives us a far saner outline. The cultural lag between native white and Indian is what disrupts and confounds Latin America. Mexico, by turning inward to the Indian, has recognized and faced the problem. She may find a solution. If she does, it will enormously aid not only her, but all Latin America as well. It will enormously aid the relations of the United States with her neighbours to the south—relations human if not financial. "The new conquest" is Gamio's name for the search, and we can only wish him every success, offering as well positive help through our anthropologists, archeologists, students of the popular arts, and our intelligent and sympathetic understanding.

"A primitive religion, a Pretorian army, a medieval church, handicraft folkways into which twentieth century mechanism is beginning to intrude, tribal organization, an educated, modernly cultivated minority—all these are found today in Mexico. The time element is the transcendent factor in the understanding of that country . . . continuity is the marrow of Mexican history beneath changing surface events." Thus Gruening sets the stage. The United States obliterated the Indian and started fresh. Mexico, Peru, and to a lesser extent other Latin American countries have been grafted upon stubborn and ancient cultures, which, from time to time, have flared into commanding civilizations. Continuity is indeed the marrow of Mexican history, the crystal through which alone she can be analyzed and understood.

From Father Hidalgo's call to the flight of Porfirio Diaz was just one hundred years. It was a century of hell. Two more decades have passed, more turbulent and bloody than those which went before, but with the underlying purpose of liquidating the lost century. For the moment, peace and stability have been achieved; the liquidation, however, is not complete. The most that we can say is that the last few years have shown a declining red balance. The account may be cast up in the following categories. Under Obregon and Calles, Mexico finally achieved:

An increased national consciousness, based on the conception of continuity.

An initial solution of the land problem.

A status for industrial labour.

A small breach in the wall of triumphant militarism.

A small gain in the struggle against disease.

A considerable gain in rural education.

A definite sovereignty over her own natural resources which foreign capital has been forced to recognize.

The divorce of the Church from economic and political power.

A renaissance of the arts, particularly painting; and a new regard for the handicrafts.

As contrasted with Russia during the same period, these gains and changes seem slight enough. At the present time, indeed, the two revolutions are headed in opposite directions. Both began in handicraft cultures, flecked with industrialism. In both manor houses were burned, and their lands reclaimed by the villagers. In both progressive labour codes were inaugurated, and trade unionism made all but mandatory. In both foreign concessionaires were held to new and stringent interpretations of property rights, while the state took title to all church lands and buildings. In both, education and the arts received strong stimulation, though in the latter category the honours are heavily with Mexico. She has produced at least two painters of the first rank, where Russia's peak to date has been a great cinema. . . . Thus we can set down parallel after parallel, but a major cleavage outweighs them all. Russia has definitely abandoned handicraft culture and welcomed industrialism to the tune of $30,000,000,000 of new investment in her Five Year Plan. She has opened her arms to mass production and the machine—though on her own terms of social control. Mass production languishes in Mexico; industrialism is not making marked headway on any terms. Handicraft culture is more sturdy today than under Diaz, with more land, more dignity, more intelligent recognition. While Russia runs to mechanical horsepower, the burros, newly blessed, foot their way over the mountains to the markets of Tepoztlan.

Whether Russia can tame wild horses of energy, where the west has failed, only time can tell. We know that Mexico can live at peace with her burros, her corncribs and her village markets. Mr. Virgil Jordan, one of the most outspoken of our business leaders, has admirably stated her case:

If it were not for storms, earthquakes and pestilences, it is probable that the system of small agricultural holdings, and of small scale handicraft manufacture, which existed between the breakdown of feudalism and the advent of the industrial revolution, was the most stable of all the forms of economic organization that have developed—although it did not supply as high a standard of living for parts of the population as has been seen since.

In Mexico, storms, earthquakes and pestilences have all taken their toll, but seldom in lethal dimensions. Have you ever heard of a Red Cross drive for Mexican relief? Mary Austin makes the argument even more local:

> Living in such fashion, the pueblos [of New Mexico] at the time Spain found them, had no rich, no poor, no paupers, no prisons, no red light district, no criminal classes, no institutionalized orphans, no mothers of dependent children penalized by their widowhood, no one pining for a mate who wished to be married. All this is so much a part of their manner of living together in communities, that three centuries of Christian contact have not quite cured them of their superior achievement.

The handicraft economy of Mexico as we analyzed it in Tepoztlan is blood brother to the above generalizations. It is economically stable and self-sufficient. There are no rich, no poor, no paupers, no sexual inhibitions beyond the reasonably tolerant folkways. (One never sees couples holding hands or flirting in the plazas, indeed one sees very few young couples at all; I never noticed a man and woman kissing; but one sees thousands upon thousands of brown babies. Romance, I fear, is neglected in favour of procreation. This is hard on poetry but good for the nervous system.) There is no local government worthy of the name, but a strong community spirit, finding expression not in after-dinner speeches and paid advertisements, but in helping a neighbour harvest his corn, and repairing the town water supply. In such communities, pecuniary standards do not apply, and integrity is not a luxury. Men are governed not by clocks but by the sun and the seasons; recreation is not a matter of paid admissions or forced disciplines, but as spontaneous as eating. The individual to survive must learn many useful crafts; he does not atrophy his personality by specializing on one. Costs, as we have seen in an earlier chapter, are lower for many articles than is conceivable under the most efficient methods of mass production, and all work is directed to specific function with a maximum economy and a minimum of waste. Over-production is as unthinkable as unemployment. Life in a handicraft community is to be lived, not to be argued about, to be thwarted by economic conditions, or postponed hopefully until one has made one's pile.

On the other side of the ledger, we find that the price of stability is the absence of progress—whatever "progress" may mean. New methods are infrequently invented; new aspirations, new desires, new material wants are all but unknown. The standard of living, while adequate, is very low, and the death-rate per thousand, particularly among infants, is scandalously high. Illiteracy is appalling, though millions of Mexican villagers speak two languages. Ignorance breeds superstition, and superstition fear. Mexicans are afraid of many harmless things, such as "los aires," and not sufficiently cautious in respect to many deadly things, such as diphtheria germs. The assets of a handicraft economy are great, but its net worth, after allowing for liabilities, is a lower figure; a figure, however, black, not red. . . . If we could but take the manifest assets of Tepoztlan and the manifest assets of Middletown, and combine them. . . .

Meanwhile there is much discussion of Middletown's exporting both its assets and its liabilities to Mexico. It is widely held that industrialization is inevitable, handicraft culture doomed, and a balanced consideration of its virtues and failings a purely academic question, if not a total waste of time. The inevitability of the mechanization of Mexico somehow puts me in mind of those prophetic curves which statisticians are wont to play with. They take the population growth of the United States, plot it, and extend the line until it reaches 300,000,000; they take American prosperity from 1922 to 1928, plot

it, and extend to 1950—when everybody will have
$10,000 a year. Similarly if the curve of industrializa-
tion from Watt to Ford is plotted, it looks like the path
of a skyrocket against the night. To keep on its course
it needs more people, more area, more natural resources.
Mexico has all three; obviously Mexico must be industrialized. Q. E. D.

But as a matter of cold fact, population in the United
States is sinking below the exuberant curves plotted a
decade ago; while a certain October 29th on the New
York Stock Exchange turned the prosperity plotters
and prophets upside down and inside out. Precisely why
is mass industrialism inevitable in Mexico, or anywhere
else for that matter? Machine civilization proper is still
incomplete over the United States; the map is spotted
with great uninfected areas in the south and west. Oases
may even be found in the New England states. It is now
moving into North Carolina, accompanied by storms of
protests from embittered southerners. Even if we drop
intelligent observation and take to curves, how long will
machine civilization require at the present jerky rate to
crawl from North Carolina to Guanajuato? The distance
is 1,800 miles.

Waiving the higher astrology of plotted graphs, what
do we actually find in Mexico at the present time that
makes for industrialization—meaning not the cultural
penetration of the "Yankee invasion" but massed factories, blast furnaces, slums—the Pittsburgh sort of
thing? Precious little. We find tier on tier of mountain
ranges bisected with frightful barrancas, as inimical to
iron horses as to huge supplies of dependable fuel and
water, without which mass production cannot function.
We find little purchasing power, no stable pecuniary demand, no vestige of that mass consumption failing which

mass production has no rhyme or reason. We find 15,-000,000 Indians who, undefeated by cannon and cross for four hundred years, are not to be capsized overnight by super-salesmen. When their simple wants have been met they go to a fiesta or they go to sleep. They have no itch for acquisition; their sales resistance is superb. What could even Mr. Bruce Barton do with such a people? For them an embittered German trader coined the phrase: *Verdammte Bedürfnislosigkeit*—damned wantlessness.

On top of the lamentable apathy of the Indians is the organized hostility of a group of Mexican intellectuals. I talked with some of their leaders for a good part of one night and found them violently opposed to the extension of industrialism—1931 model—in Mexico. Certain members of the group hold important positions in the government. Said one of them bitterly: "I have been in towns which were practically depopulated. What had happened? American investors who wanted to try a futile experiment in raising rubber or coffee needed workers. . . . American, French, German investors who needed hands. Whole towns were depopulated against the wishes of the townsfolk in order to supply contract labourers to foreign concessions. . . . Well, that is one way of improving, teaching, giving the results of western culture to the Mexican people."

The machine needs capital—millions of it. Mexican citizens have very little capital, and foreigners are still in fear of article 27. Until the full implications of that amazing document are made clear—a matter of decades perhaps—capital simply will not flow into the country in sufficient quantity to finance industrialization. Mexico might, like Russia, lift herself by her bootstraps, and create capital out of natural resources and labour, but that requires a centralized socialism beyond her grasp at the present time.

Most Mexicans cannot read. To operate machines, or consume their products on a scale profitable to the manufacturer, requires a literate population—which is why Russia "liquidated illiteracy" before she inaugurated the Five Year Plan. It will be many years before the little white schoolhouse liquidates illiteracy in Mexico, even to a practicable minimum.

Finally, I am not at all convinced that the Mexican can be adapted without fearful convulsions to wholesale mechanization. There are those who say he makes a good machinist, but I fear they are drawing dubious conclusions from the fact that he is a good craftsman and works nimbly with his hands. I went to enormous lengths to inspect every piece of machinery I could find in Mexico —this being a hobby of mine—and I make solemn affidavit that not even in Russia have I seen such an abnormal proportion of bankrupt plumbing systems, ill-advised electric wiring, ruthlessly neglected motor cars, safety-pin railroading. So far as two eyes are to be trusted, I would say that Mexicans are the world's worst machinists; the whole metallic discipline is alien to their temperament. What do you and I do when, driving along a country highway at thirty-five miles an hour, we suddenly enter a village? We slow down to twenty or less, particularly if the street is full of pedestrians and animals. What does a mestizo do? He throws his throttle wide open, and jumps from thirty-five to sixty. Riding behind him I invariably close my eyes and pray. Why does he do this? Because he has no mechanical sense. He thinks he is still riding a horse. On horseback he is wont to dig in his spurs and come galloping into the village street, a fine figure of a man, and no damage done. Burros, pigs and children can cope with horse acceleration. He carries this pattern over into a steel machine, the equivalent of forty horses. Instead of rowelling the brute, he steps on the accelerator. It is naive, it is understandable, but it is criminally dangerous.

The most that one can see in the immediate future is a new factory here and there, a mechanized plantation or two for sugar, henequen, bananas in the tierra caliente, a steady but reasonable growth in light and power plants, and enough new automobiles to supply the new highways. Highways in Mexico, due to the fantastic grading, are very costly, and only a few kilometers can be built a year. The homicide rate will mount, of course, but fortunately most villages will remain unconnected for decades to come. Less than three per cent of them are now on any kind of motor road.

Turning to cultural penetration in the form of American sports, radios, jazz, words, habits, subdivisions, billboards, Rotary clubs, plus-fours, Arrow collars—the above conclusion must be modified if not indeed reversed. White Mexicans in the cities have shown a hearty appetite for such commodities. Intellectuals protest, but the stream has been accelerating for the past decade. Certain tributaries, as we have noted earlier, are manifestly excellent; even more are manifestly corrupting. In the Yankee invasion so defined lies Mexico's real problem. Such is her chief menace from the machine age.

The future for industrialism in the sense of mass production is not rosy, for which we may thank whatever gods there be. As a result Mexico has unparalleled opportunity to evolve a master plan whereby the machine is admitted only on good behaviour, and not bolted raw as North Carolina now bolts it. Fortunately there is a definite movement in this direction. I have referred to a group of intellectuals dubious about mass production. I can go further and present the National Plan for Mexico.

Carlos Contreras, the driving force behind the plan, is an architect educated at Columbia and the Sorbonne. He started his agitation eight years ago. In 1925, he presented to President Calles "A National Planning Project for the Republic of Mexico." In 1927, he published a magazine, *Planificacion*. In January, 1930, the first national planning conference was held in Mexico City, under the auspices of the Ministry of Public Works, with some fifty papers by engineers, architects, economists, doctors. The keynote read: "Our object is to plan a united, homogeneous and beautiful Mexico—and an independent, respected and prosperous Mexico, in which the life of man will be complete, filled with noble interests, dignified, and as happy or happier than in any other part of the world. . . . Know in order to foresee; foresee in order to work." Meanwhile Contreras had been given a programme department in the government with a staff of engineers and draftsmen. His first work was the reorganization of the port of Vera Cruz. President Ortiz Rubio has promulgated a "Law of General Planning of the Republic" which provides for a central conning tower in the government, comprehending and coordinating topography, climate, population, social and economic life, national defence, public health. Under its mandates, Contreras and his staff are endeavouring to set up the following specific programmes:

1. The division of Mexico into natural economic regions, or functional zones; determining the best crops, the best industries for each area.
2. A master plan for the Federal District.

3. A plan for the future development of railroads, highways and communication lines.
4. A plan for the hydrographic system of the Valley of Mexico.
5. A plan for sea ports.
6. A plan for air ports.
7. A plan for the use of waters, primarily in the interest of irrigation. (Mexico has very few navigable rivers.)
8. A plan for afforestation and national parks.
9. A plan for federal buildings throughout the republic.

When a project is worked out by the Programme Department, it is presented to the president. If he approves, he has the power, *without legislative check,* to condemn property and put the project into immediate operation. No government agency, furthermore, can undertake any major work of construction without the approval of the Programme Department. Contreras dreams no longer but has double-barrelled executive sanction behind him. At a nod from the president, his blueprints can be turned into cement, breakwaters, irrigation ditches and tall pine trees. Outside of the Russian Gosplan, I know of no such far-reaching and powerful agency, since the collapse of our own War Industries Board in 1919. Mexico has the framework of a genuine machine to control the machine; to strain industrialism through a sieve of just enough and no more. Before my enthusiasm runs away with me I must remind myself and you, kind reader, that many noble projects with the highest sponsorship have put up their heads in Mexico in the past decade, only to be decapitated. The sponsor leaves hurriedly for parts unknown, or the next government budget finds him without funds. Meanwhile, Mr. Carlos Contreras, I envy you your job.

This book is but the account of a wayfaring economist in a land he does not know much about, but which interests and stimulates him enormously. Because of that interest and stimulation, perhaps he will be forgiven if he makes bold to tender his advice for the planning of Mexico's future, particularly its economic future. He should be forgiven too because of his youth. He is a parvenu cousin with only nine generations in North America behind him; a comparative newcomer on the continent.

ADVICE TO VILLAGERS

You have in your possession something precious; something which the western world has lost and flounders miserably trying to regain. Hold to it. Exert every ounce of your magnificent inertia to conserve your way of life. You must not move until you can be shown, by the most specific and concrete examples, that industrialism and the machine can provide a safer, happier, more rewarding existence. No such examples now obtain anywhere on earth. The most likely place to look for them, if they are ever to be attained, is Russia. The United States for the moment has nothing to offer you save its medical and agricultural science. Hold to your corncribs, to your economic security. Hold to your disregard of money, of pecuniary thrift, of clocks and watches, of hustle and bustle and busy emptiness. Hold to your damned wantlessness. Hold to your handicrafts and the philosophy of your handicrafts, and watch them jealously in the face of tourists and ignorant exporters. When they debase the work of your hands they debase you. Remember the code of the craftsmen in the great civilization from which you descend. You have their honour to keep.

Hold to your implacable hatred of the latifundia; give not an inch of your land, and strive continually for more

Diego Rivera 1931

BOSTON PUBLIC LIBRARY

land if once it was an authentic part of your community. But remember this: Land, bare land, without knowledge, seeds, water or fertilizer to cultivate it, avails you nothing. Land is to use, not own, as your ancestors taught. Today I think more important than any quest for land is that knowledge, those tools and irrigation ditches. Support your rural schools, send your sons to schools of agriculture, learn to read, learn to know your crops and the best harvests for your valley. When you are sick, ask help from the school-teacher instead of the herb-doctor.

And if I were you, when and if the new highway comes looping over the mountains into your village street, I would buy all the boxes of extra-sized carpet tacks I can afford. Declare cuatequitl and buy them co-operatively; I will give you an address in Mexico City and the postman will bring them to you. Mestizo chauffeurs must be cured of the bronco-buster complex.

ADVICE TO GOVERNMENT AND INTELLECTUAL

To the American ear the bracketing of the above sounds strange indeed. North of the Rio Grande, no intellectual would demean himself by associating with any branch of the government, while to call a politician an intellectual is practically a fighting word. We keep the categories pure. It was not so in the days of Thomas Jefferson and Alexander Hamilton. Mexico, for all its gun toters, pursues a wiser course. Its best brains are drifting in—also, alas, out of—political office. One need only mention such names as Manuel Gamio, Dr. Jose Zozaya, Carlos Contreras, Carlos Chavez, Moises Saenz. Painters, musicians, architects, doctors, archeologists, scientists are continually on the government payroll. There is no such haughty cleavage as obtains in the United States. I proceed, accordingly, with a joint address.

There are two main tasks before you, clearly interlocked, both of which you have begun. You must build your future in a full comprehension of the cardinal importance of the Indian, his inheritance, his psychology, his craftsmanship, his peculiar virtues; and you must strive for economic self-sufficiency for both the nation and its internal regions, a self-sufficiency not one hundred per cent perhaps, but enough to save you from the mad plunges of the business cycle in the outside world. To very few nations would this advice be other than absurd. It so happens that you are blessed with a large share of self-sufficiency already in your village economy, and with natural resources almost sufficient to close the circle. You have, for instance, both the raw cotton and the cotton-mill plant to satisfy, without a great deal of new investment, this cardinal requirement. You have the soil for practically every sort of foodstuff. You have nearly all the minerals, oils, fibres, drugs, timbers. Certain machines and instruments of precision you will do better to import—automobiles, for instance, and electric devices. You should feed, clothe, house yourself, and thus establish the first great line of defence. This is more vital than the increased exports which you are also seeking. The trimmings and the comforts are legitimate fields for importation in your particular case.

To come to terms with the Indian and his traditions, you must follow up the groundwork already laid in archeology, anthropology, ethnology, and rural sociology. You need many more studies like Gamio's *Teotihuacan* and Redfield's *Tepoztlan*. You need Frances Toor and her *Folkways*. As yet, in spite of a brilliant beginning, you do not half know your country. Foreign students may help, but yours should be the driving force. This task could be accomplished many times over with what you now spend on a ludicrous military system. One hundred airplanes in the pink of condition and a small, efficient state police will do more to discourage revolutions than a million armed men. Your army has no other excuse for existence.

To come to terms with economic self-sufficiency you need primarily agricultural education, and secondarily capital. The first you are shamefully neglecting, the second your citizens do not possess. Which brings us back to the military budget. There is capital in that budget to build the necessary modicum of textile mills, shoe factories, packing plants, canneries, which self-sufficiency demands. Whether it should be lent to regulated private enterprise or conducted as a government trust, I leave to you. Or you might admit, under control, foreign capital, allowing it a reasonably generous return—say ten per cent. But hold bitterly to the principles if not all the provisions of article 27 and article 123.

When and if you embark on a programme of further industrialization, jump clean over that murky intermediate period of reeking factories and roaring industrial districts. You can lead the Russians at this point. It is a period antiquated, unnecessary and scandalously inefficient. Head directly—as we in America are clumsily heading, weighed down by our past mistakes—for *decentralized industry,* small plants in the open country fed by cheap electric power, where workers have each his truck garden. Ask Henry Ford about the relative merits and costs of the two systems. Decentralization, furthermore, is ideally adapted to maintaining and encouraging the handicrafts. Electric lights, small motors, power-driven tools can aid potters, weavers, leather

[323]

workers, silversmiths. Your big investment will be for a
national spinal cord of electric power. Little plants with
small investment will tap this central stream. Yoked to
the power programme will be of course the irrigation
programme. Both depend on falling water. While jumping to decentralization it will also be well to jump to
Henry Ford's other favoured programme: high wages—
as high as Indians will accept without walking out—and
short hours. These, he finds, are more efficient than the
tradition—which Americans are outgrowing—of starvation wages and the sixty-hour week.

It is perfectly obvious by now that villages too long
impounded in the hacienda system cannot properly cultivate the land you give them, whereas free villages take
care of themselves. Some can be reclaimed by education
or agricultural credit, and made into functioning free
villages. Determine the number. Many are beyond immediate redemption. For these I suppose you must allow
the hacienda to come back, but on the strictest terms—
perhaps even as government-directed collective farms
like those of Russia. I suggest you make the foreman
pass a test in scientific agriculture. The ultimate objective, of course, is a nation of free villages, but you cannot have it all at once, or under the present provisions
of the land law. All your villagers know how to co-
operate; they were doing it long before the landing of
Cortez. In this you have a priceless asset; a ground rich
and ready made for co-operative associations of producers and consumers. Cultivate that ground. The lack of it
is now bringing ruin on my country's agriculture.

Analyze the Yankee invasion, take what is genuinely
helpful, boycott the rest. A few sports, phrases, notions
of efficiency; a few useful mechanisms can do no harm.
But why make Mexico City, or Guadalajara, or—the

thought blanches me—Oaxaca, into a second-rate Memphis, Tennessee? Be yourself, hombre. And how about consulting a good psychiatrist concerning that inferiority complex? You, with such a country and such a history?

And oh, Mexico, be careful of tourists in Buicks; they are the most ignorant and careless of all earth's wayward children. Unchecked they will litter your country with newspapers and lunch-boxes, they will bawl for hot dogs, they will ruin your roadsides, debase and destroy your popular arts, confuse your villagers with their shiny gadgets, bring your innkeepers to an early grave. Let them in gingerly, and when they become impossible, raise a hearty bandit scare. Why not keep a few battalions of trained bandits on hand for such emergencies? And may I ask why in the name of all that you and I hold dear—we have much in common—you allow great leering signboards on the Cuernavaca road, a road almost too noble for mere men to drive upon?

I do not need to remind you that your country needs unification, education and a greatly improved public health service. I should like to emphasize again, however, the transcendent importance of the new planning board and the planning law. It is, with rural education, the most hopeful movement in the nation today. Do not let it die for lack of funds, lack of intelligent interest, above all, lack of political integrity. Which reminds me: In Russia when a government official is caught stealing public property he is stood against a wall and shot, preferably before the day is done. I commend this procedure to your attention.

ADVICE TO INVESTORS AND FOREIGNERS—PARTICULARLY
    THE AMERICAN COLONY·

Diaz is dead.

ADVICE TO MIDDLETOWN

You, my fellow citizens, do not desire to return to a handicraft economy, and one would not want you to. You could not if you wished. But there are certain features of the early American way of life as typified in Mexico which, if you could acquire them, would make you more human and more happy. As your unemployed tramp from factory to factory, you might begin thinking about a modicum of regional self-sufficiency—Mr. J. Russell Smith has sketched the basic plan; about more in the way of economic security, not in dollars but in goods. Even now your jobless are drifting back to the farms, but the farms are sinking too; they are largely innocent of corn-cribs. You ought to know by now that business leadership is bankrupt, that "prosperity" was but a flash in the pan, and that mechanical civilization can never give you what you want on the policy—or lack of it—heretofore pursued. The billion wild horses can be tamed only by a deliberate master plan which keeps over-production and unemployment in an iron grip. Mexico has already embarked on that great adventure.

It is almost time that you recovered from infantilism in your habits of recreation, your tinkering with mechanical toys, your watching of circus athletes, and got back to genuine enjoyment with something of the fiesta spirit in it. You would have more fun if you developed handicrafts, first as hobbies for your hours outside the mill and office, and then, who knows, for some of the more gifted of you, as a major occupation, using the backbone of cheap electric power which is coming fast in America. Mass production has a useful function in severely restricted fields. Big business has not learned to keep to those fields. In a genuine civilization there is room for mass production, for small-scale production, for handicrafts. I have no confidence whatever in the theory that cultures based on hand work and machine work are mutually exclusive.

And why do you hustle around so fast, as though a hornet were forever behind your ear? Do you arrive anywhere with all this scrambling? Have you time to live as you gulp your coffee and rush to the station, or to the garage, and back again? Mexico takes no back talk from clocks. It is an art which you too some day must learn; for it is the art of living.

It is fitting, I think, to end this chapter and this book with the dream of one Mexican for his own people. He happened to be a Maya Indian; he happened to be my friend; and a part of his dream he converted into tangible reality. Shortly after writing the words which follow he was shot to death. Whatever one may think of the man—his name was Felipe Carrillo Puerto—the policy here embodied must never die.

With their own communal lands, with good roads, with schools in every hamlet, with a self-sustaining diversity of farm products, with a social organization in each village that will serve spiritual and social needs, with the cultivation of more than one export crop, with co-operative consumers' and producers' organizations, with a cultivation of the handicrafts, the native music and dances, with a deliberate introduction of every scientific improvement, we will, in a single generation, have a new Yucatan. We will have a Yucatan that will preserve all that is rich, beautiful and useful in the traditions of the Mayas, and at the same time one that will have absorbed all that can be used of the new and modern in science. We will cherish our soil, harbour our group life, grow and develop into a free and strong people, an example to Mexico and even to the world.

SELECTED BIBLIOGRAPHY

Ernest Gruening: *Mexico and Its Heritage*. New York:
    Century. 1928
The most scholarly modern book on Mexico, with
detailed accounts of phases of the revolution, a definitive chapter on health, and probably the fullest bibli-
ography since Bancroft.

Robert Redfield: *Tepoztlan, A Mexican Village*. Uni-
    versity of Chicago. 1930
A trained anthropologist's detailed study, excellently
written, of the way of life of a free Aztec village,
based on residence in the village from November, 1926
to July, 1927. The source of much of the concrete
evidence in this book.

Carleton Beals: *Mexico, An Interpretation*. New York:
    Huebsch. 1923
A newspaper correspondent who has been in and out
of Mexico for thirteen years interprets the revolution
with profound understanding of its political intricacies,
and a somewhat dogmatic radicalism.

Carleton Beals: *Mexican Maze*. Philadelphia: Lippin-
    cott. 1931
A more impressionistic and disillusioned book than the
above, full of good stories and highly colored descriptions. Large collection of Rivera's sketches.

Hubert C. Herring and Katharine Terrill, editors: *The
    Genius of Mexico*. New York: Committee on Cul-
    tural Relations with Latin America. 1931
Lectures delivered before the annual summer seminar
which Mr. Herring conducts in Mexico. Contributions
by Moises Saenz, Manuel Gamio, Mary Austin, Ches-

ter Lloyd Jones, Paul U. Kellogg, Samuel Guy Inman, Rene d'Harnoncourt, and many others.

T. Philip Terry: *Guide to Mexico*. Boston: Houghton Mifflin. New edition 1930

Except for such details as the dimensions of the ruins at Chichen Itza, the importance of those at Monte Alban, and the author's warnings against venomous reptiles and drafts, I believe that this enormous mass of information is substantially correct. Especially good is the treatment of Latin-American Spanish, on which the same author has written an excellent textbook. Allow for his admiration of Porfirio Diaz.

Frank Tannenbaum: *The Mexican Agrarian Revolution*. New York: Macmillan. 1929

An American radical sociologist studied the intent and execution of the revolutionary land reforms, with many statistics, when these reforms gave promise of being more fundamental than they have since turned out to be. When revolutionary emphasis shifted to rural education he made a field study of that subject, and wrote a book on it, soon to be published.

La Mendicidad en Mexico. Mexico: Public Charities. 1931

As a background for this case study of city beggars are studies of Mexican labour, public health, living costs, etc. Prepared with the assistance of Dr. Eyler N. Simpson.

Manuel Gamio: *La Poblacion del Valle de Teotihuacan*. Mexico: Department of Anthropology. 1922. 3 volumes

A study similar to Redfield's, and even more complete, of a less typical town—the site of probably the greatest pre-Aztec city on the plateau, which had degenerated into hacienda villages. Written by the archeologist who restored the ruins and reorganized the community. The introduction in English summarizes the material.

[330]

Manuel Gamio: *Forjando Patria*. Mexico: Porrua
  Hermanos. 1916
A Mexican leader's ideal for his own people.
Jose Vasconcelos and Manuel Gamio: *Aspects of Mexi-
  can Civilization*. University of Chicago. 1926
Discusses international relations and attempts to refute
Mexican racial inferiority.
Joaquin Isquierdo y Croselles: *Geografia de Mexico*.
  Granada: Edition Urania. Undated, probably 1929
Natural resources and other data for the country as a
whole and state by state. Photographs, occasional
good stories, and most original typography.
Anita Brenner: *Idols behind Altars*. New York: Payson
  and Clarke. 1929
Dramatic evidence of pagan practices, excellent sum-
mary of the art renaissance stimulated by the revolu-
tion, and considerable scattered material on history,
sociology, colonial art, and personalities.
Susan Smith: *Made in Mexico*. New York: Knopf. 1930
An excellent book for children about Mexican handicrafts and popular arts.
Ruben M. Campos: *El Folklore Literario de Mexico*.
  Mexico: Secretariat of Education. 1929
Collection of legends, stories, songs, extending from
1525 to 1925.
Charles Macomb Flandrau: *Viva Mexico!* New York:
  Appleton. 1908
A book by the literary brother of a coffee hacendado,
which, slight and impressionistic as it is, has become a
classic for the humour and truth of its picture. Inim-
itable description of the bourgeois Mexican.
Madame Calderon de la Barca: *Life in Mexico*. New
  York: E. P. Dutton (Everyman's Library). Out of
  print
Letters from the Scotch-American wife of the first
Spanish ambassador to the republic of Mexico, from
1839 to 1842, full of humour, indiscretion, and acute

observation. Many items of the description are still valid, and the rest are history.

Hubert Howe Bancroft: *History of Mexico*. New York: The Bancroft Company. 1914
A revision and condensation of his history published in 1888. See also volumes 9 through 14 of his complete works. The revision exhibits a strong Diaz reflex.

Alexander von Humboldt: *Political Essay on the Kingdom of New Spain*. New York: John Black. 1811. 2 volumes
Humboldt's observations on the geology, flora and fauna, natural resources of Mexico remain at many points unsuperseded. Competent scientists ought to check and amplify his work.

W. H. Prescott: *The Conquest of Mexico*. New York: E. P. Dutton (Everyman's Library). 2 volumes
Remains the best critical and comparative history of the conquest, although it was completed in 1843, by a historian who had never visited Mexico and was hampered in his documentary studies by failing eyesight.

Bernal Diaz del Castillo: *The Discovery and Conquest of Mexico,* translated by A. P. Maudslay. New York: Harper. 1928
The best eye-witness's account of the conquest, in a new translation from the original manuscript. The account in its censored form was heavily used by Prescott.

Bernardino de Sahagun: *Historia General de las Cosas de Nueva España*. Mexico: A. Valdes. 1829. 3 volumes
By one of the early missionaries, who wrote it in Aztec, transliterated into Roman characters, giving invaluable material about life and customs before the conquest.

A. Hyatt Verrill: *Old Civilizations in the New World*. Indianapolis: Bobbs Merrill. 1929
Popular volume by a representative of the Museum of the American Indian, which brings into focus the whole

picture of prehistoric migrations over the two Americas, and which may suffer in accuracy as a result of its wide scope.

Eduard Seler: *Gesammelte Abhandlungen zur Amerikanischen Sprach- und Alterthumskunde*. Berlin: A. Asher. 1902-8. 5 volumes
Valuable for its illustrations and for reference on specific ruins, by an indefatigable scholar who made both documentary researches and lengthy expeditions.

Herbert J. Spinden: *Ancient Civilizations of Mexico and Central America*. New York: American Museum of Natural History. 1917
A short summary by one of the leading authorities on Maya archeology.

Herbert J. Spinden: *Maya Art*. Cambridge: Peabody Museum. 1913
A semi-technical work, beautifully illustrated.

Ignacio Marquina: *Estado Actual de los Principales Edificios Arqueologicos de Mexico*. Mexico: Secretariat of Education. 1928
This and other volumes in the same series contain admirable photographs, elevations, and descriptions of various ruins unearthed in Mexico.

Tulane University Expedition: *Tribes and Temples*. New Orleans: Tulane University. 1926. 2 volumes
Report of expedition into Maya territory in 1925 by the archeologist, Franz Blom, with the sociologist and novelist, Oliver LaFarge.

Carl Lumholtz: *Unknown Mexico*. New York: Scribner. 1902. 2 volumes
Explorations in the country of the Tarahumares, Yaquis, Apaches—the Mexican northwest.

Gregory Mason: *Silver Cities of Yucatan*. New York: Putnam. 1927
Journalistic account of expedition to scout out new ruins. Valuable introduction by Herbert J. Spinden.

Magazine and pamphlet material:

Frank Tannenbaum, editor: *Mexico—A Promise. Survey Graphic,* May, 1924
Articles by Calles, Carrillo, Gamio, Rivera, Carleton Beals, and others. Published at a period of greater revolutionary optimism than the present.

Carlos Contreras: *National Planning Project for the Republic of Mexico. City Planning,* July, 1925
First draft of the national plan now being executed officially.

Walter Lippmann: *Church and State in Mexico. Foreign Affairs,* January, 1930
A clear statement of the American part in the Church controversy of 1926 and its settlement.

Paul S. Taylor: *Mexican Labor in the United States.* University of California. 1929
Migration records for the period from 1920 to 1928, with errors in both Mexican and U. S. official figures pointed out and corrected.

T. T. Waterman: *Bandelier's Contribution to the Study of Ancient Mexican Social Organization.* University of California. 1917
Careful proof of the democratic nature of the Aztec government.

Herbert J. Spinden: *Maya Dates and What They Reveal.* Brooklyn Museum. 1930
Theory that the Maya calendar was worked out with reference to lunar and solar eclipses. Rather technical.

See also files of the monthly official publication of the Mexican department of statistics: *Estadistica Nacional,* and the quarterly *Mexican Folkways,* edited in Mexico City by Frances Toor, with the co-operation of the secretariat of education.

INDEX

INDEX